IMAGES
of America

JOHNSTON COUNTY REVISITED

On the Cover: This rare image shows a reunion of some of Johnston County's last Confederate veterans at a Fourth of July picnic in Selma in 1919. The bottles on these makeshift tables are most likely from the Selma Hayo-Cola Bottling Company. John Harrison Parker is the vet holding the bugle—the instrument he carried and played during the Civil War. (Courtesy of James Carlton Parrish.)

IMAGES
of America

JOHNSTON COUNTY REVISITED

K. Todd Johnson and Windy Thompson

ARCADIA
PUBLISHING

ISBN 978-1-4671-2362-4

Published by Arcadia Publishing
Charleston, South Carolina

Printed in the United States of America

Library of Congress Control Number: 2014958699

For all general information, please contact Arcadia Publishing:
Telephone 843-853-2070
Fax 843-853-0044
E-mail sales@arcadiapublishing.com
For customer service and orders:
Toll-Free 1-888-313-2665

Visit us on the Internet at www.arcadiapublishing.com

To Thomas Wingate Lassiter—journalist, photographer, historian, and longtime supporter of the arts and humanities in Johnston County

Contents

Acknowledgments

This book started writing itself over 100 years ago. Many people over those years have had a hand in collecting the photographs that tell the story of Johnston County. We would like to take a moment to thank all of you.

We are indebted to Terry Hobgood at the Benson Museum of Local History, Pam Baumgartner at the Clayton Library, Betty Pope at the Kenly Public Library, and Lewis Mullen of Selma for providing photographs that we have included in our book.

We would like to thank the volunteers and staff of the Johnston County Heritage Center, and before that, the Johnston County Room of the Public Library of Johnston County and Smithfield. Unless otherwise noted, images appear courtesy of the heritage center. The collection began in the 1960s, and in the last 60 years, many hands have been busy collecting, documenting, preserving, and curating these incredible photographs that tell our county's history. For all of your efforts, we say thank you. And for the efforts of future staff and volunteers who will continue to collect photographs, we applaud you because it is important to continue telling our story.

Finally, I would like to thank Todd Johnson for asking me to coauthor this book with him. I love old photographs and have spent the last several years volunteering at the heritage center, working with many of the photographs we selected for this book. I have learned a great deal about Johnston County, and I have learned how little I know about Johnston County. And I have learned the amount of work it takes to put together a book. Todd, thanks for the opportunity to do all of these things and have so much fun.

—Windy Thompson

INTRODUCTION

If a picture is worth a thousand words, this little volume of pre-1970 photographs should amount to several dissertations. The title of one tome might be, "How Johnston County Has Changed in the Last Half Century." In the *State* magazine on September 8, 1956, Bill Sharpe described the typical Johnstonian of the 1950s: "He is mostly rural and either farming or connected with related enterprise. He is likely plebeian but does not lack for landed aristocracy; slow to embrace change, yet proud of his progress; and a habitual joiner of movements for betterment. He is inward-looking, which is to say provincial. He loves to attend meetings and travel, visit, and fish. Politics is a serious matter and often revolves around the schools. He is religious—his rural and small-town churches are numerous and flourishing."

Farming is still important, but it no longer employs the majority of the population. In the 1950s, a total of 56 percent of the people worked in farming; today, fewer than 1,000 persons (out of a population of about 178,000) are employed in agricultural pursuits, and the majority of the workforce drives to jobs outside the county. A provincial mind-set persists to some extent, but there are so many newcomers and natives who left and returned in retirement that such a mentality is becoming negligible. Sharpe's comment about the integral ties between politics and education was close to the mark. For almost a century, tremendous sums have flowed from county coffers into public schools each year, and debate over how these funds are spent continues. In the area of religion, there is a marked decline—some 65 percent of the population claim no church affiliation.

The county's long-standing racial divide is evident in these pages, especially in schools and churches. Until the Jim Crow caste system was challenged in the 1950s, it was understood that white and black children would attend separate schools and participate in separate public events. Much to county school superintendent H.B. Marrow's credit, however, Johnston did not have the huge disparity between white and black school facilities found in many other Southern locales. In the 1920s, Marrow led the way in closing over 100 one- and two-room schools and oversaw construction of modern brick buildings in towns and rural communities alike. Black schools received special funding and challenge grants from Northern philanthropists, but county taxpayers covered the lion's share of capital expenditures for both races. Under the leadership of Marrow's successor, the venerable Evander S. Simpson, another consolidation movement in the late 1960s made it possible for schools to be fully integrated and the county to qualify for a state-supported technical college.

Smithfield Herald editor-publisher James M. Beaty opposed consolidation 100 years ago, insisting that removing a school from a rural community was tantamount to taking its soul. Every community should have a church and a school, he felt, and, as Sharpe pointed out, "he preferred that the church be Baptist." The success of this denomination is often attributed to Beaty's tireless work. Although Johnston was one of the last North Carolina counties to have a county farm agent (1914), many local farmers already knew about crop rotation, diversification, purebred livestock, and other scientific farming practices because Beaty had been educating them on improved agricultural methods through the columns of the *Smithfield Herald* since the 1880s.

We hope you enjoy meeting the towering figures, the colorful individuals, and all the regular, everyday folk (many of them nameless) whose faces grace the pages of this Johnston County photo album.

—Todd Johnson

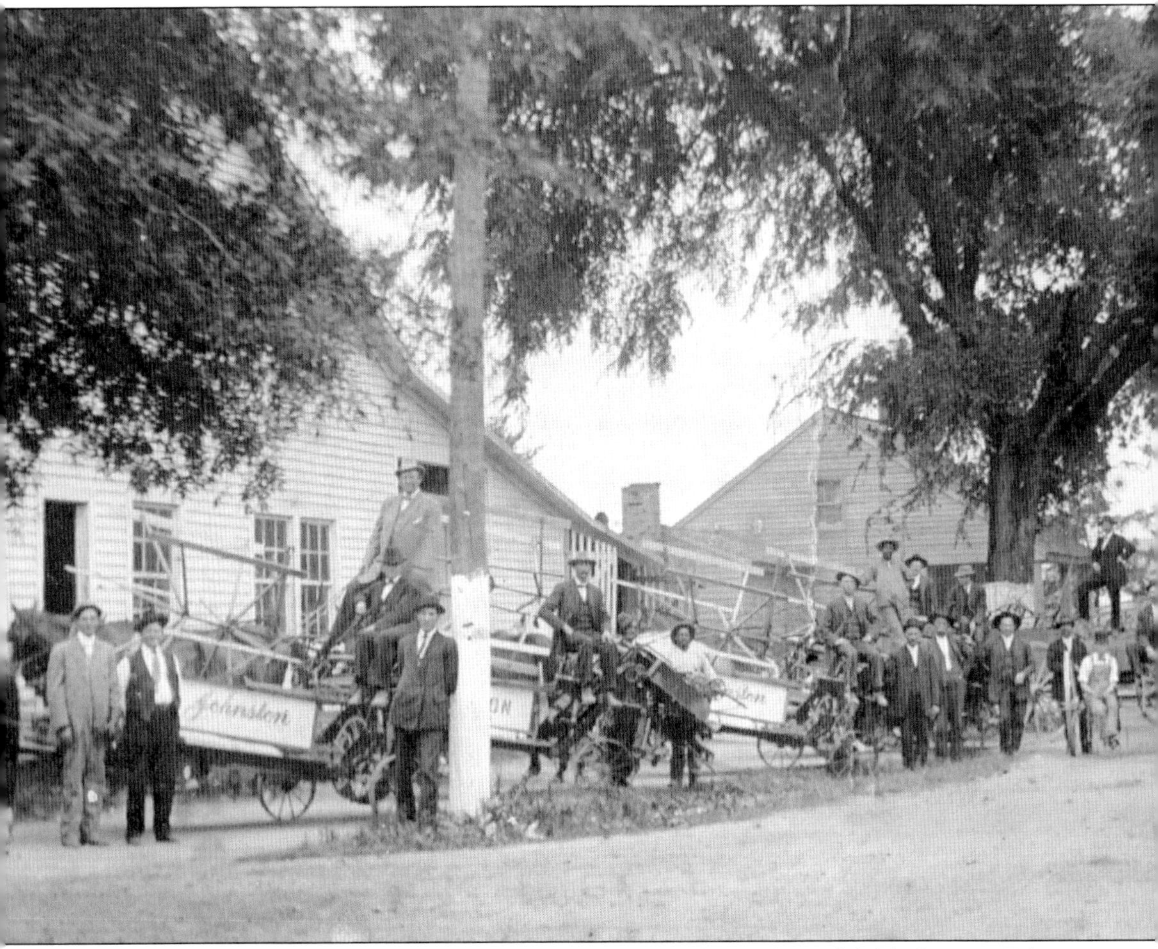

Around 1920, these farmers and merchants gathered in front of Smithfield's Banner Tobacco Warehouse on Johnston Street (behind present Howell Theater) with a display of grain reapers from Johnston Harvester Company in Batavia, New York. (Courtesy of the Johnston County Heritage Center.)

One

Rural Life

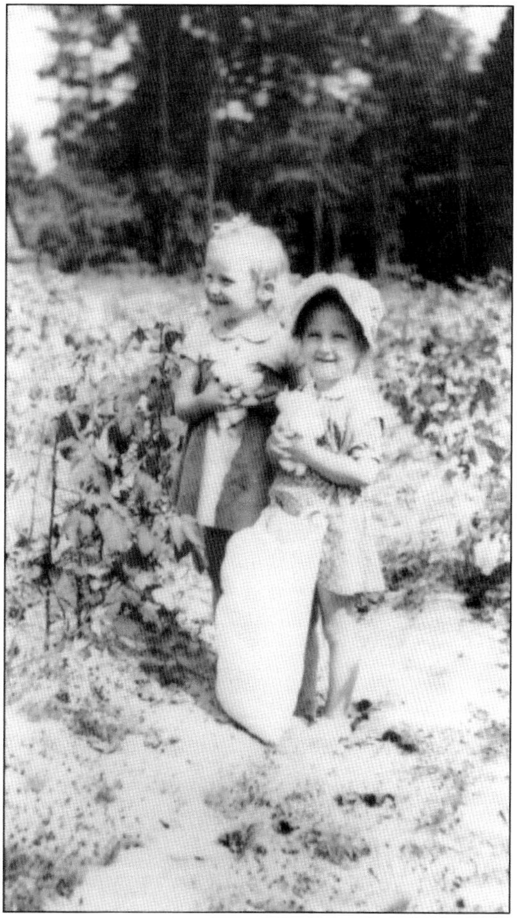

Linda Edwards (left) and Sylvia Royall (right) of the Brogden community of Boon Hill Township are captured on camera doing their part to help with the cotton harvest around 1942. (Courtesy of Sylvia Royall Pearce.)

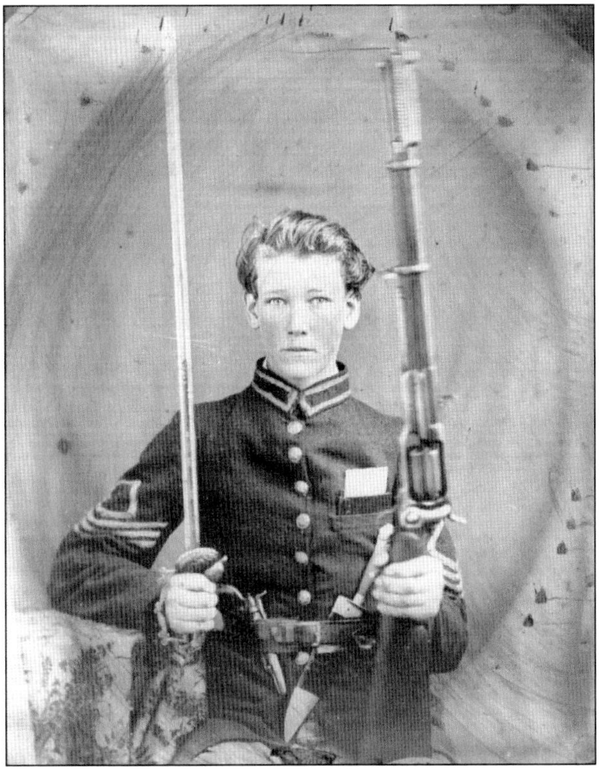

Charles Stevens Powell, later known as Sheriff Powell, was only 18 when he enlisted in the 24th North Carolina Infantry Regiment in 1861. He served with General Lee in Virginia and West Virginia and later helped defend Wilmington, the lifeline of the Confederacy. He fought at Bentonville in 1865, and during a brief stay in Kenansville, he and his fellow soldiers were fed and entertained by a group of young girls. He never forgot one particular teenaged girl, Edith Millard, and after the war he sought her out and eventually made her his wife.

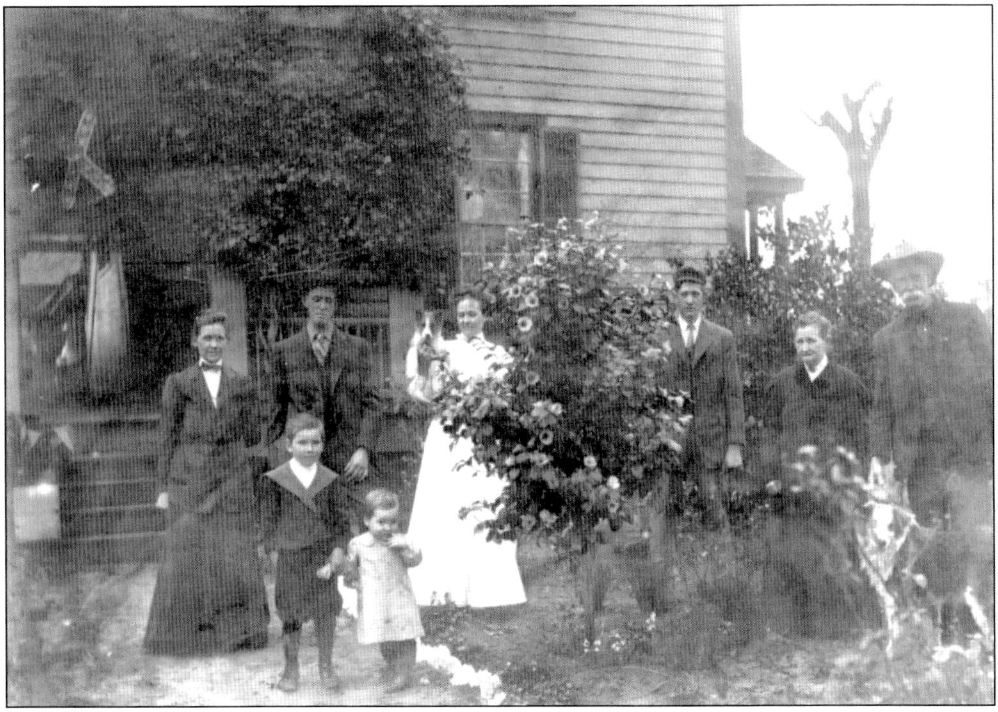

C.S. and Edith Millard Powell (at right) are at home with children and grandchildren about 1910.

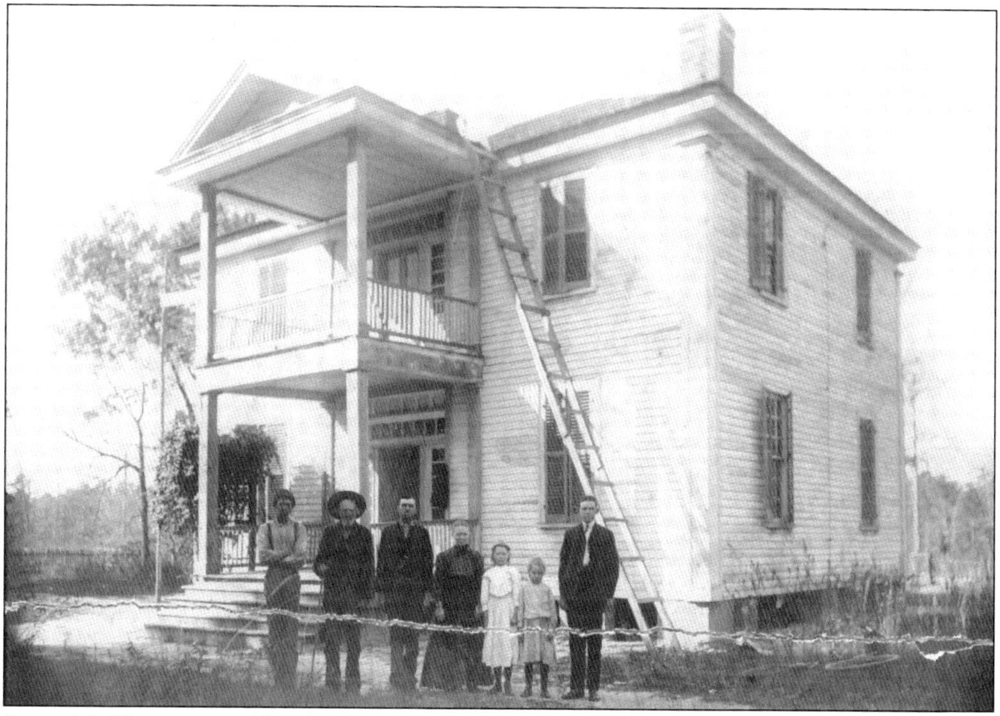

Samuel I. Thornton and his family pose in front of their home in Bentonville Township in the early 20th century. This house was formerly the home of John and Amy Harper and served as field hospital during the Battle of Bentonville in March 1865. It is now open to the public as part of the Bentonville State Historic Site.

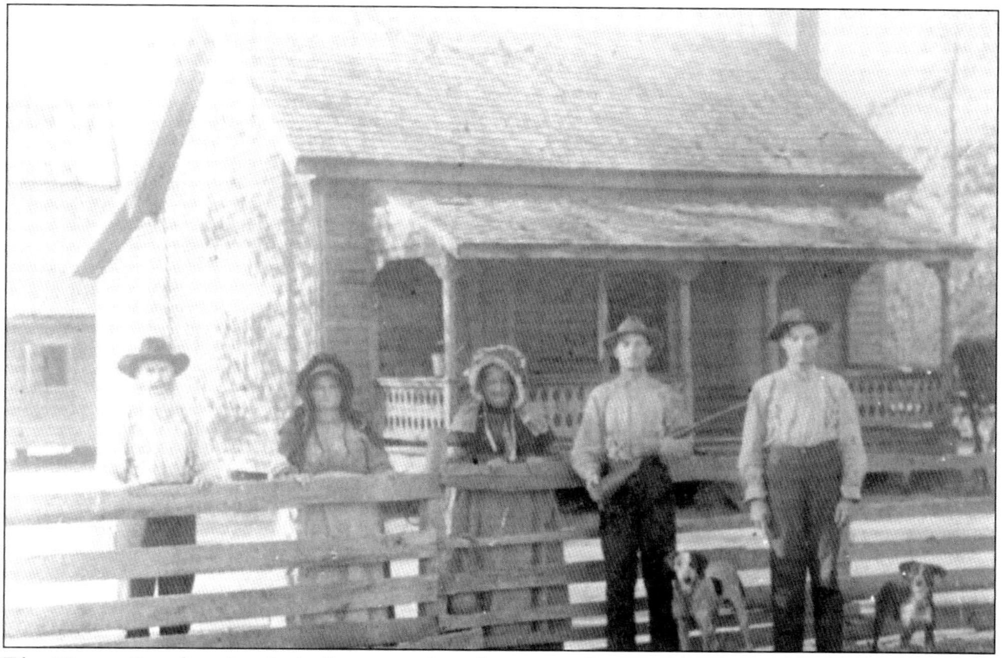

The Cicero Barefoot family is shown at their farm near Benson about 1900, as the boys prepare for a hunting expedition. (Courtesy of Benson Museum of Local History.)

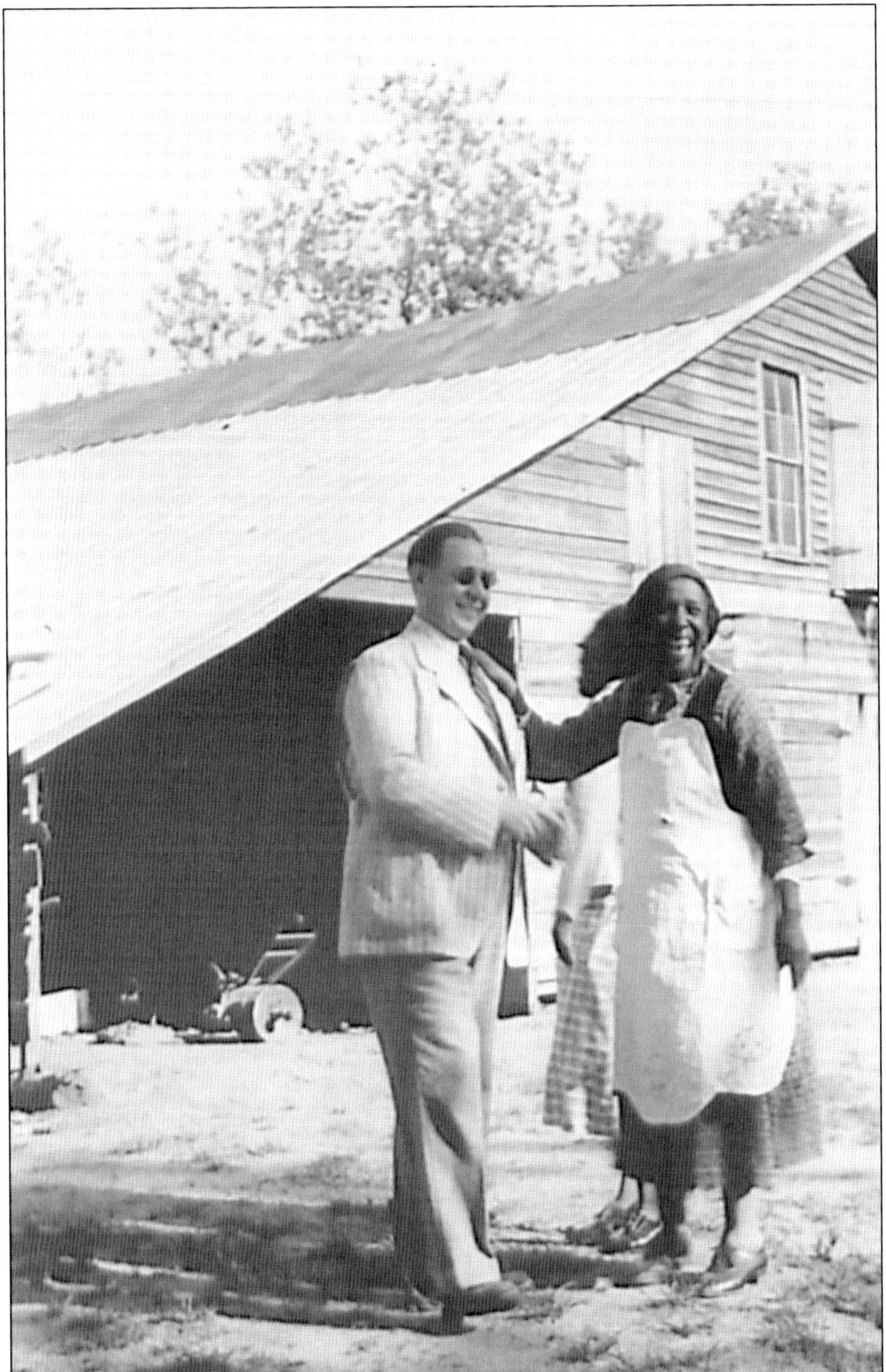

H. Smith Richardson, son of Vick Chemical Company founder Lunsford Richardson, receives a warm welcome in the 1940s from his grandparents' former slave, Sylvia Richardson Holder, as he returns to the plantation where his father grew up. (Courtesy of UNC, Chapel Hill, H. Smith Richardson Papers, Southern Historical Collection.)

Former slave Sylvia Richardson Holder of O'Neals Township is demonstrating her wood-splitting skills for a photographer who came in the 1930s to document the family history of her former owners. (Courtesy of UNC, Chapel Hill, H. Smith Richardson Papers, Southern Historical Collection.)

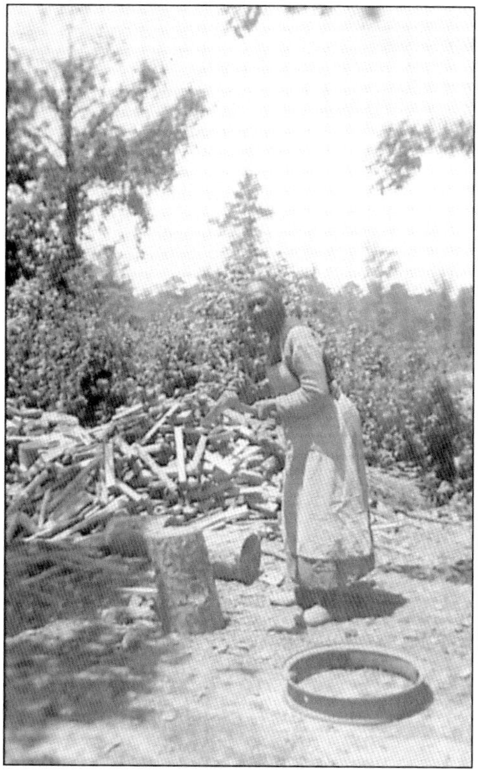

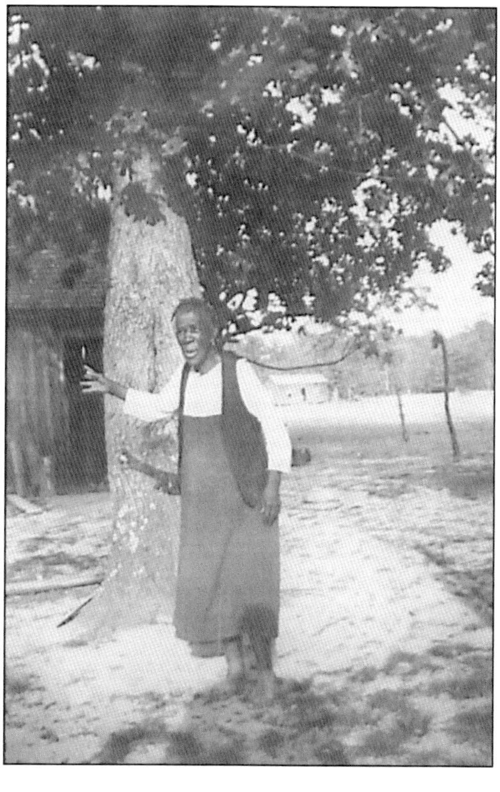

In the 1940s, Sylvia Holder shows her old master's grandson the cabin where she lived as a slave. (Courtesy of UNC, Chapel Hill, H. Smith Richardson Papers, Southern Historical Collection.)

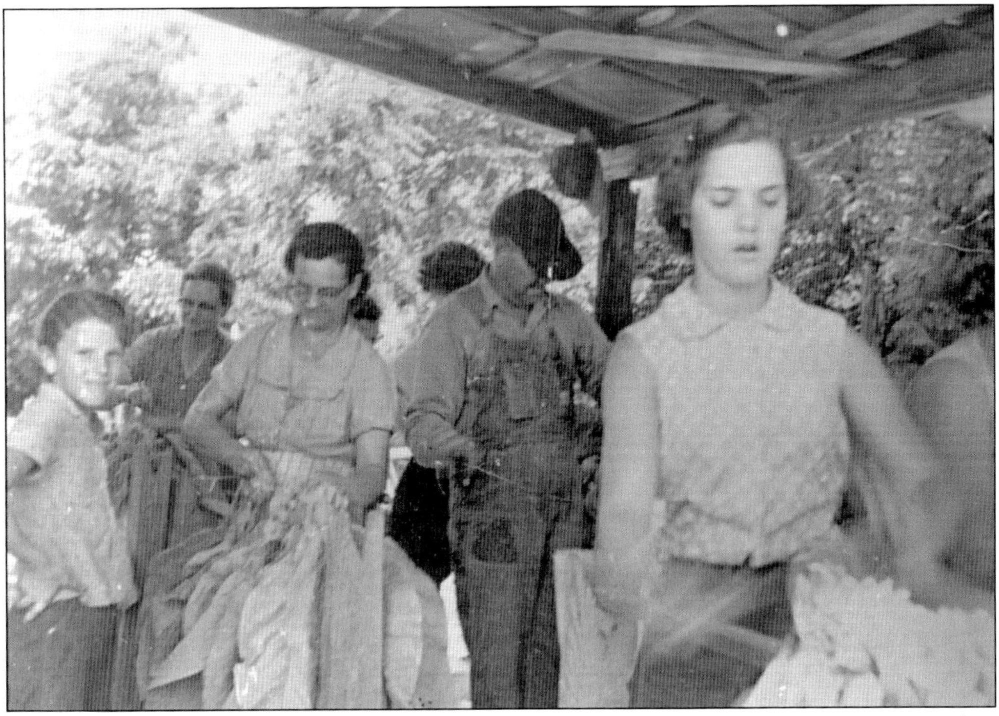

Jasper "Jap" and Nicy Dunn, Ella Adams, and others are shown barning tobacco in Meadow Township in the 1950s. (Courtesy of Benson Museum of Local History.)

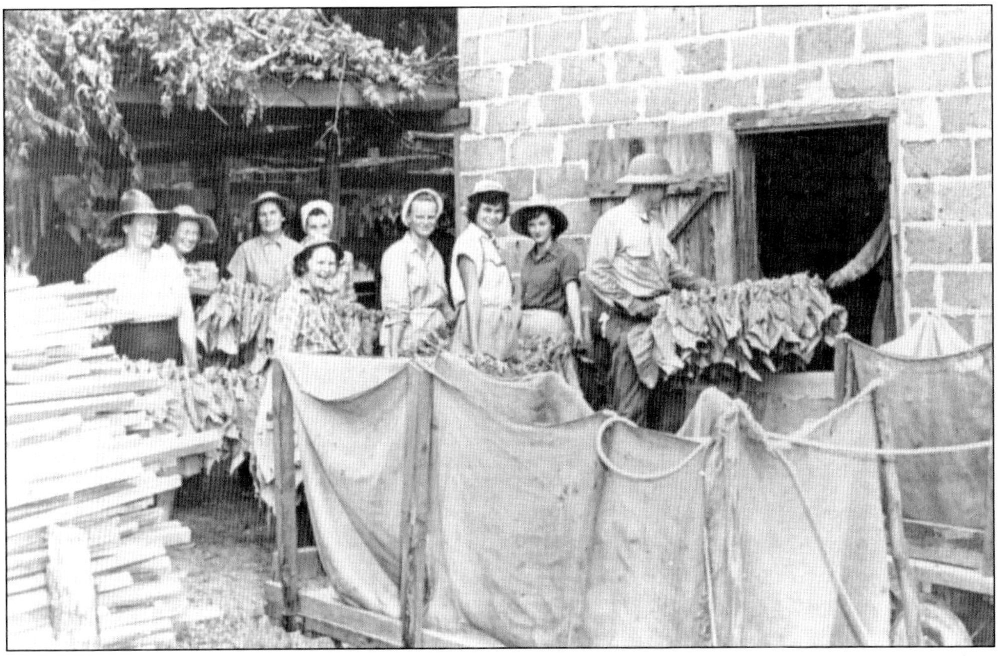

This tobacco-barning scene shows several cheery workers on the Lee farm in Clayton Township around 1950. Pictured here are, from left to right, John Price, Edith Lee, Lola Mae Lee, Daisy Puckett, Fay Lee, Edith Lee, Edna Cole, Shirley Puckett, and Jack Lee. (Courtesy of Benson Museum of Local History)

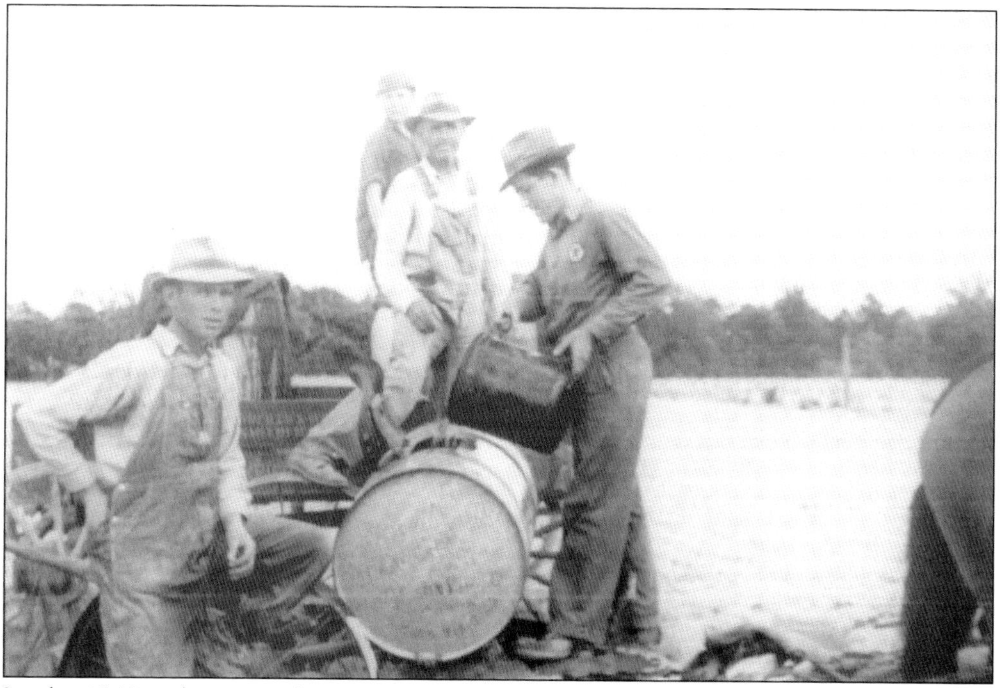

In the 1940s, planting tobacco was a labor-intensive undertaking. Gilbert Thompson (left) watches as Eldridge Thompson adds water to their horse-pulled tobacco planter in the Brogden community. The other two men are unidentified.

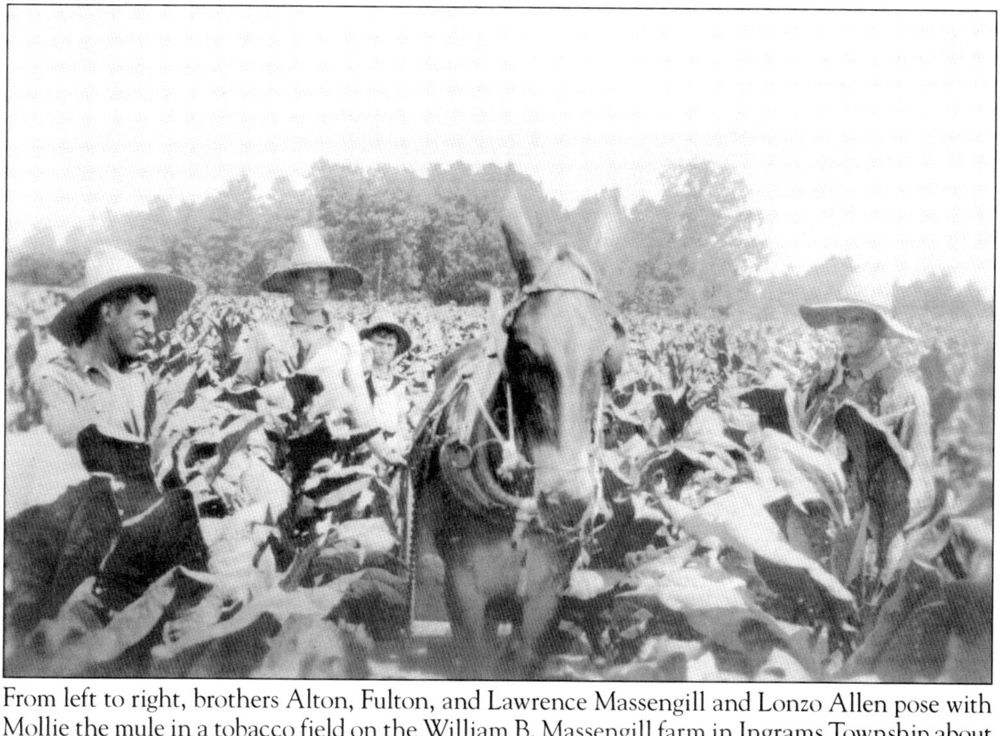

From left to right, brothers Alton, Fulton, and Lawrence Massengill and Lonzo Allen pose with Mollie the mule in a tobacco field on the William B. Massengill farm in Ingrams Township about 1920. (Courtesy of Stanton Massengill.)

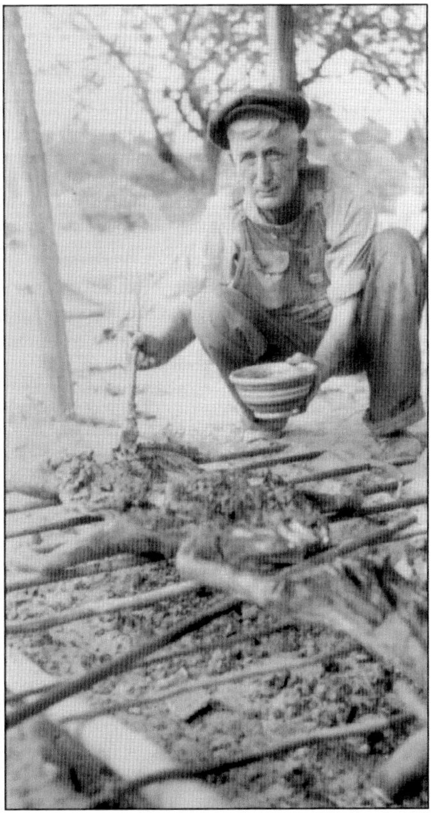

Walter Royall bastes a pig cooking on a ground pit in the 1940s. (Courtesy of Sylvia R. Pearce.)

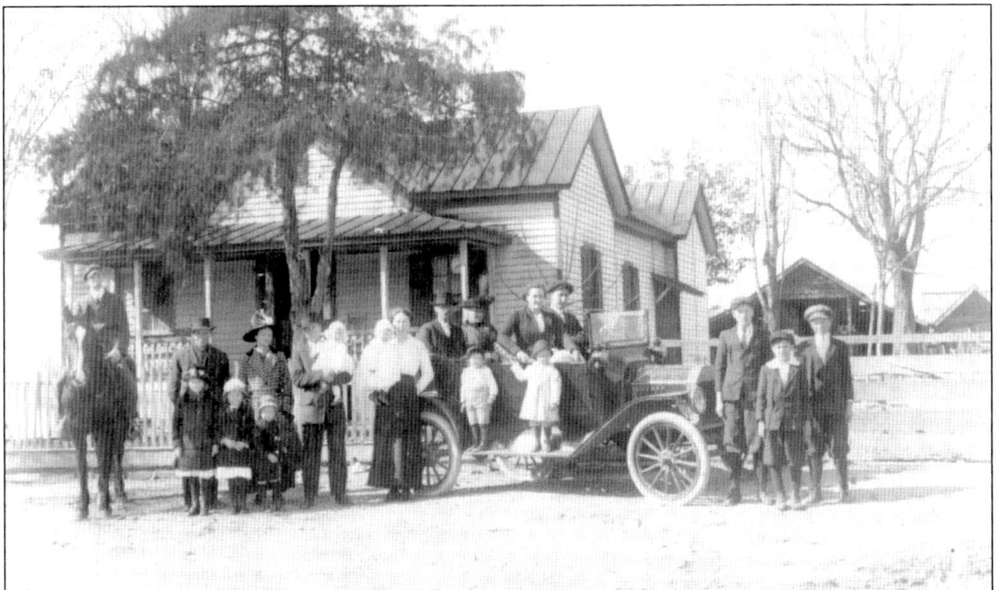

Ernest E. and Edith Parker are chauffeured in the back seat of a touring car in front of their home near Hopewell Church in Smithfield Township about 1915, flanked by children and grandchildren. Horses and horse-drawn conveyances were still the primary mode of transportation at this point, but the automobile was quickly gaining popularity.

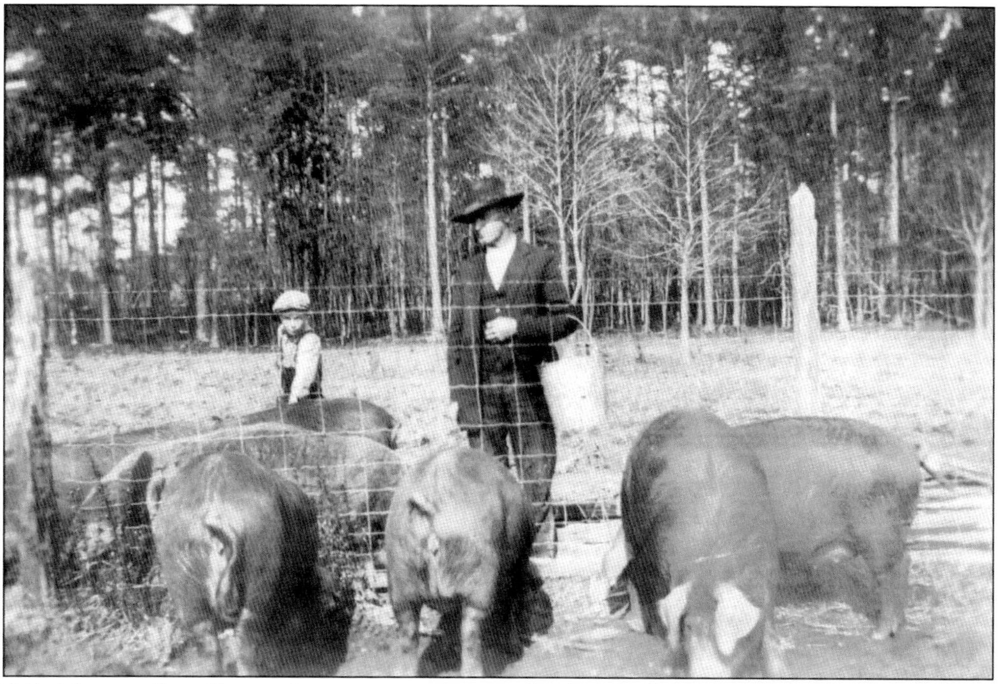

Billy Massengill and his son Lawrence tend to purebred Duroc hogs on his farm near Blackman's Crossroads in the 1920s. (Courtesy of Stanton Massengill.)

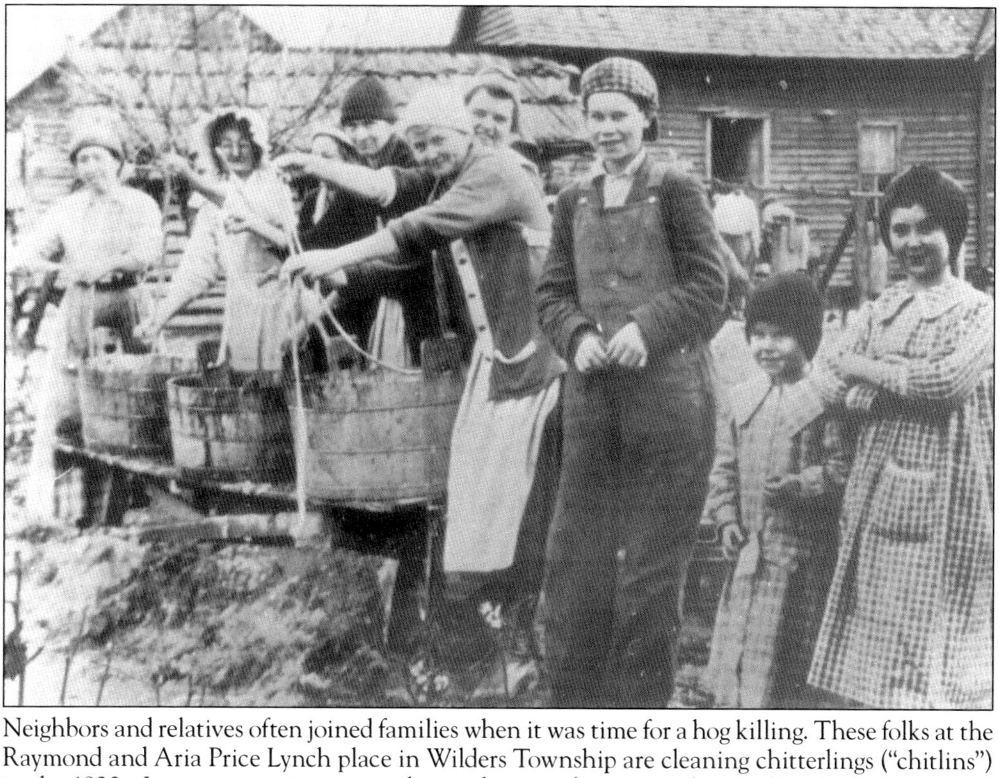

Neighbors and relatives often joined families when it was time for a hog killing. These folks at the Raymond and Aria Price Lynch place in Wilders Township are cleaning chitterlings ("chitlins") in the 1920s. It seems surprising to see happy faces performing such a smelly job.

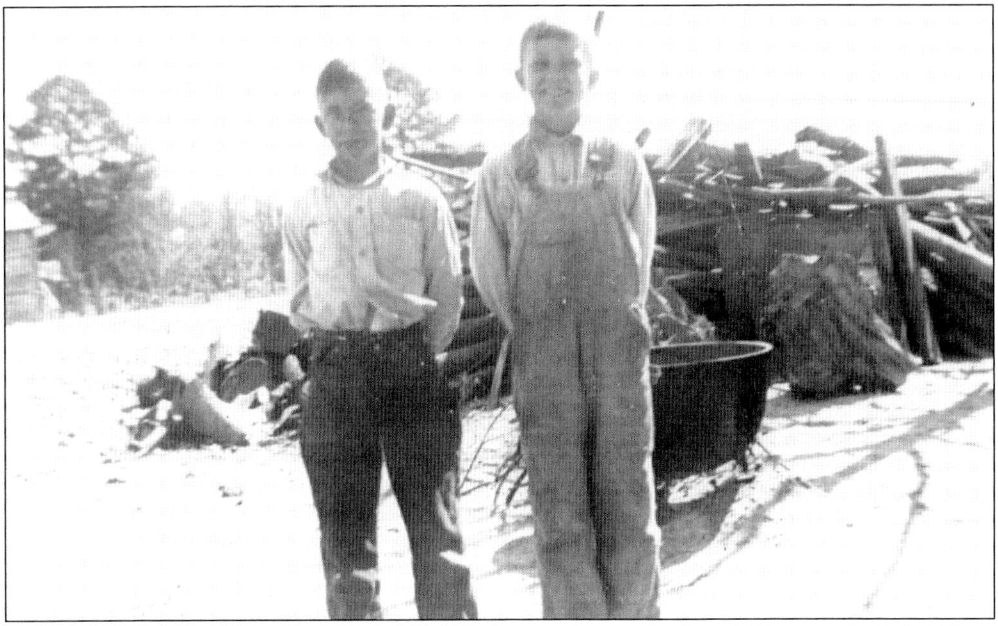

Firewood and iron pot are all in place for wash day as Chester (left) and Clarence (right) Abbott pose for this shot on Selma's Walnut Street in the early 1940s.

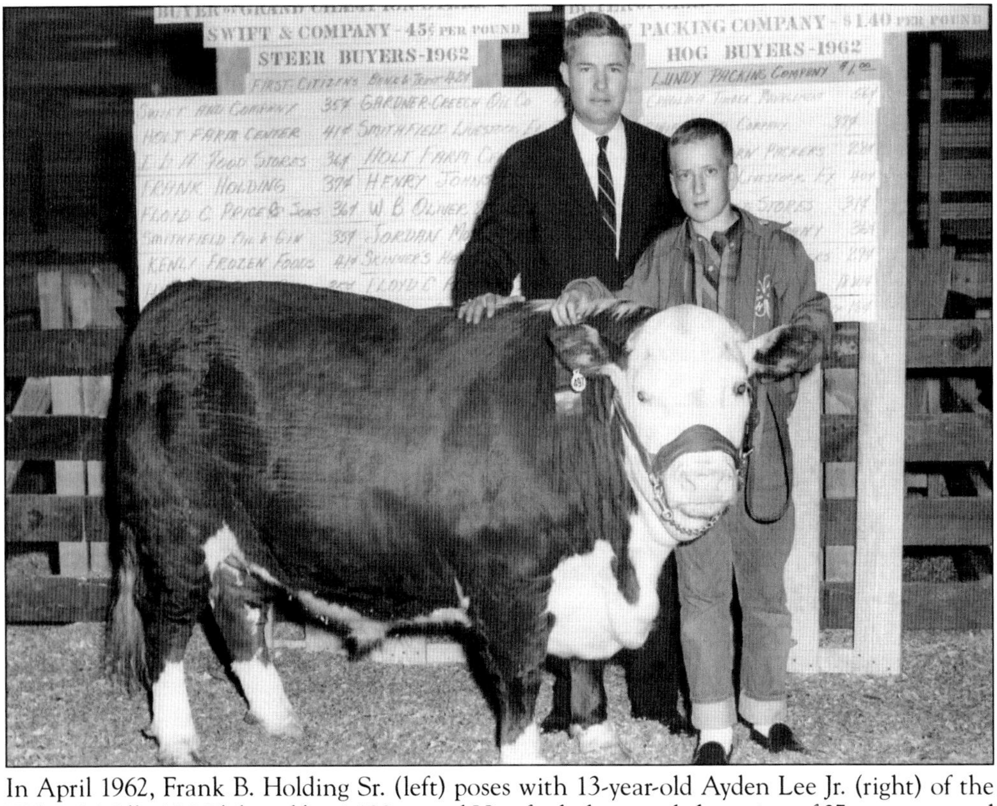

In April 1962, Frank B. Holding Sr. (left) poses with 13-year-old Ayden Lee Jr. (right) of the Wilson's Mills 4-H Club and his 1,180-pound Hereford, the grand champion of 27 steers entered in the 16th annual Johnston County Livestock Show. (Photograph by Reuben Johnson.)

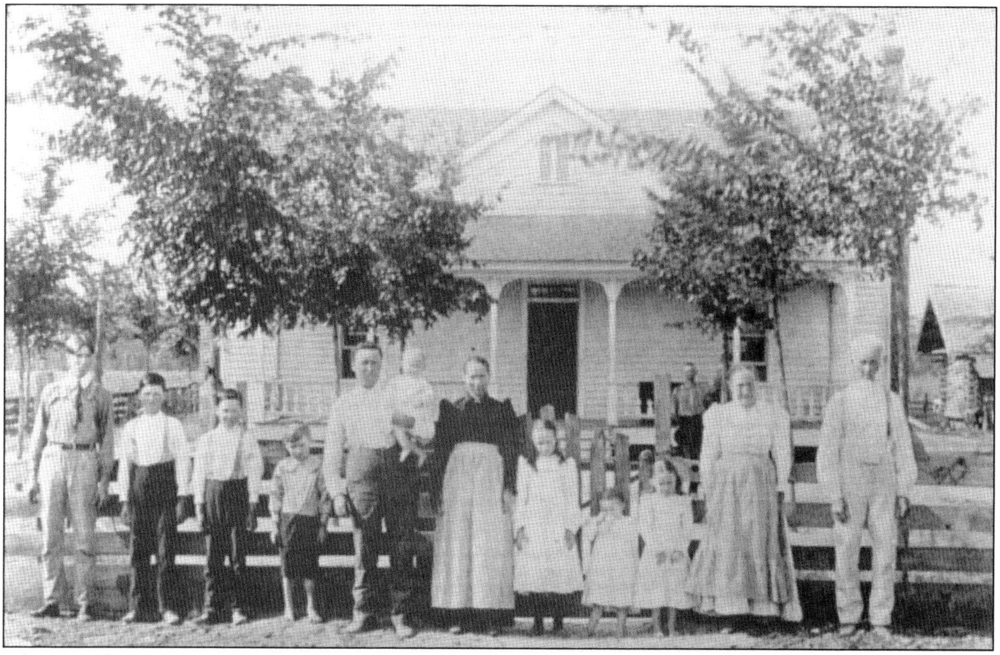

The Joseph Martin and Mary Eliza Smith McLamb family lined up for this shot in front of their home near Benson about 1902. The baby in Joseph McLamb's arms is believed to be daughter Luma, who became Johnston County's first female elected official when she won the register of deeds office on the Republican ticket in 1928. (Courtesy of Benson Museum of Local History.)

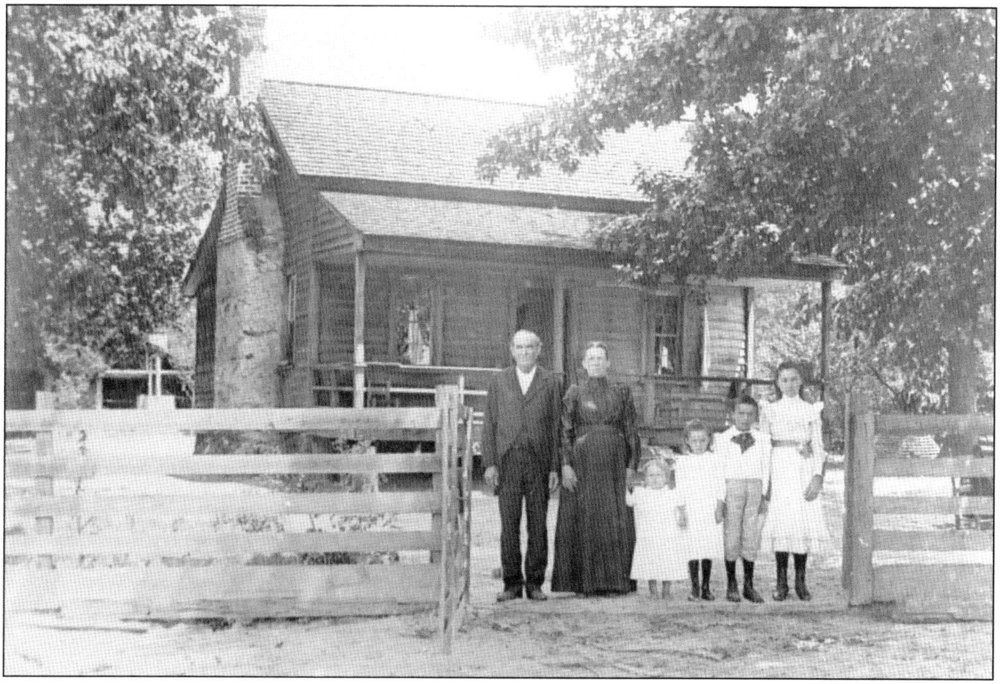

The Henry and Leacy Rose Morgan family is pictured here in their Sunday best in front of their Benson-area home around 1903. The children are, from left to right, Alma, Lucy, John Henry, and Julia, arranged in stair-step fashion. (Courtesy of Benson Museum of Local History.)

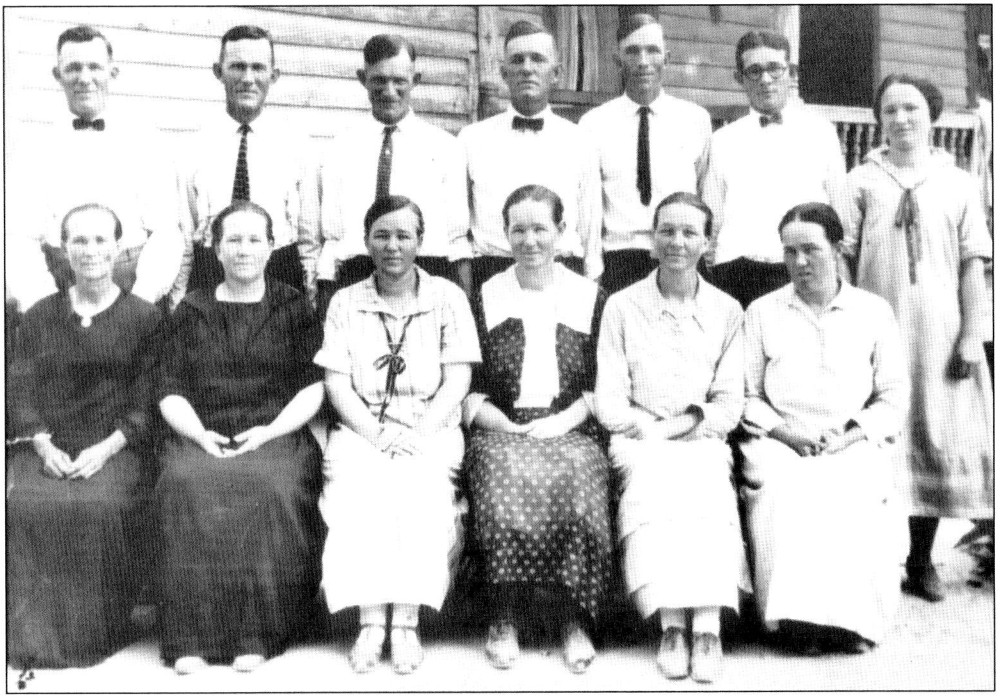

Johnston County has a rich heritage of family reunions. Pictured here in 1918 are the 13 daughters and sons of Dempsy and Kizzie Overby Daughtry. The Daughtry reunion has been held near the Brogden community every September for almost 100 years. Shown are, from left to right, (first row) Frances Woodard, Laney Creech, Lucy Braswell, Ransey Braswell, Sally Braswell, and Bena Thompson; (second row) Richard, Joe, Walter, Robert, Dempsy, and Durwood Daughtry and Kizzie Creech.

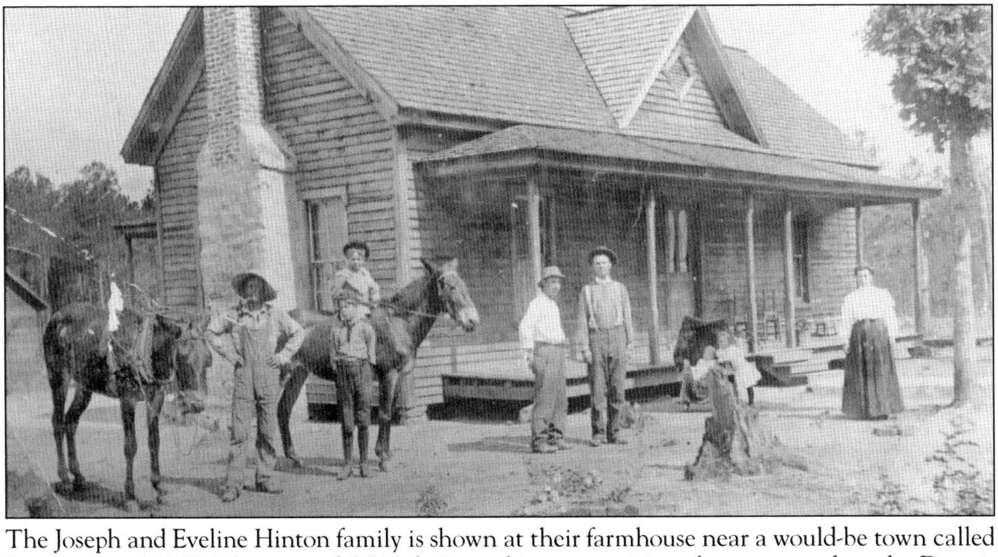

The Joseph and Eveline Hinton family is shown at their farmhouse near a would-be town called Dixie, around 1900. This area of O'Neals Township was envisioned as a town when the Dennis Simmons Lumber Company built a tram railway from Kenly around 1910 and began a huge sawmill operation. After eight years of feverishly harvesting the area's virgin timber, the company closed down its Johnston County operation, and dreams of Dixie were gone with the wind.

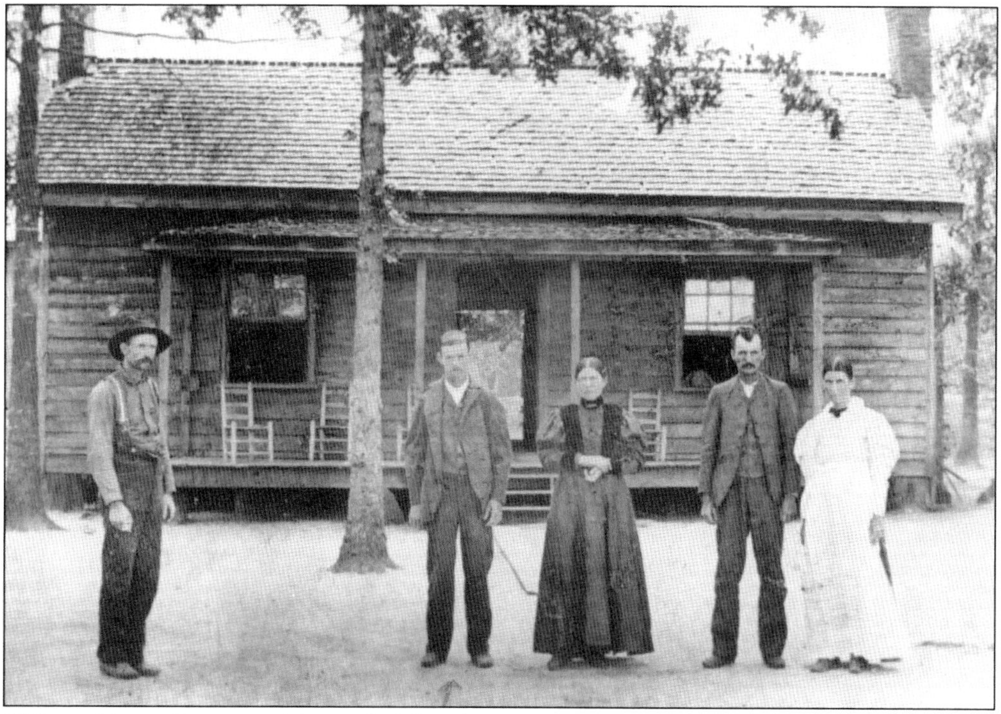

William Henry Batten and his wife, Mary (at center), are entertaining Sunday visitors Elisha Grant (left) and Thomas and Martha Wellons (right) at their home near Micro in July 1897.

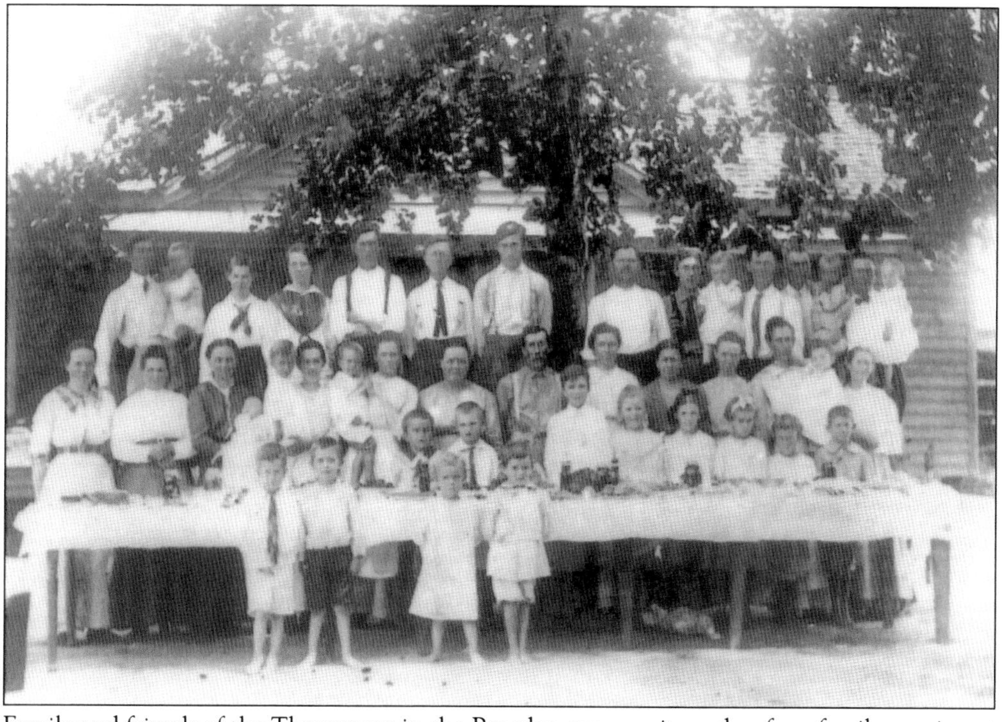

Family and friends of the Thompsons in the Brogden community gather for a family reunion at the Thompson farm in 1916. Seated at center are Richard and Callie Thompson.

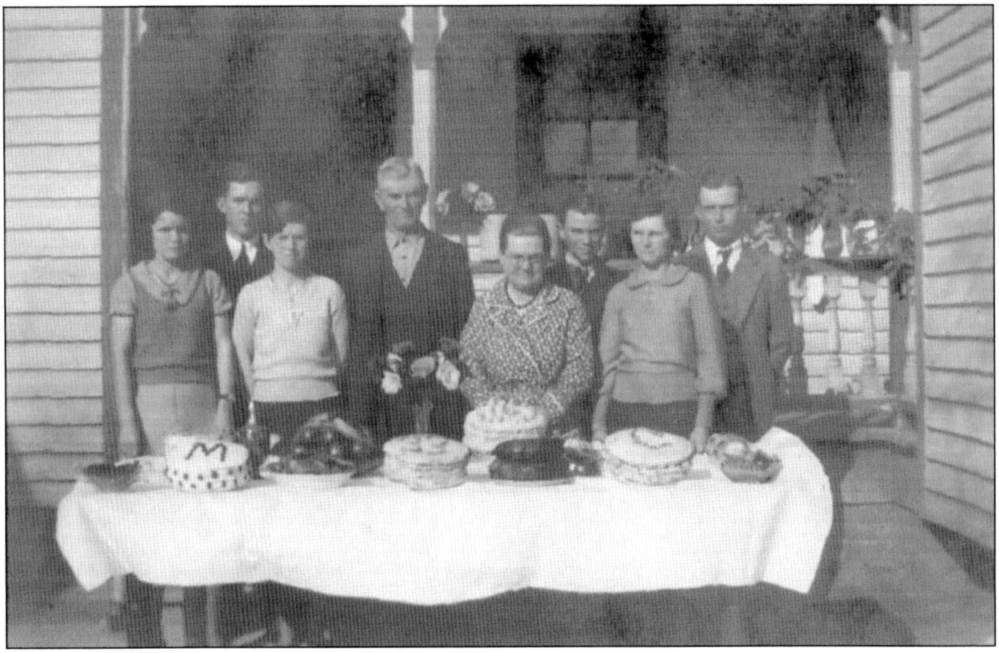

William Bennett "Billy" Massengill Jr. (fourth from left) and his wife, Sarah Cornelia "Neely" (fifth from left), of Ingrams Township are flanked by children Alton, Lawrence, Fulton, Pernella, Gladys, and Daisy in this 1933 family reunion photograph. The elder Massengill was a sturdy, self-sufficient farmer who embraced scientific agriculture earlier than most Johnstonians. He made practically everything used on the farm and grew plug tobacco and crafted coffins for his neighbors. Like most Johnston farmers in the 19th and early 20th centuries, he was staunch Primitive Baptist. (Courtesy of Stanton Massengill.)

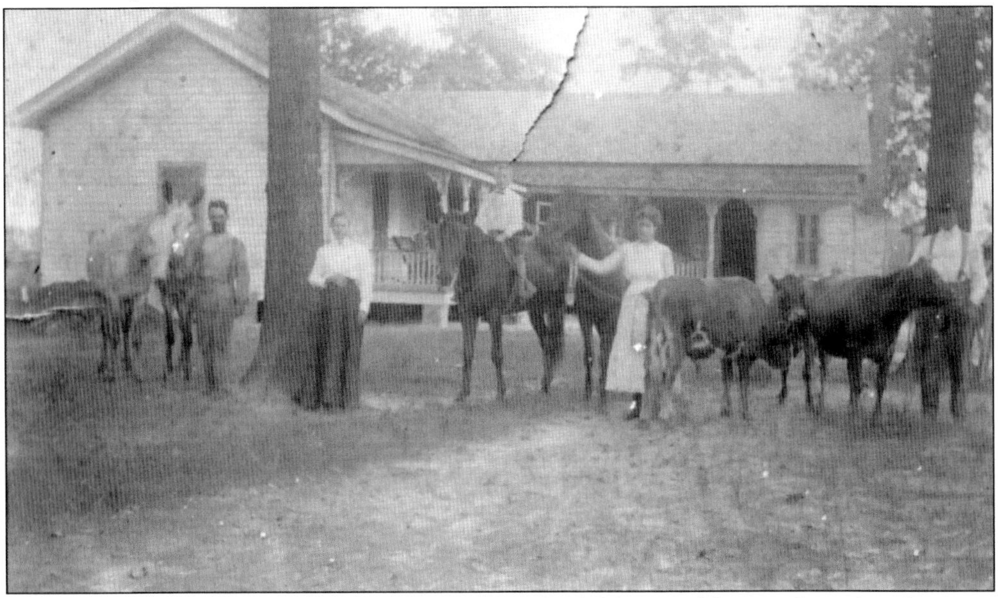

Ben and Effie Casey, shown at left, are posing with children and livestock at their home in Smithfield Township around 1910. The farm was on present-day Swift Creek Road, near Johnston Regional Airport. (Courtesy of Margaret Powell Benton.)

Members of the David and Mary Johnson Wood family of Cleveland Township gathered for this photograph around 1910 when Mary Elizabeth Wood Lyon came from Raleigh for a visit. (Courtesy of Judy Coley Reibel.)

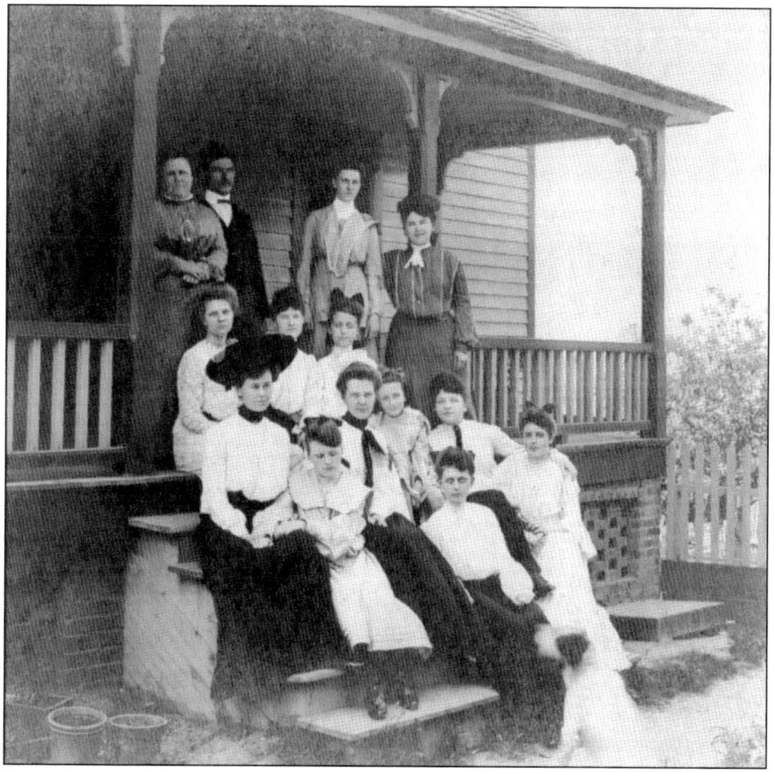

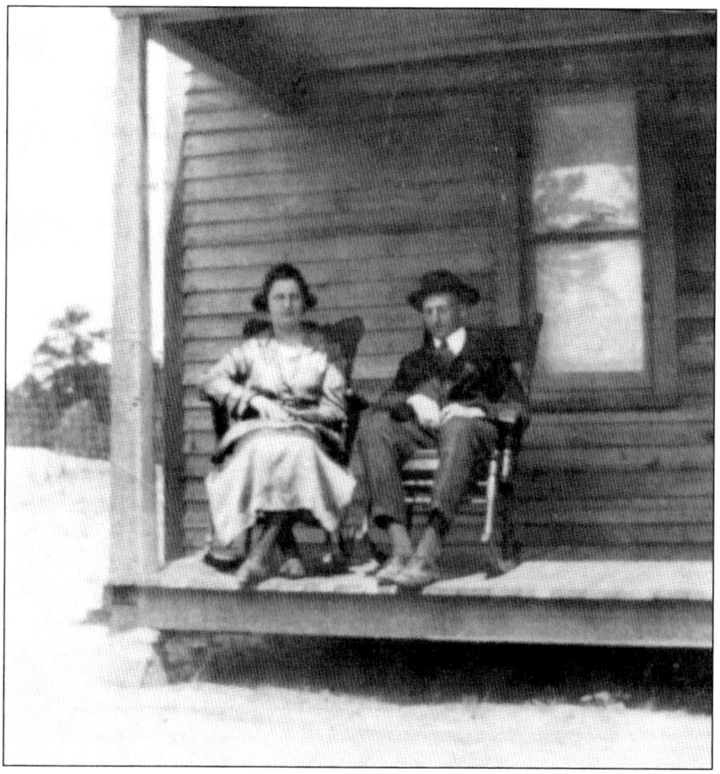

Ora Collins (left), a teacher at Rehobeth School in Elevation Township, was relaxing with Victor Clifton (right) on the Clifton family's porch about 1916 when this photograph was taken. Collins was one of several teachers who boarded at the Clifton home in the early 20th century. Many of the teachers came from the mountains of North Carolina.

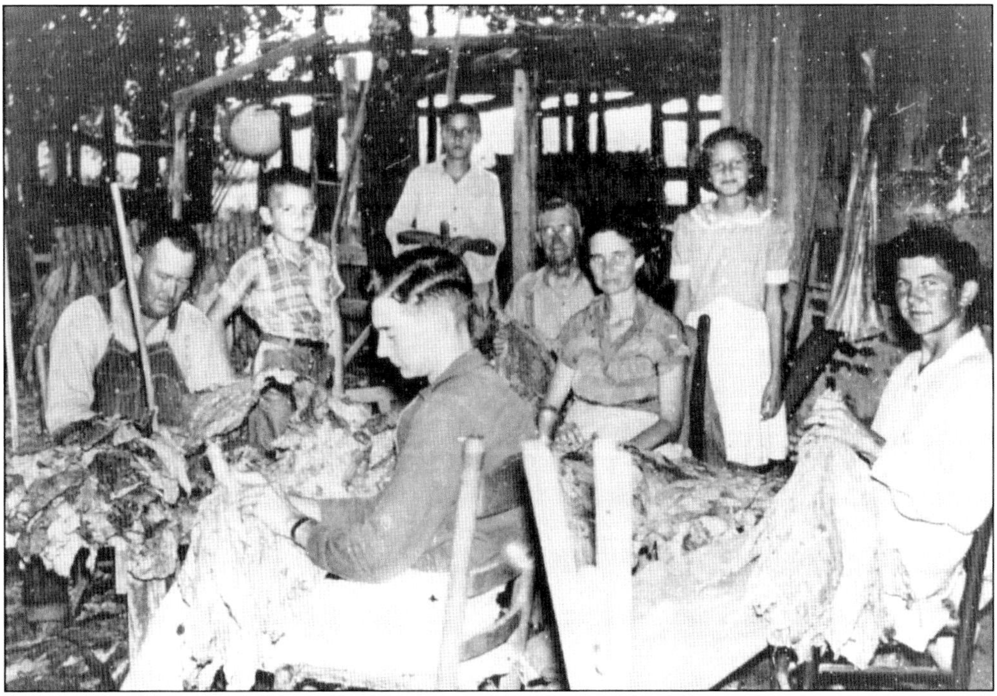

Grading tobacco is a family affair for this unidentified group in the 1940s or 1950s. The cured leaves had to be sorted based on quality and tied in bundles before being taken to market.

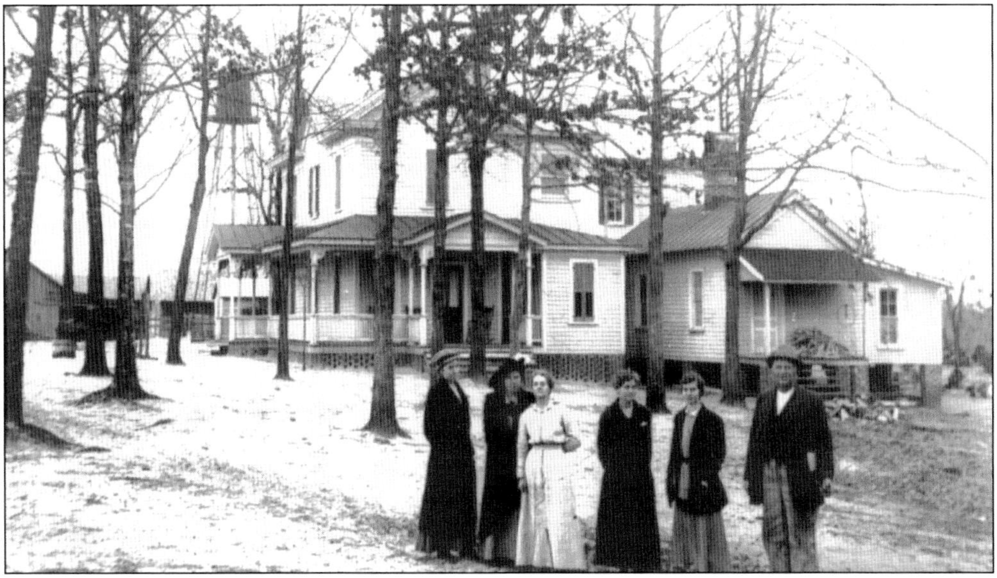

John H. B. Tomlinson (far right) posed with, from left to right, sisters Lizzie Smith and Emma Tomlinson; his wife, Edith Turner Tomlinson; and daughters Helen and Mary Louise at his Woodsdale Farm in 1916. The farmhouse still stands on Wellons Road near Smithfield. Long before there was a chamber of commerce, Tomlinson invited prospective investors from the North to his home, where he entertained and took them hunting and fishing.

Two

SMALL-TOWN LIFE

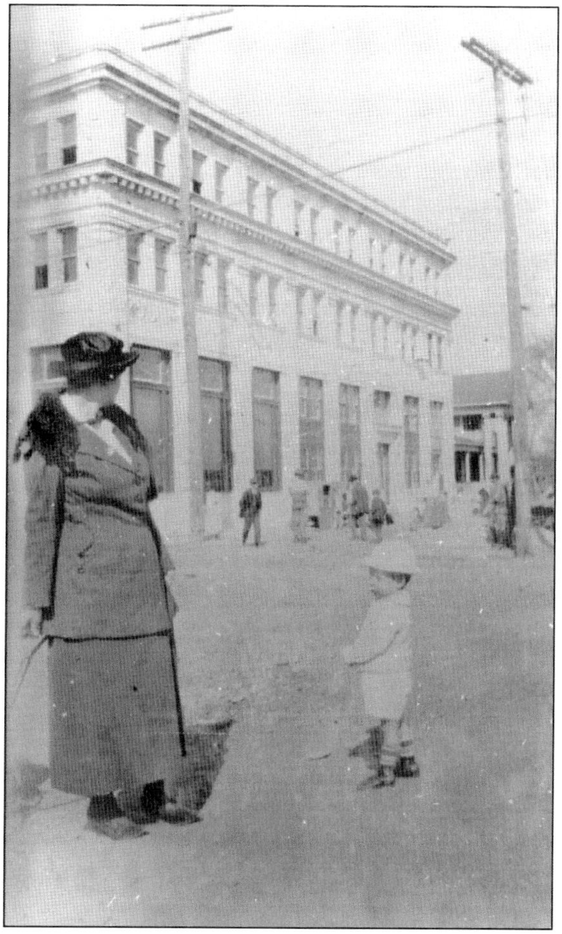

Felicia Whitaker Warren and her son cross Benson's Main Street in the early 1920s, when the town's streets were still unpaved. First National Bank, later First Citizens and now home to the public library, is shown in the background. (Courtesy of Benson Museum of Local History.)

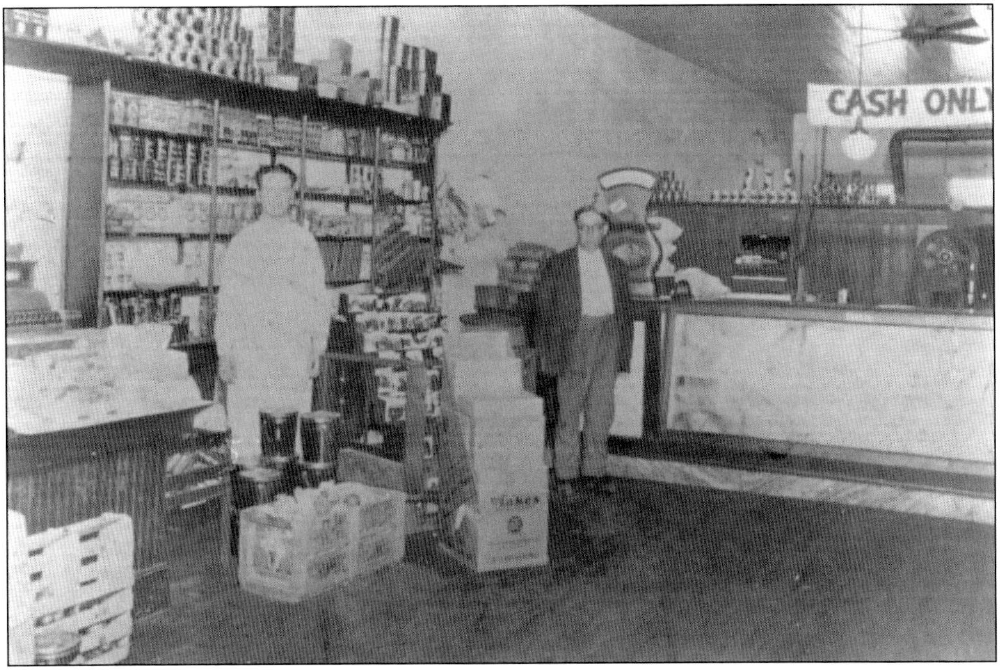

Benson's Town Market, owned and operated by Jeff and L.O. Matthews, has plenty of floor space to spare in this Depression-era photograph. (Courtesy of Benson Museum of Local History.)

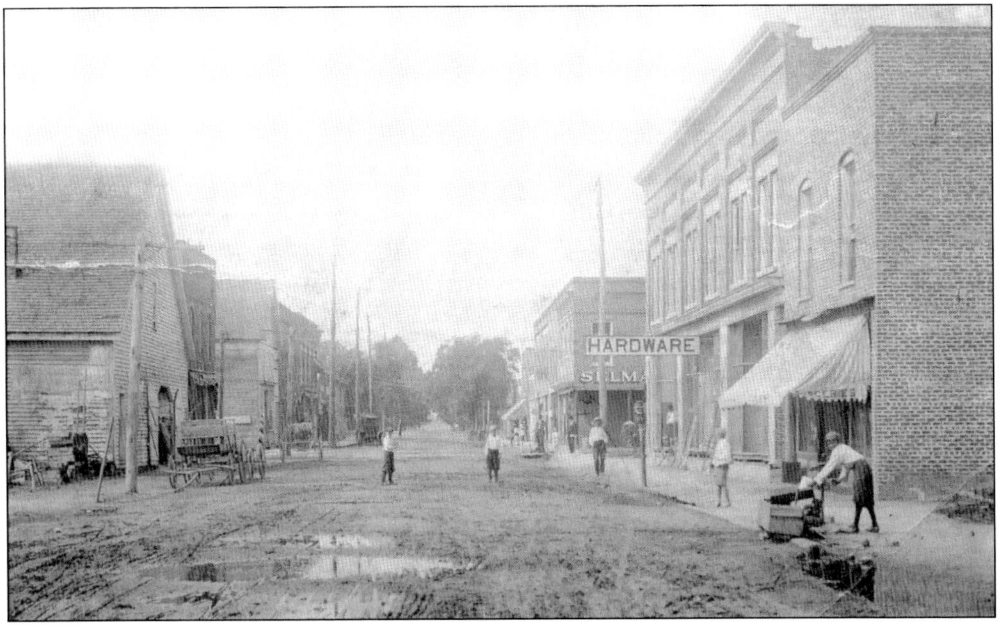

Boys in knickers and newsboy caps are avoiding mud puddles on Selma's unpaved Raiford Street around 1910. Wide, tree-lined streets are seen in the distance. (Courtesy of Lewis Mullen.)

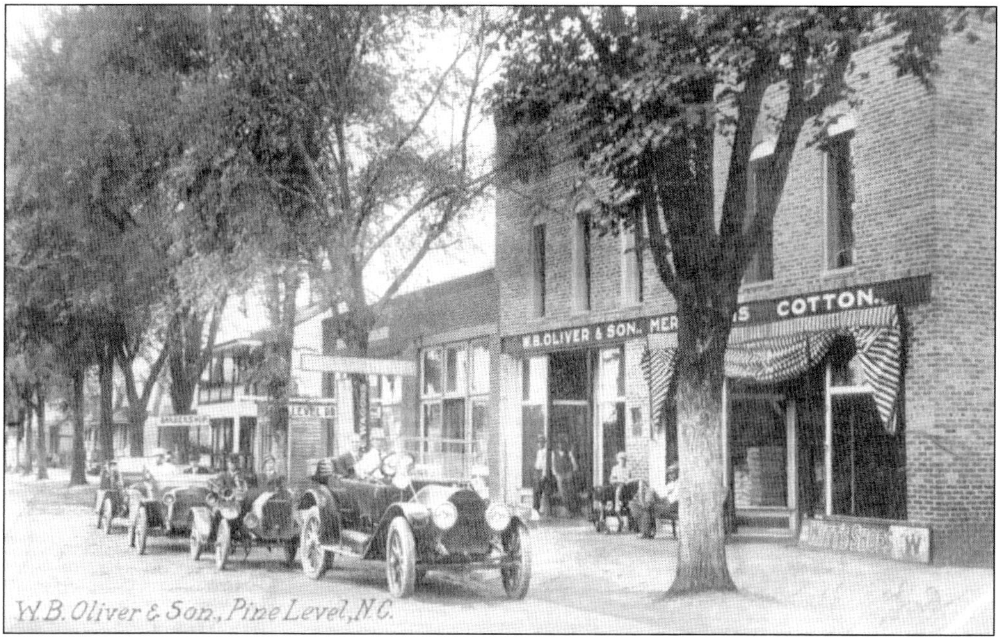

Pine Level had a small but prosperous commercial center on the eve of World War I, when this photograph was taken. William Berry Oliver was a founder of the town in the post–Civil War era, and his son Doc Berry Oliver and other heirs kept the family farm supply business going for 114 years, closing in 1980. W.B. and his brother Tom Oliver were involved in turpentine production in their early years, hence the town's name.

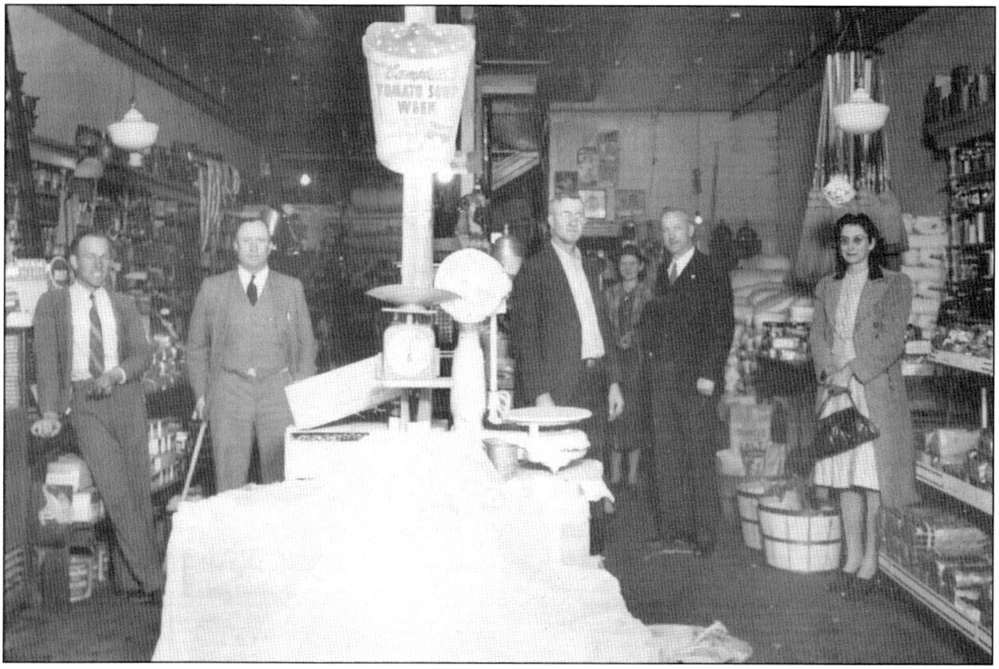

This photograph was taken inside the J. Dobbin Bailey Store in Kenly in the 1940s. Pictured here are, from left to right, Frank Woodard, Johnny Wiggs, Will Pierce, J. Dobbin Bailey, and two unidentified women. (Courtesy of Kenly Historical Association.)

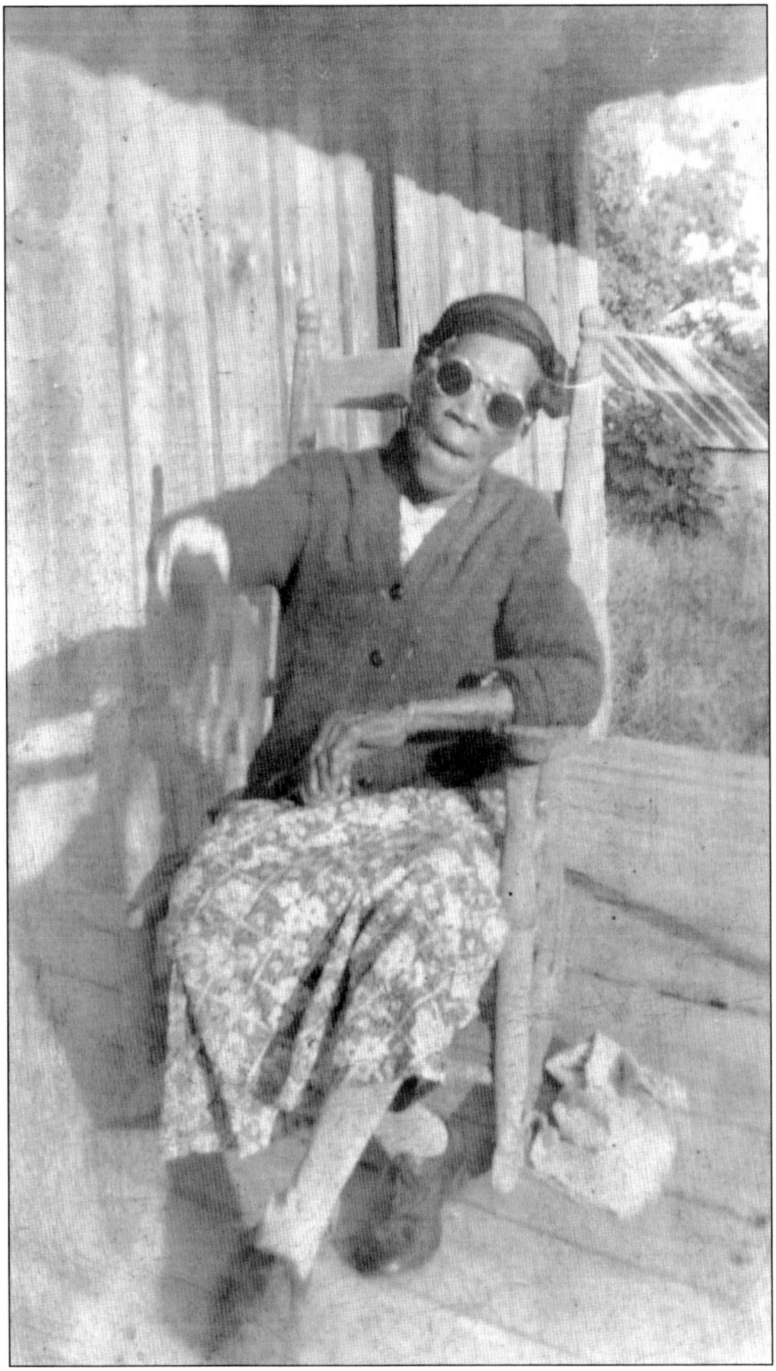

In the 1930s, Jenny Sanders was a neighbor of James Bryan Creech when he was a child growing up in Four Oaks. He was fascinated by her tales about Yankee soldiers who came through in 1865. She especially never forgot how they knocked out the end of a molasses barrel with the butts of their rifles and made the kitchen floor very sticky. In this photograph, she is sitting on the side porch of her small unpainted house, engaged in one of her friendly debates with her neighbor across the street, attorney Charles Lee.

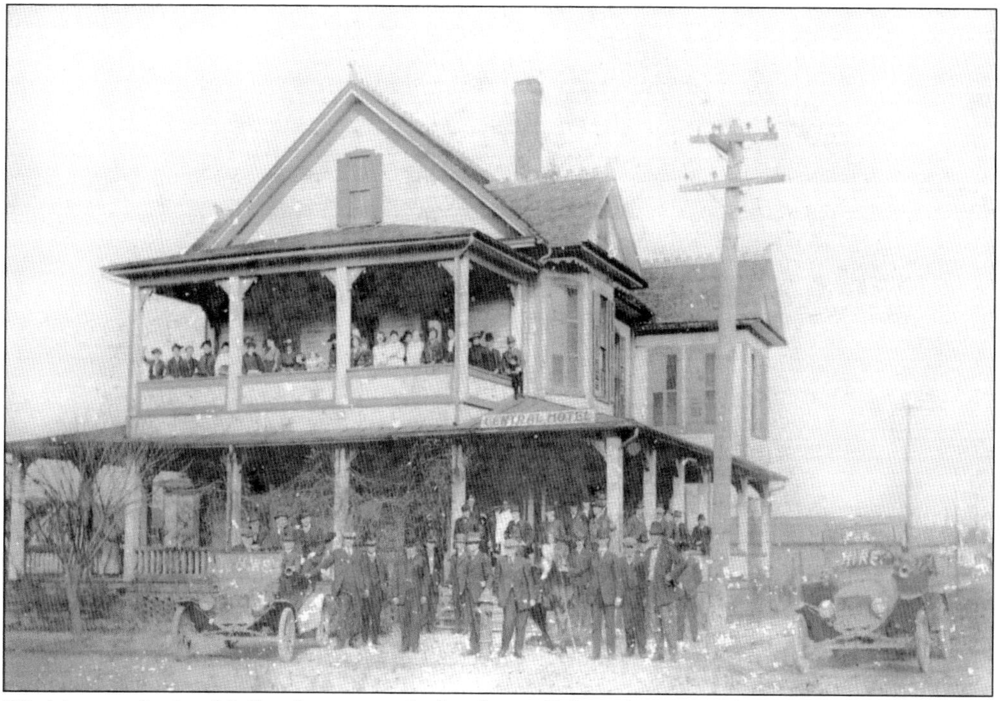

Washington Irving Holland poses with family, staff, boarders, taxi drivers, and others at his Central Hotel in Selma around 1920.

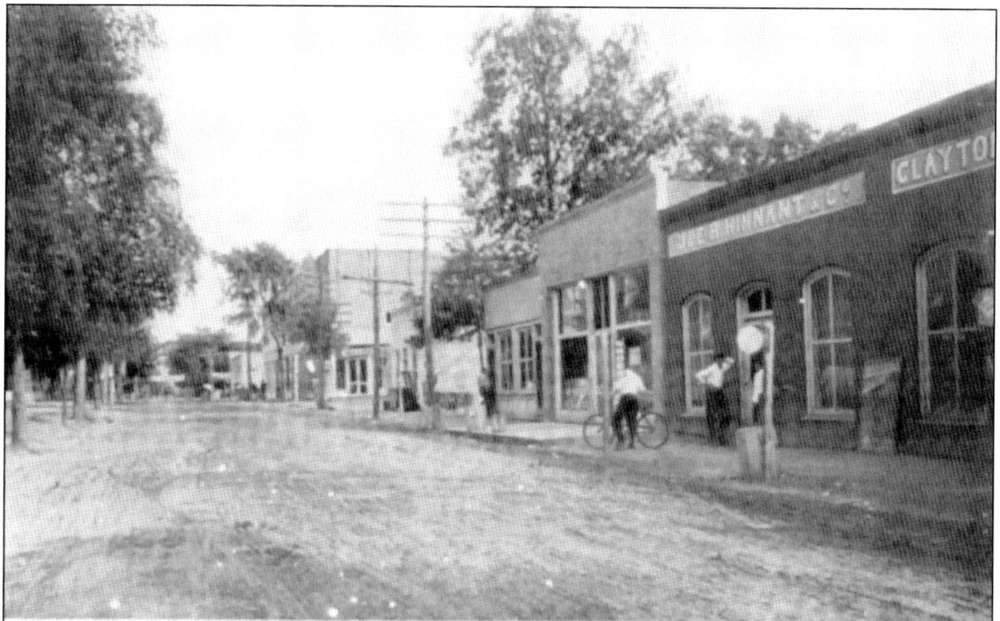

Main Street, Clayton, N. C.

Clayton's tree-lined Main Street, like streets in all other Johnston County towns before the 1920s, was still unpaved when this photograph was taken in 1912. What set this town apart from the rest was its designation as the richest small town in the United States at the turn of the 20th century.

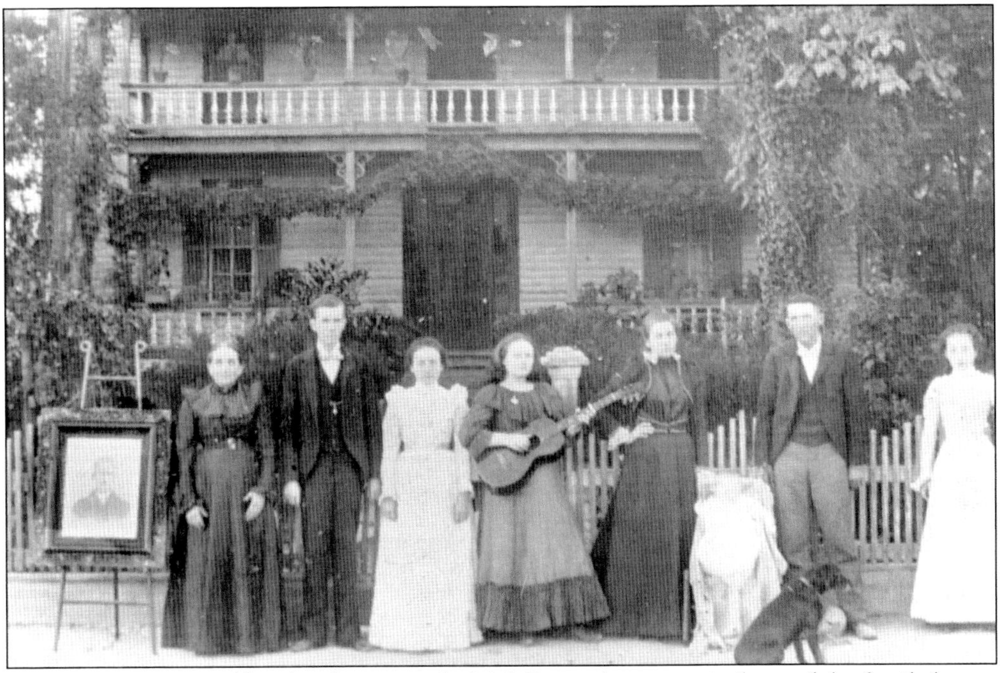

Catherine Benson and her family pose with A.M. Benson's portrait in front of the family home, located in the town that bears their family name. After Benson was chartered in 1887, the Bensons sold 45 acres to the town for $1. (Courtesy of Benson Museum of Local History.)

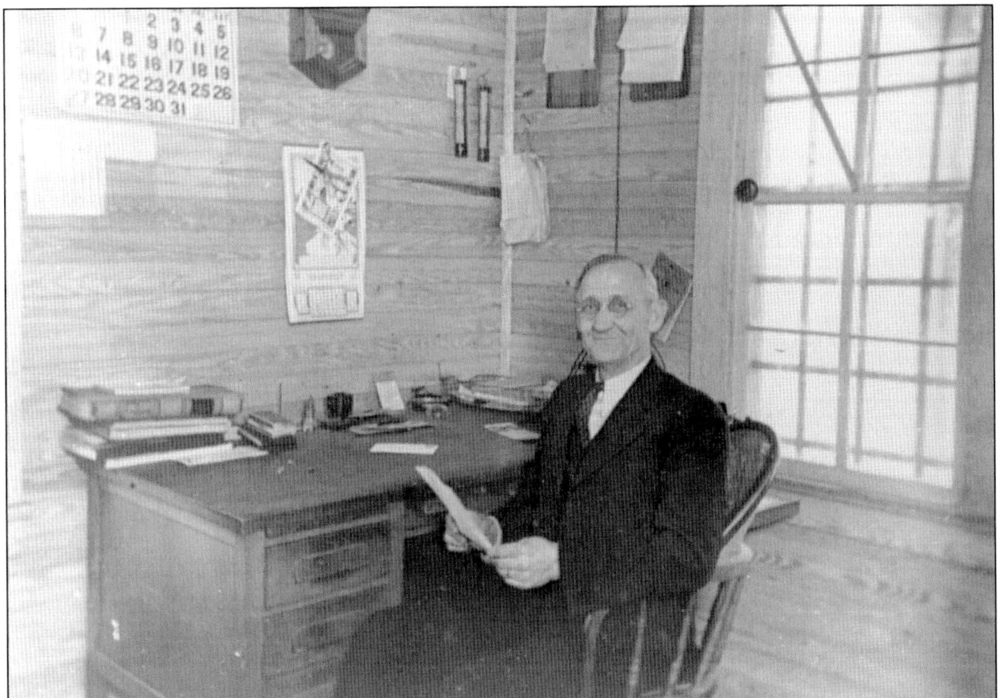

Benson farm supply merchant J.H. "Bud" Godwin is pictured here in his office in 1935. (Courtesy of Benson Museum of Local History.)

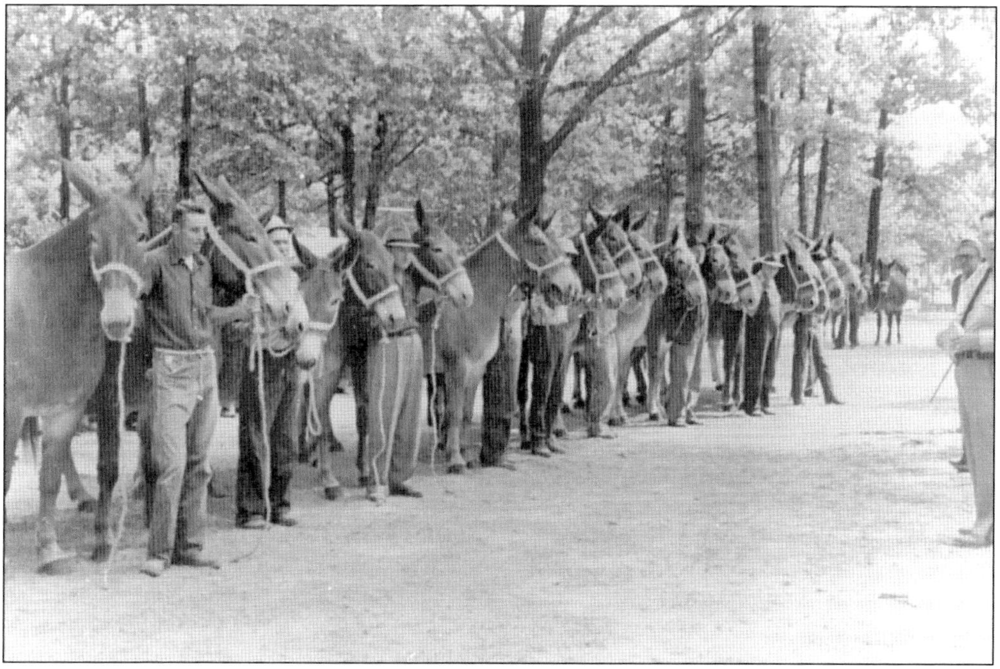

Benson's largest annual festival, Mule Days, began in 1950 and continues to draw thousands every September. This 1950s image shows mules lined up for judging. (Courtesy of Benson Museum of Local History.)

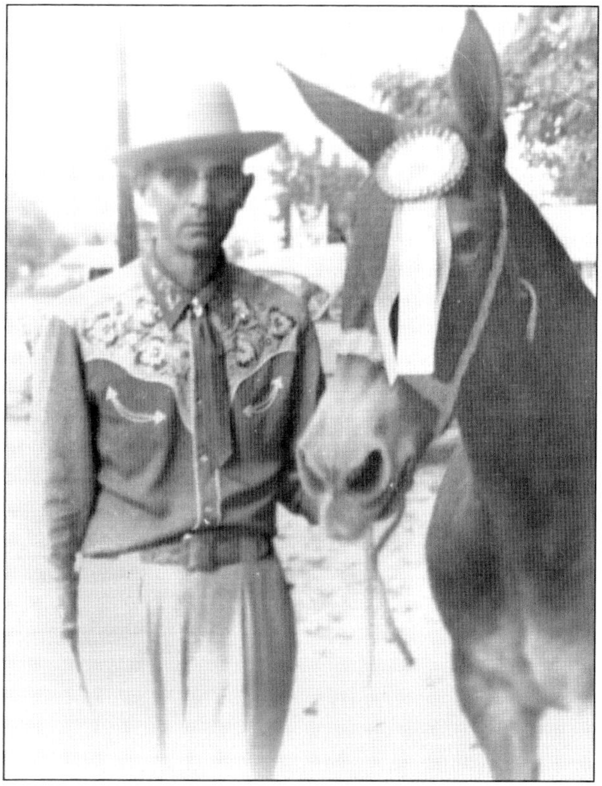

Mule Days cofounder Nowell Smith is shown with his prize-winning mule during an early Mule Days event in Benson in the 1950s. (Courtesy of Benson Museum of Local History.)

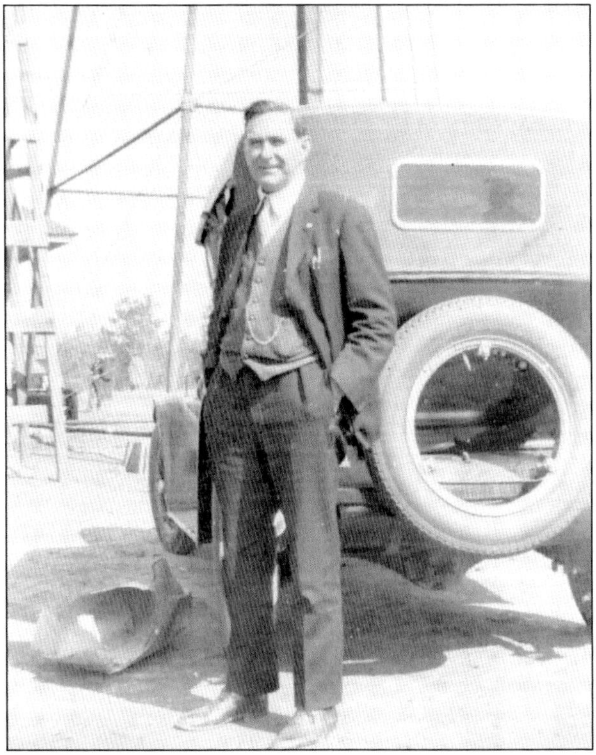

Micro was proud to have on its high school faculty in 1925–1926 Dr. Benjamin Marvin Shacklette, a graduate student at Duke University, who poses here near the water tower. He was a Baptist minister who served as president of several small colleges in Missouri, Kansas, and Kentucky before finding his way to Johnston's tiniest town. Louise Moser wrote in her high school scrapbook that his chief virtue was religion, he was always telling stories, and his favorite expression was "put it over." She also cited two passages of scripture under his name: 2 Timothy 2:15 and 1 Thessalonians 5:28.

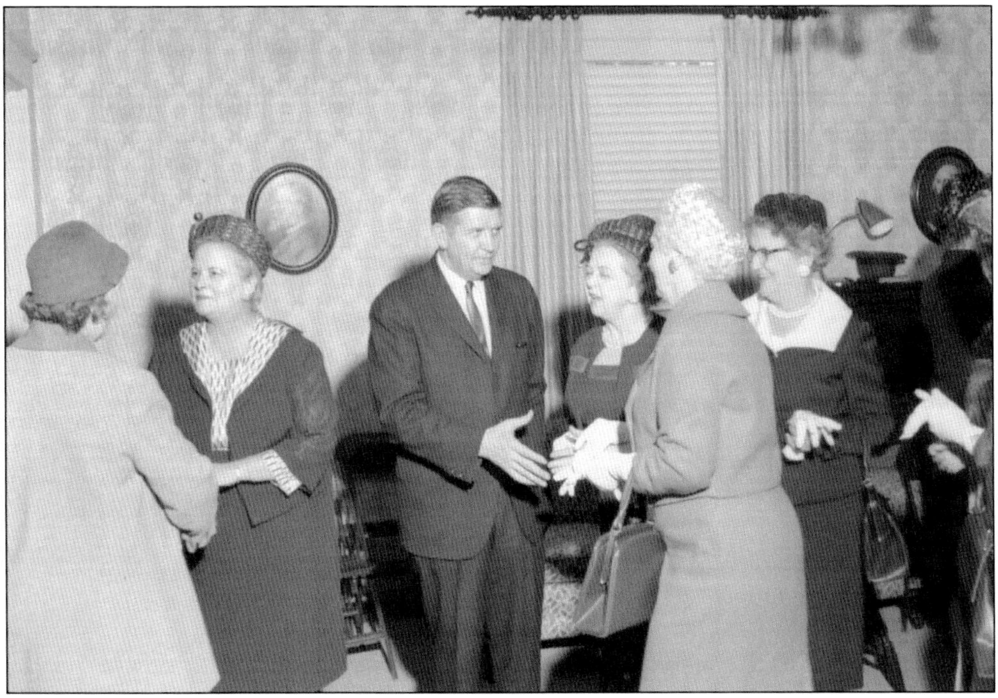

North Carolina governor Terry Sanford is charmed by some of Clayton's finest ladies during this reception at the Clayton Woman's Club in 1962. (Photograph by Charles Barden; courtesy of Hocutt-Ellington Memorial Library.)

Ashley Horne II (right) entertains a female guest at the Horne mansion in Clayton around 1910. (Courtesy of Hocutt-Ellington Memorial Library.)

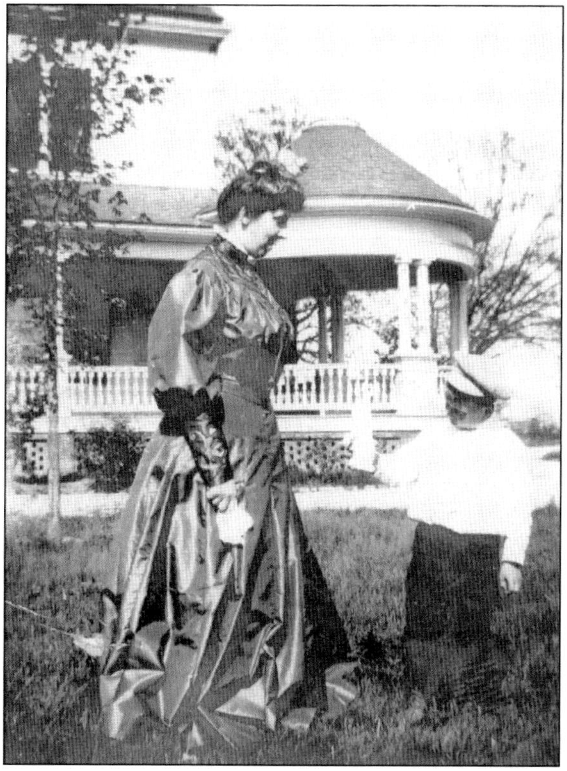

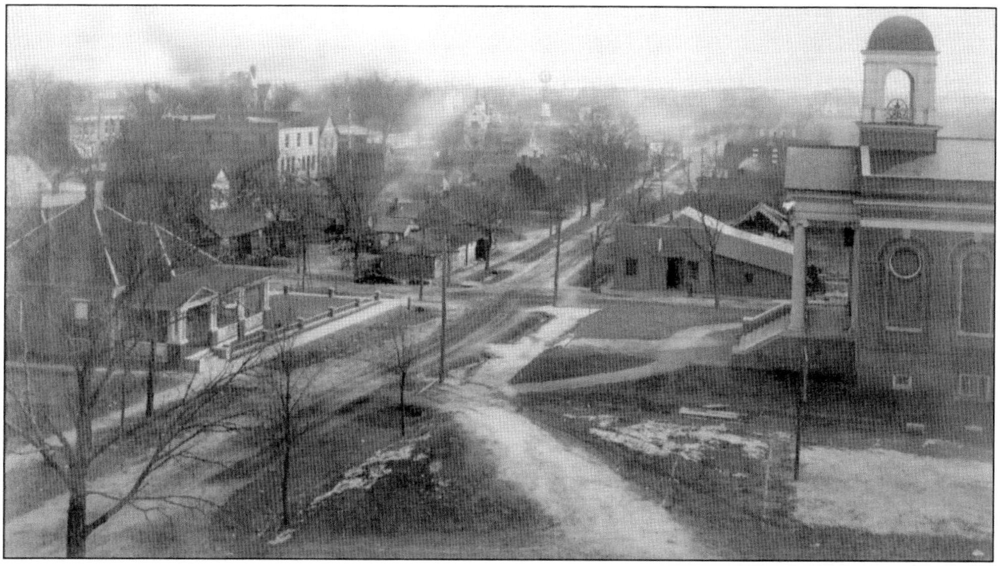

This bird's-eye view of the intersection of Second and Church Streets in Clayton shows the newly completed Horne Memorial Methodist Church, named in honor of its largest benefactor, Ashley Horne. He insisted the church be named St. James, but the wishes of a grateful congregation prevailed following his death in 1913. The stained-glass windows in the sanctuary were made by Tiffany Studios in New York and shipped to Clayton by train in 1916, shortly before the firm closed. The imposing Horne residence is visible in the background of this photograph, which was taken from the roof of Clayton High School. (Courtesy of Hocutt-Ellington Memorial Library)

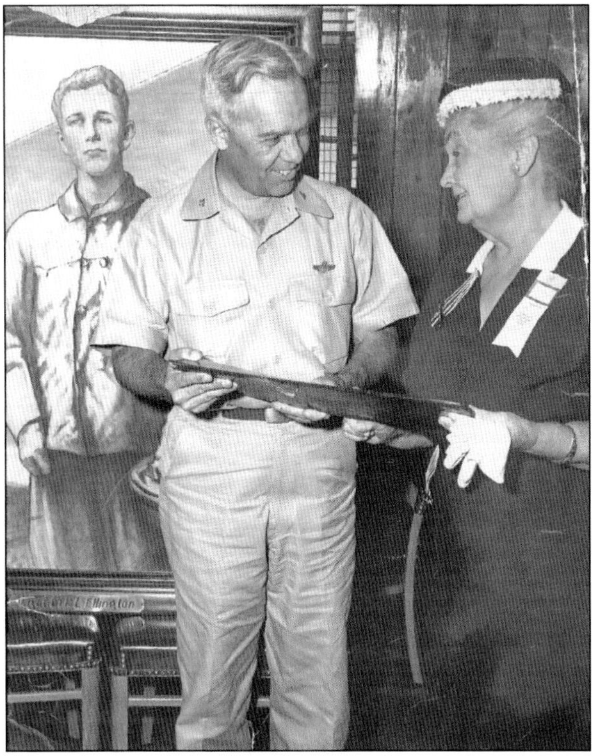

Lucille Ellington Hocutt of Clayton receives a grand tour of Houston's Ellington Air Force Base, named for her brother Eric, while attending the Southern Baptist Convention in 1958. "Miss Lucille" was an iconic personality in Clayton for much of the 20th century, as was her esteemed husband, Dr. Battle A. Hocutt. She provided land for the public library, which bears her and her husband's family names. (Courtesy of Hocutt-Ellington Memorial Library.)

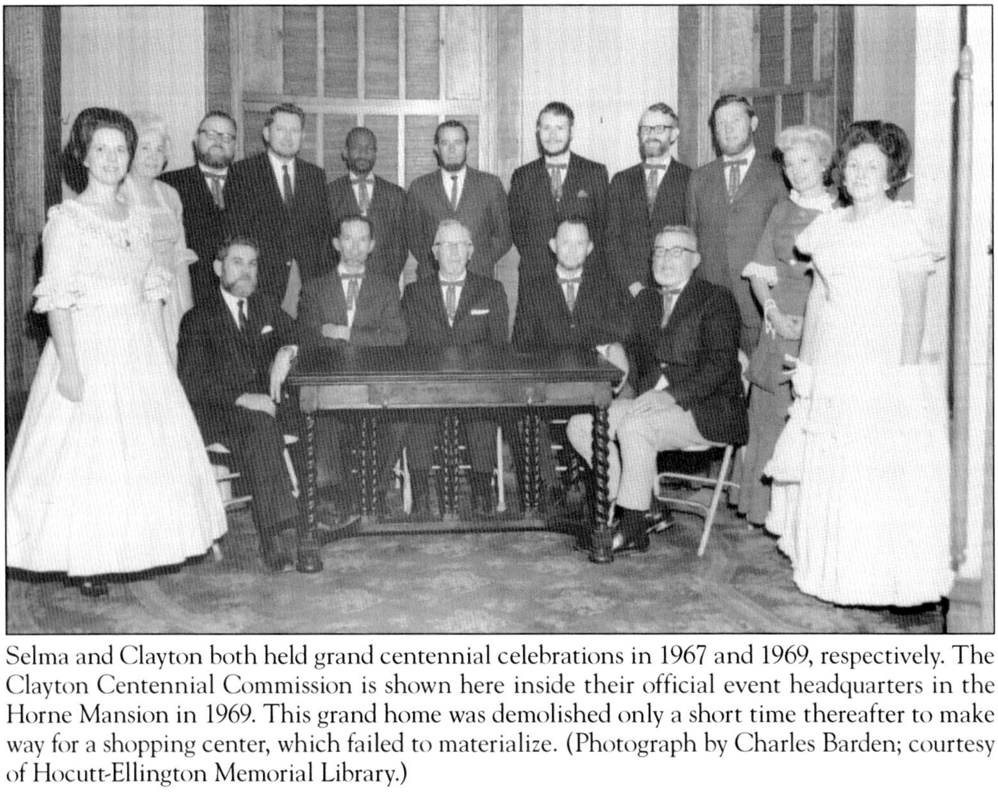

Selma and Clayton both held grand centennial celebrations in 1967 and 1969, respectively. The Clayton Centennial Commission is shown here inside their official event headquarters in the Horne Mansion in 1969. This grand home was demolished only a short time thereafter to make way for a shopping center, which failed to materialize. (Photograph by Charles Barden; courtesy of Hocutt-Ellington Memorial Library.)

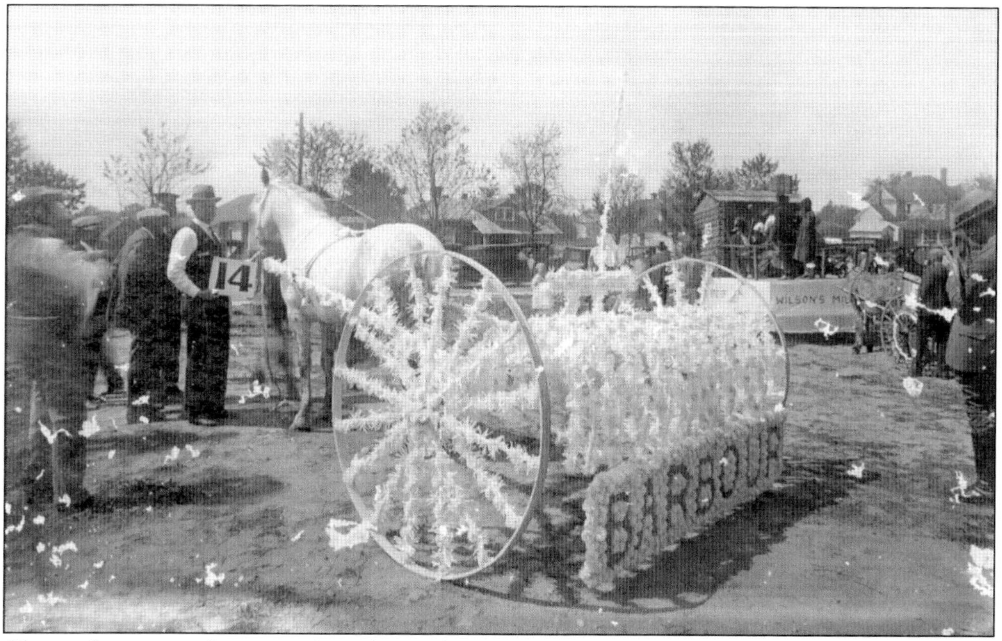

Clayton farming implement and supply merchant J. Dwight Barbour lines up for what is believed to be a 1920s Fourth of July parade in Smithfield. (Courtesy of Hocutt-Ellington Memorial Library.)

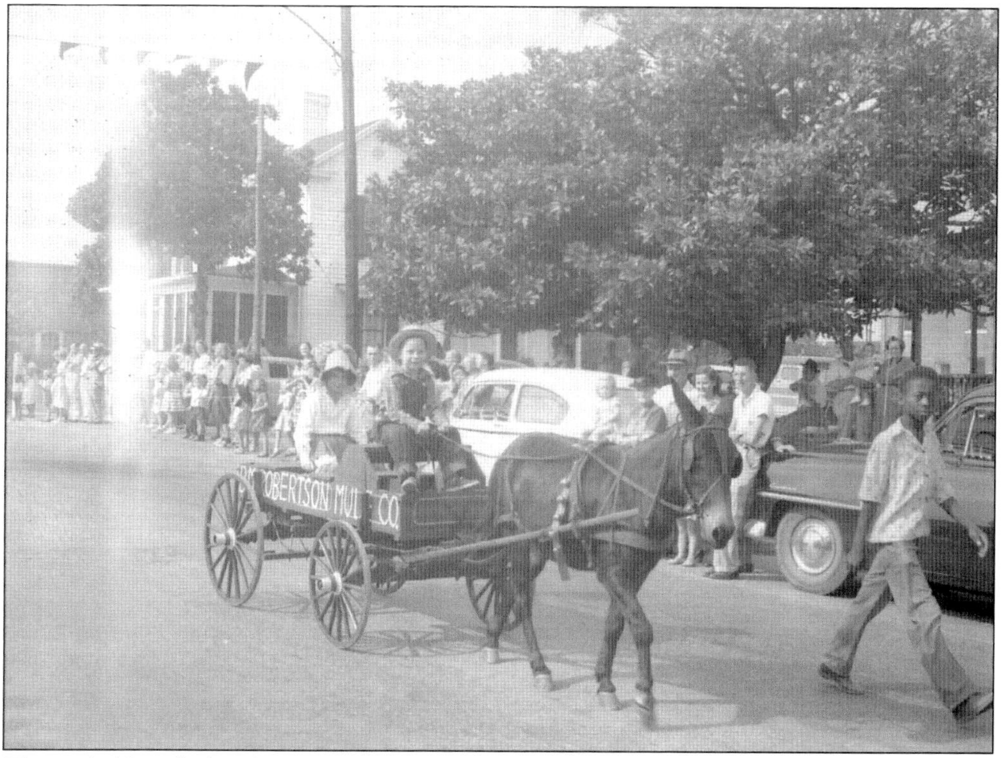

These children help Clayton folks celebrate their agricultural heritage during the annual Cotton Festival Parade in 1953. (Photograph by Charles Barden; courtesy of Hocutt-Ellington Memorial Library.)

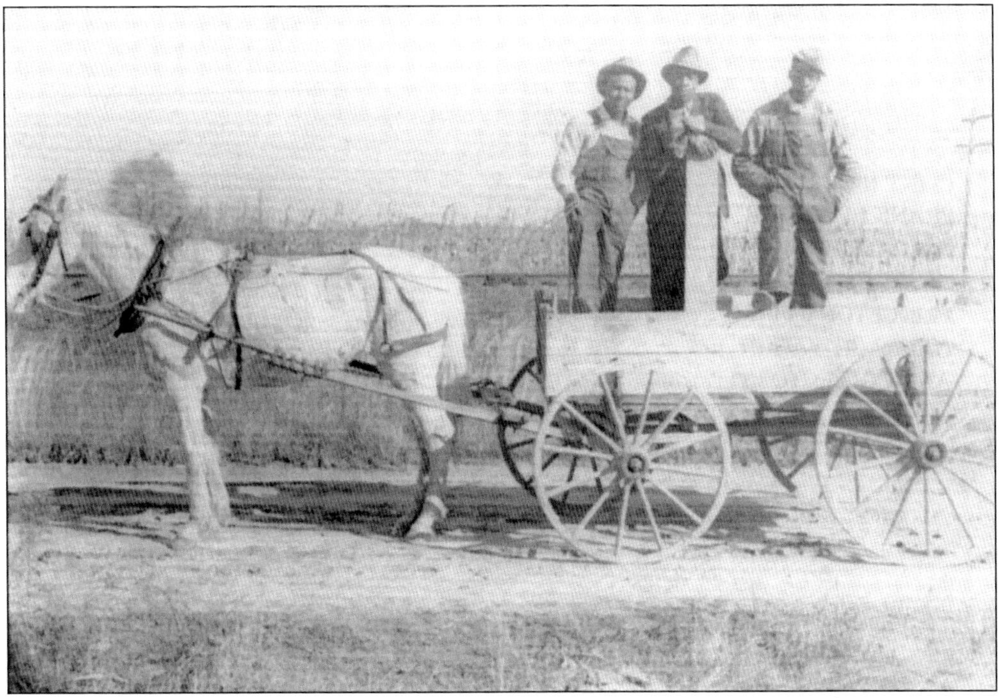

From left to right, Clint Noble, Frank Everette, and Jim Campbell are pictured on Princeton's first garbage wagon in 1937.

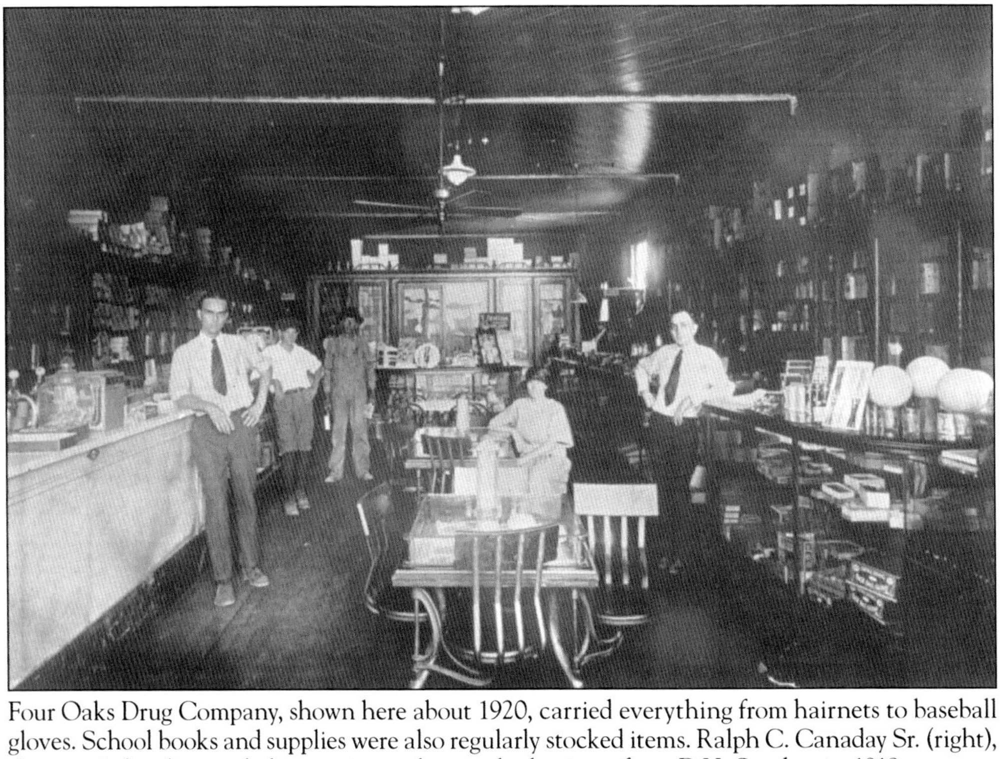

Four Oaks Drug Company, shown here about 1920, carried everything from hairnets to baseball gloves. School books and supplies were also regularly stocked items. Ralph C. Canaday Sr. (right), the town's first licensed pharmacist, took over the business from D.H. Sanders in 1918.

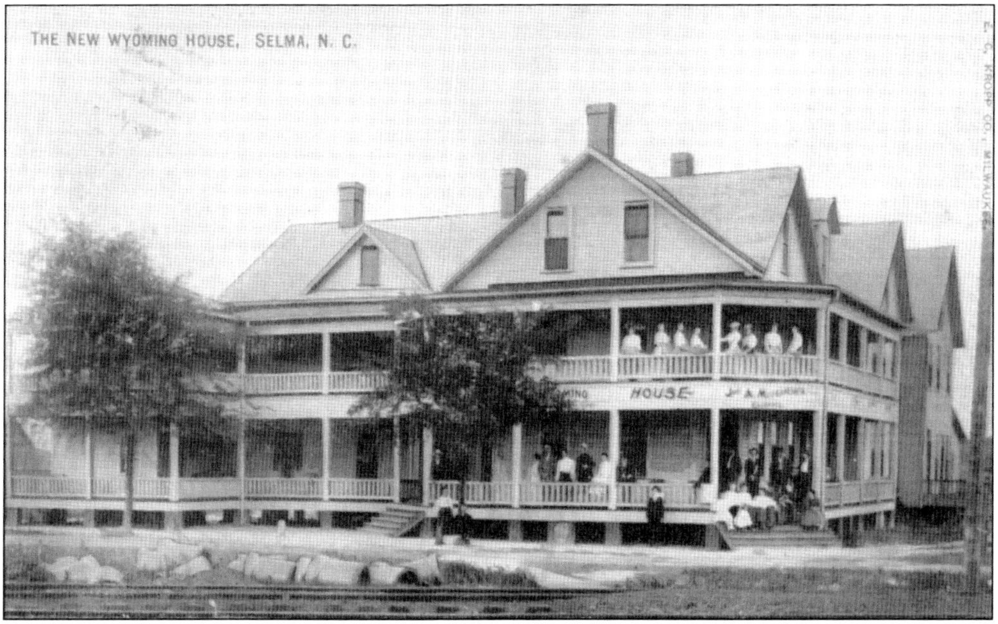

This postcard image from 1910 shows the sprawling Wyoming House, owned and operated by John A. Mitchener, next to the railroad tracks in Selma. Businessmen, politicians, and other prominent men who were frequent guests here enjoyed listening to Mitchener's many tales, especially one about a rock with a tongue that wagged.

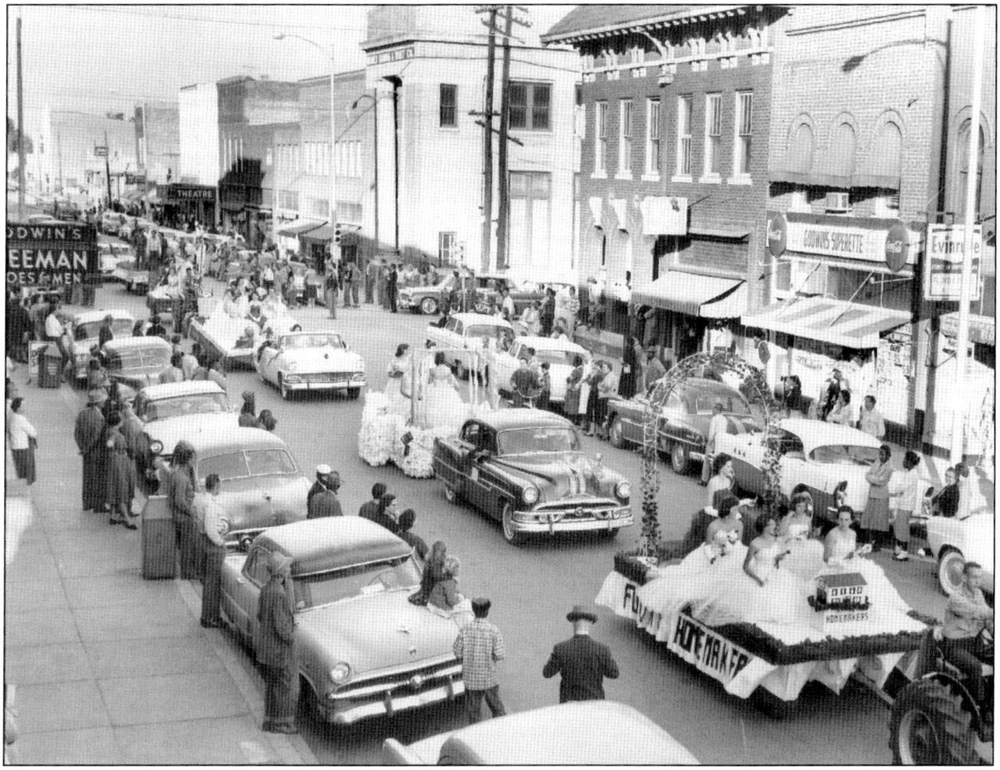

This 1950s parade in Selma is believed to be a Selma High School homecoming event.

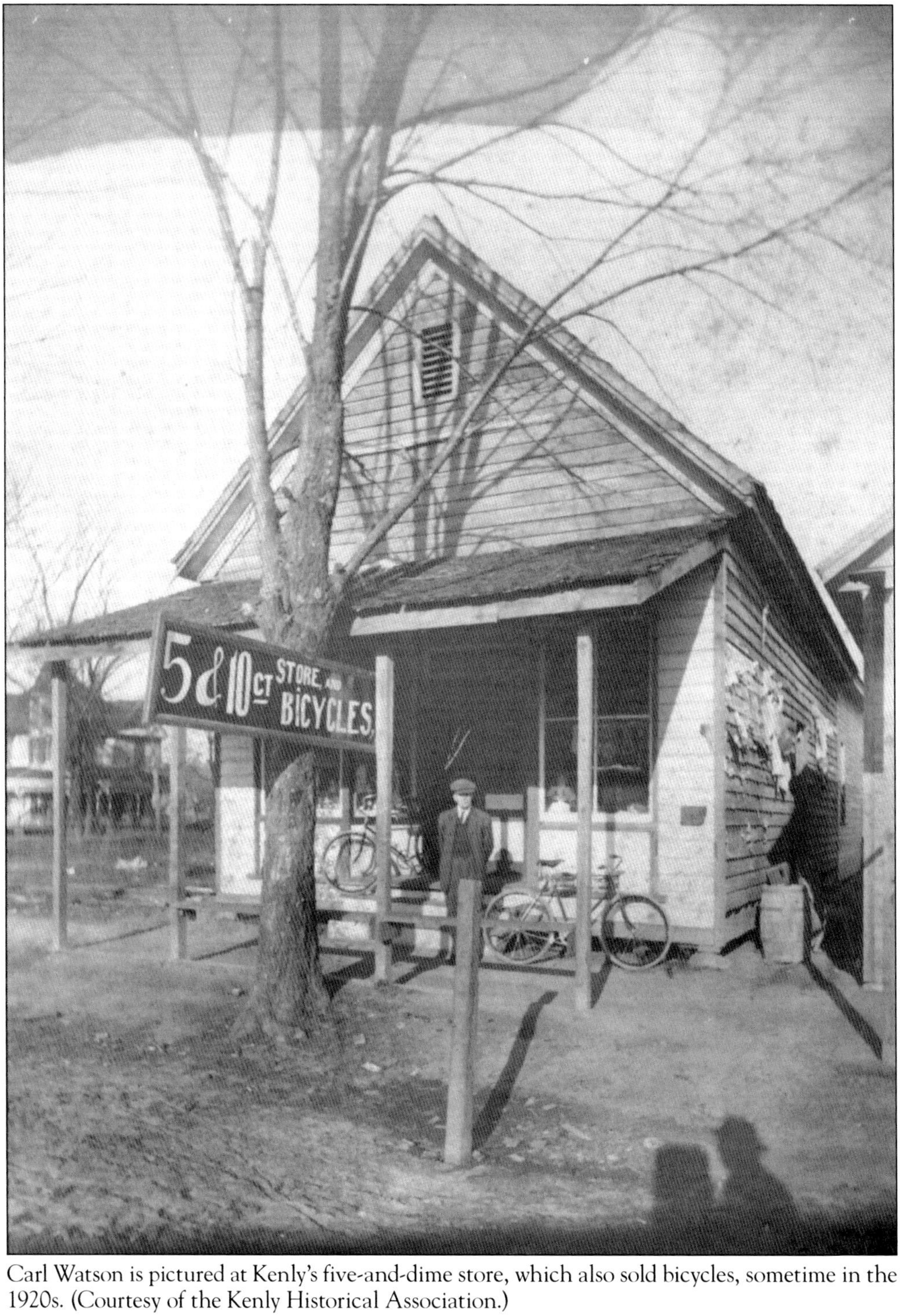

Carl Watson is pictured at Kenly's five-and-dime store, which also sold bicycles, sometime in the 1920s. (Courtesy of the Kenly Historical Association.)

Three

County Seat

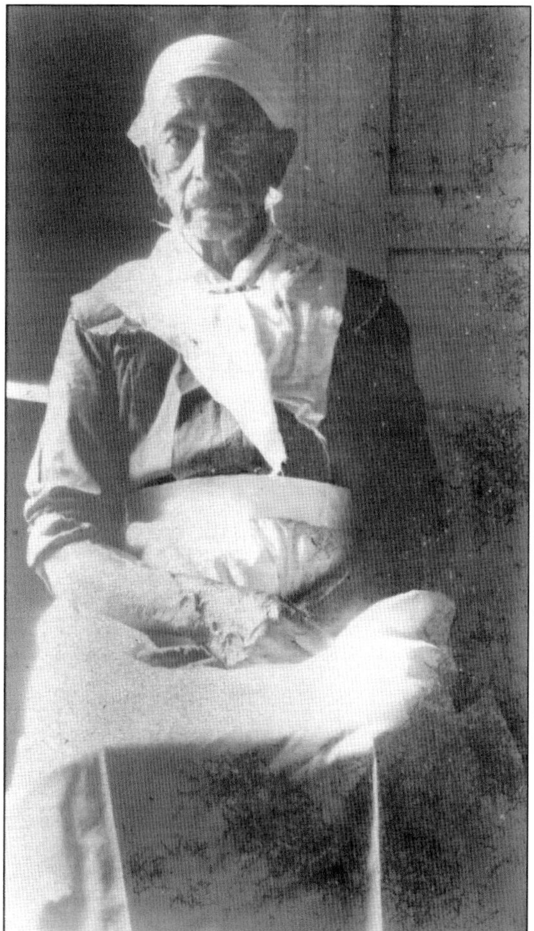

This rare photograph shows Fanny Morgan, one of many former slaves who worked in Smithfield in the late 19th and early 20th centuries. Her contemporaries cooked sumptuous meals, cleaned houses, boiled laundry in big iron pots and scrubbed on washboards, ironed, raised children, midwifed, and provided other vital services for the well-to-do as they struggled to provide for themselves and their own families. Lucy Sanders Hood wrote on the back of this photograph, "Aunt Fanny Morgan-Negro and Indian-blessed all our chicken."

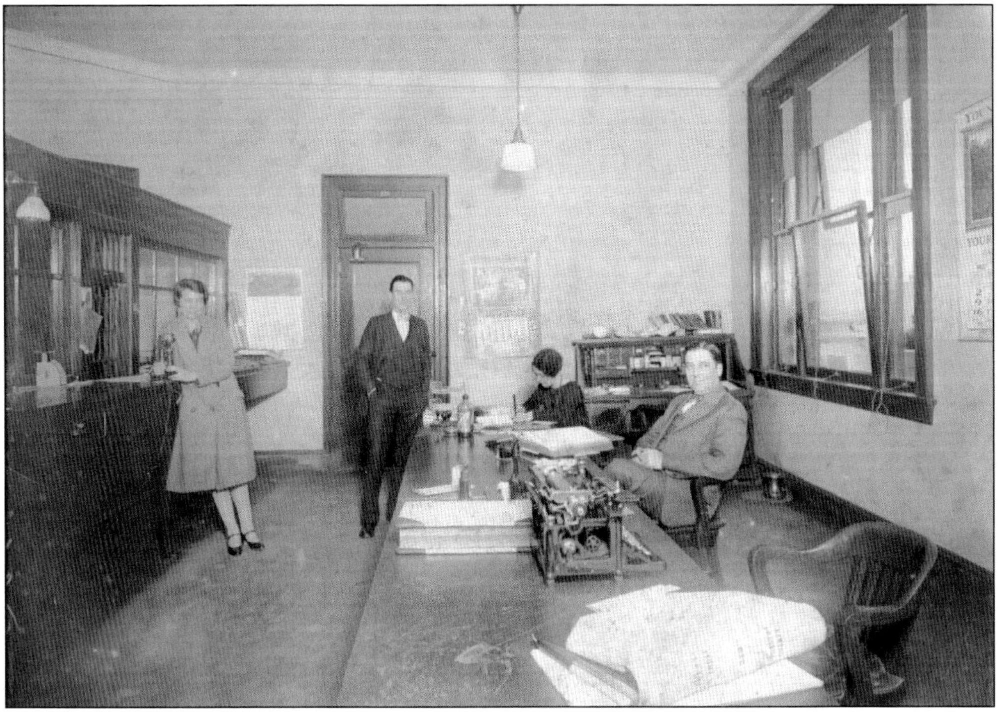

This photograph of the Johnston County Register of Deeds Office in January 1927 was found in the belongings of Cora Belle Ives, who worked in the nearby law office of Judge F.H. Brooks. The young man near the doorway is believed to be Neil Barnes of Clayton, register of deeds.

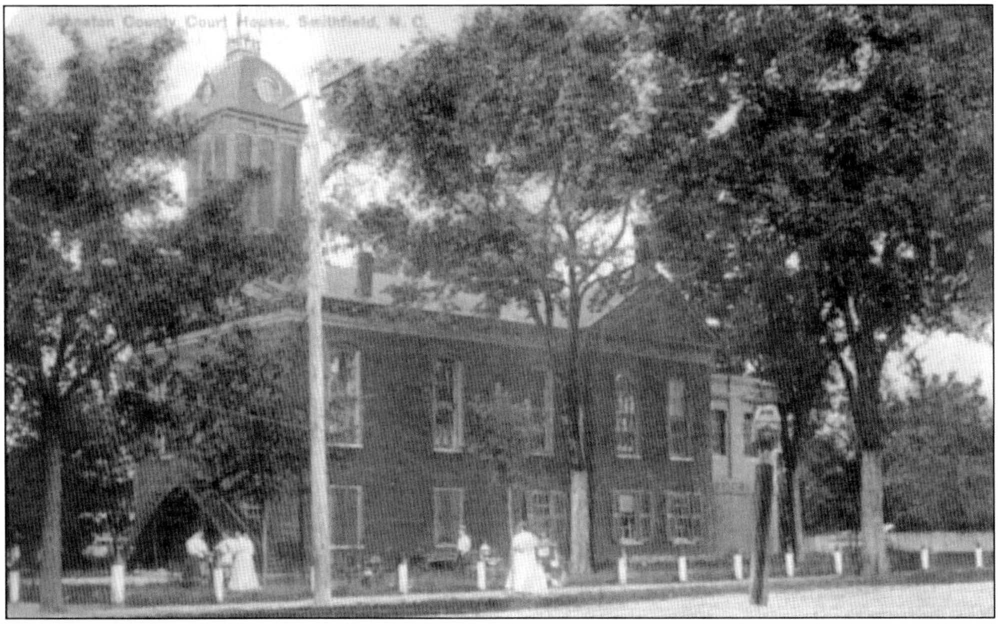

This postcard image from 1909 shows the old Johnston County Courthouse, built in 1843 and demolished in 1921 to make way for the present courthouse at the corner of Smithfield's Market and Second Streets. At the time of the Civil War, this building and the adjacent jailhouse were the only brick structures in town.

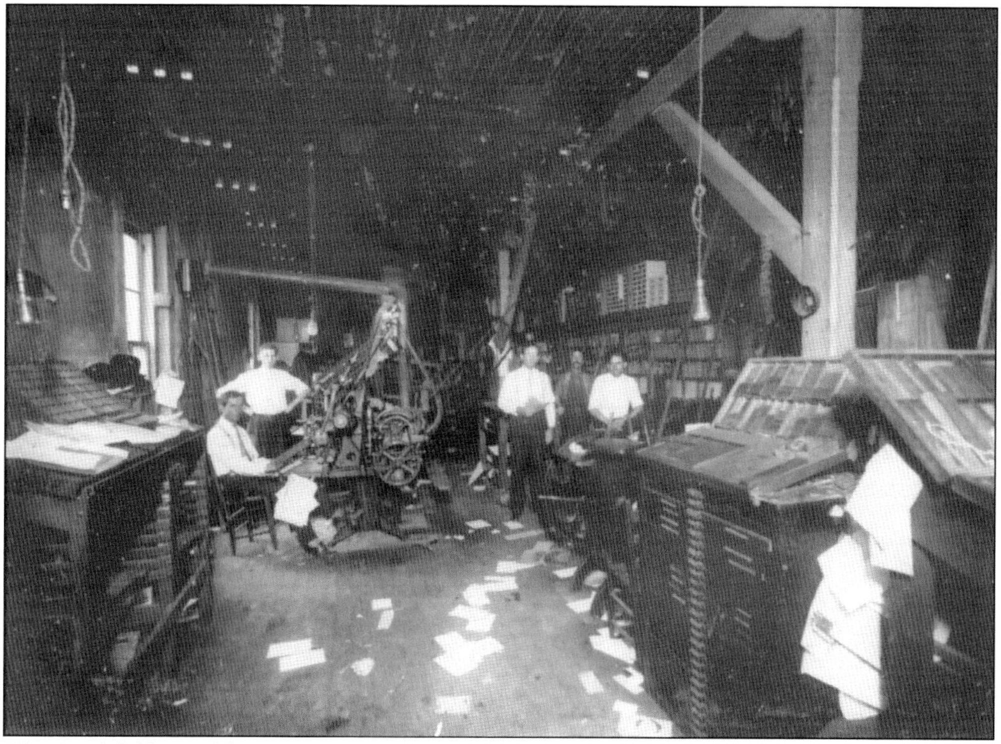

The *Smithfield Herald* newspaper office was locate in the Stevens Building on North Second Street when this lantern slide was made around 1920. Pictured here are, from left to right, Luther Stancil (seated at linotype machine), Ira Medlin (a later shop foreman and part-owner of the paper), Thomas J. Lassiter (editor), John West (pressman), and Louis Ellis (shop foreman). Stancil later became editor of Selma's *Johnstonian-Sun*.

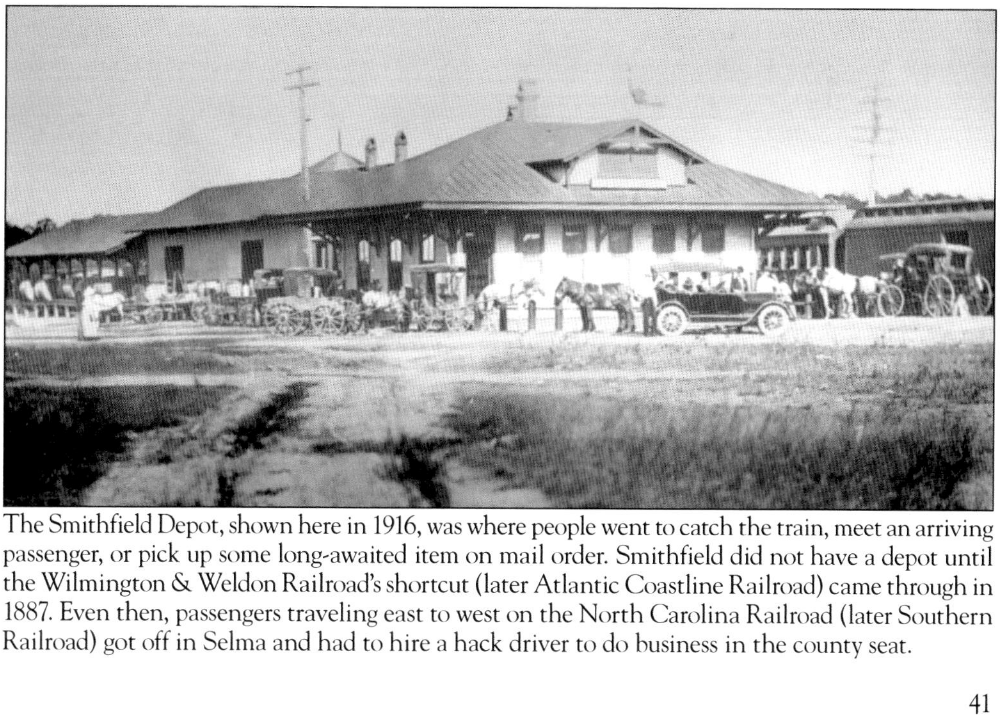

The Smithfield Depot, shown here in 1916, was where people went to catch the train, meet an arriving passenger, or pick up some long-awaited item on mail order. Smithfield did not have a depot until the Wilmington & Weldon Railroad's shortcut (later Atlantic Coastline Railroad) came through in 1887. Even then, passengers traveling east to west on the North Carolina Railroad (later Southern Railroad) got off in Selma and had to hire a hack driver to do business in the county seat.

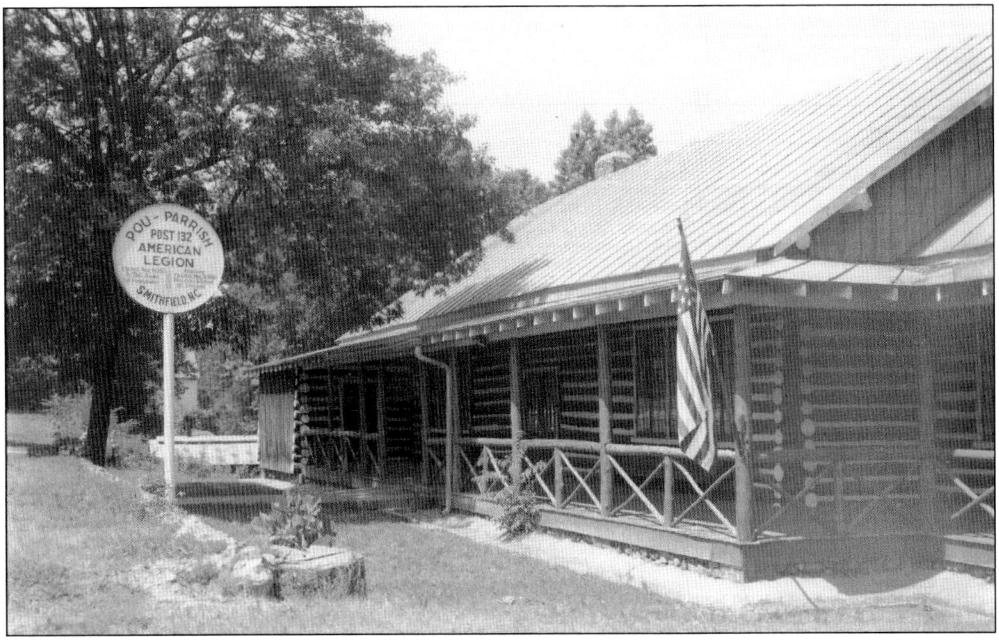

The American Legion Hut, located at the southwest corner of Smithfield's Front and Market Streets near the Neuse River, was built during the Great Depression with funding from the federal Works Progress Administration. During World War II, USO dances were held here for soldiers stationed nearby. It is now home of the Neuse Little Theatre.

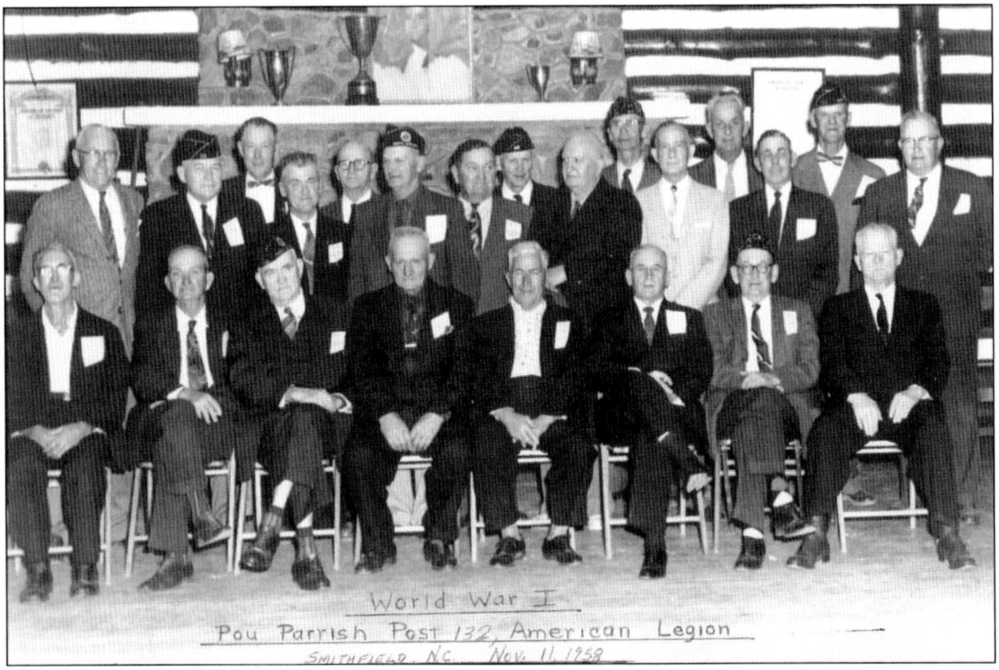

These distinguished gentlemen are World War I veterans who gathered in 1958 at the American Legion Hut in Smithfield. They are members of the American Legion Pou-Parrish Post No. 132. There is a statue in the northwest corner of the Johnston County Courthouse that memorializes World War I veterans who died in the war.

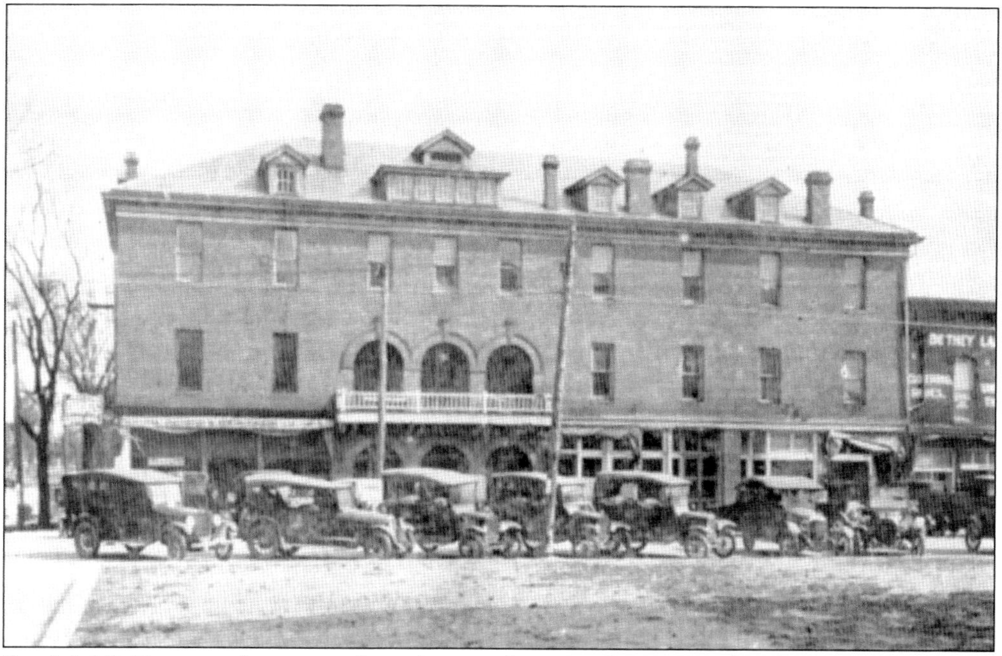

Smithfield's Tuscarora Inn, across from the courthouse, is shown in its heyday in the early 1920s. Built in 1902, it was outdated by the 1930s, so the Gabriel Johnston Hotel was constructed on Fourth Street to provide more modern accommodations to tobacco buyers and other businessmen. The Johnston and Stephenson Drug Store occupied the corner storefront.

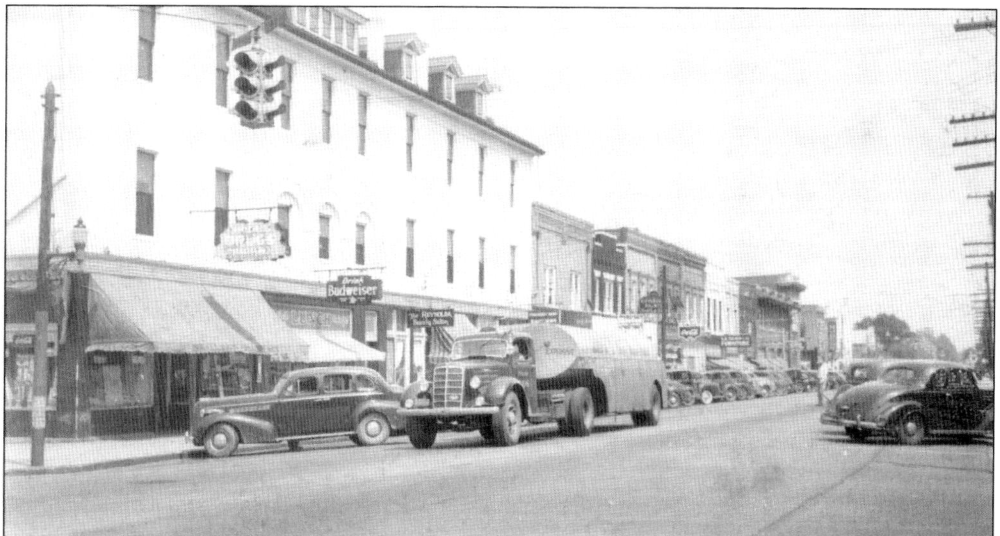

Smithfield photographer Dorothy Hooks took this photograph of the old Tuscarora Inn in the 1940s, after its redbrick exterior was painted. Johnston and Stephenson Drug Company had given way to Stallings Pharmacy. The bus stop was behind the building, and tickets were sold in the drugstore. It was here that Ava Gardner bought a ticket in 1941 and boarded a bus for her Hollywood screen test in New York. Druggist Jimmy Creech was working that day and remembered she sat alone on a bench out front until the bus arrived. No one would have guessed this was a Hollywood star in the making.

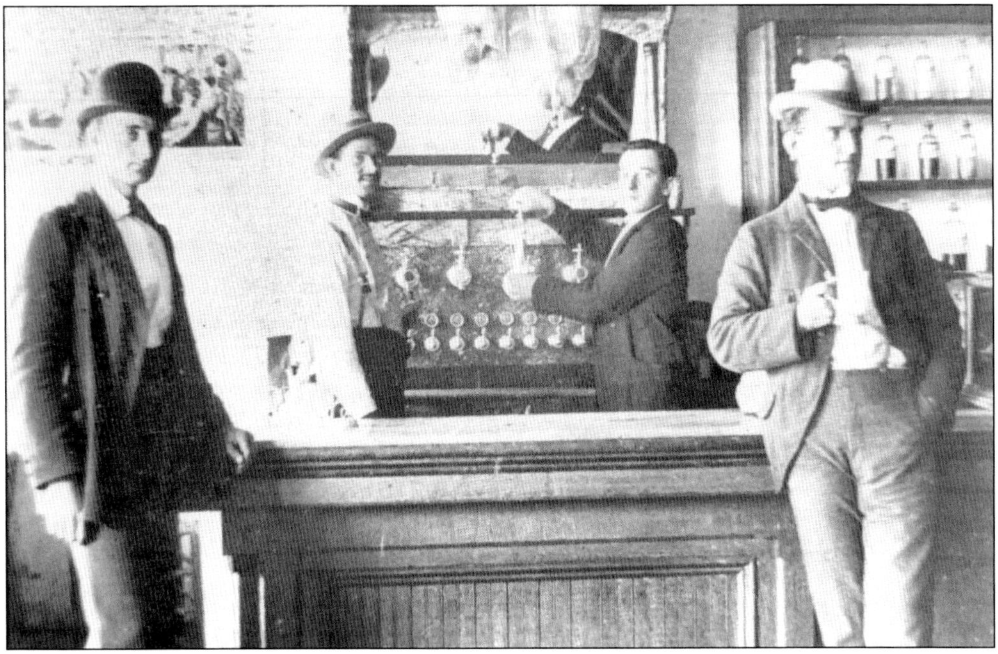

Charlie Kirkman (third from left) is operating the soda fountain in his drugstore across from the courthouse around 1898. Pictured here are, from left to right, undertaker R.O. Cotter, an unidentified employee, Kirkman, and attorney F.H. Brooks. Kirkman died tragically in 1908, when he fell from a burning building.

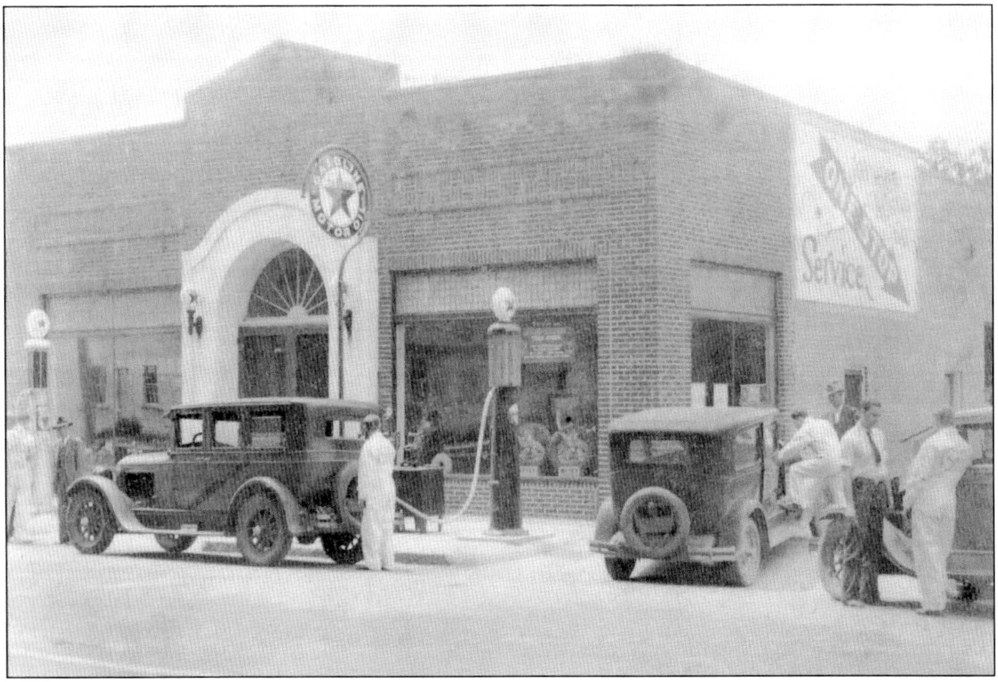

Johnson Motor Company's Texaco station on Johnston Street in Smithfield is pictured here in the 1930s. The gas pumps are on the sidewalk, and drivers parked their cars on the street to put gas into their tanks.

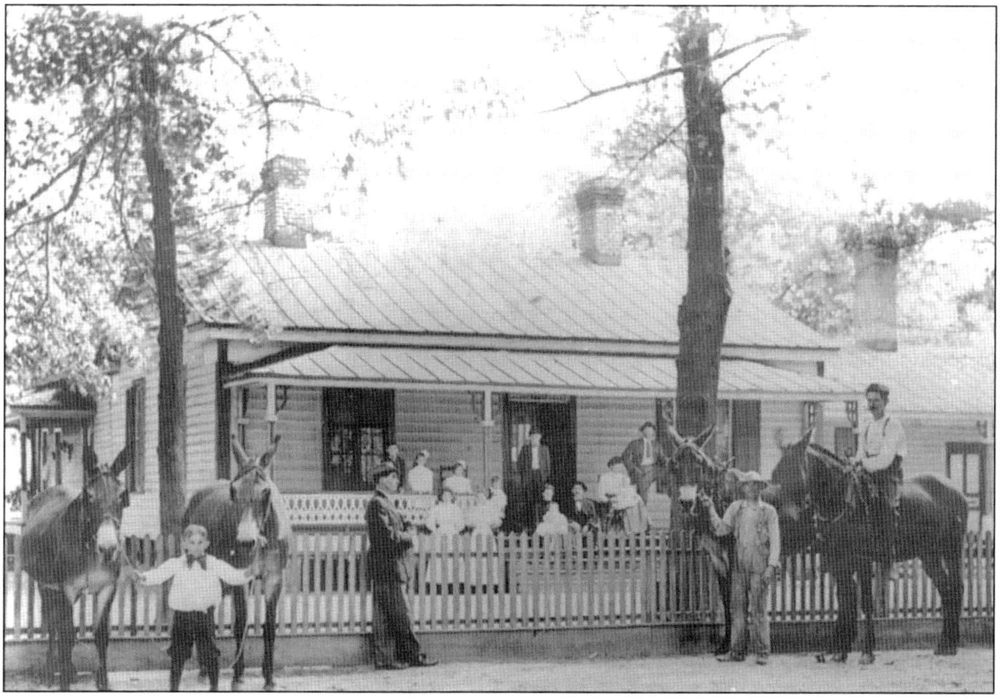

The Joseph C. Jernigan family is shown here around 1910 in front of their freshly painted home at the northeast corner of Fifth and Davis Streets in Smithfield's historic Brooklyn section. This home, still standing, is referred to as the Stephenson-Jones House in honor of its earliest owners.

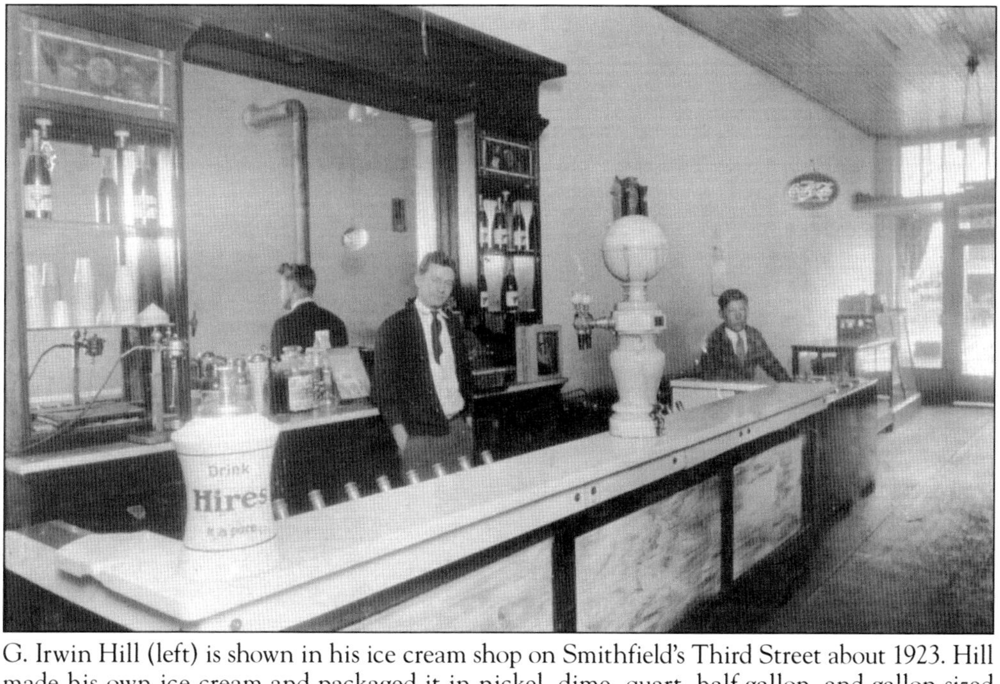

G. Irwin Hill (left) is shown in his ice cream shop on Smithfield's Third Street about 1923. Hill made his own ice cream and packaged it in nickel, dime, quart, half-gallon, and gallon-sized containers and made ice cream sandwiches as well. He operated this popular business until one year before his death in 1964. (Courtesy of Lucy Hill Worley)

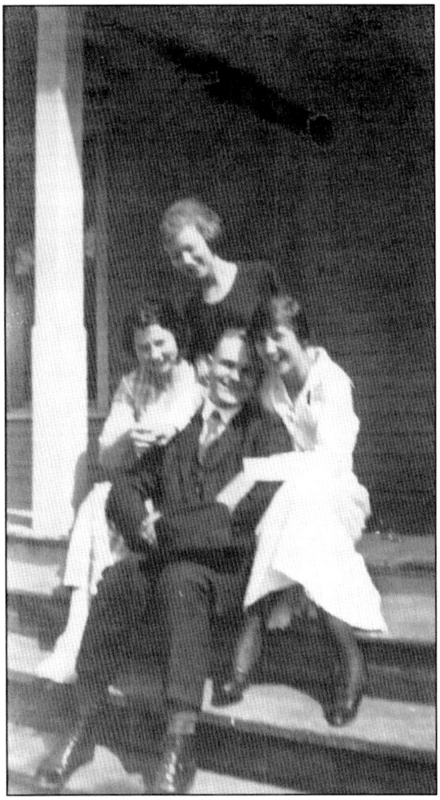

Dr. Carl Vann Tyner is flanked by, from left to right, an unidentified nurse; his wife, Nina; and nurse Ruth Schmick on the porch of Smithfield Memorial Hospital, located at the southeast corner of North Second and Bridge Streets in the early 1920s. Tyner was a Wake Forest College graduate, a surgeon in New York's Bellevue Hospital, and a member of the Medical Corps during World War I before being recruited to open Johnston County's first hospital in 1920. He left for Leaksville, North Carolina, in 1924. Schmick, an Army nurse, came with Dr. Tyner from New York and later married a local man, Ed L. Woodall. The house, acquired by Four Oaks Bank and torn down for a parking lot, was formerly Mary Woodall Myatt's boardinghouse.

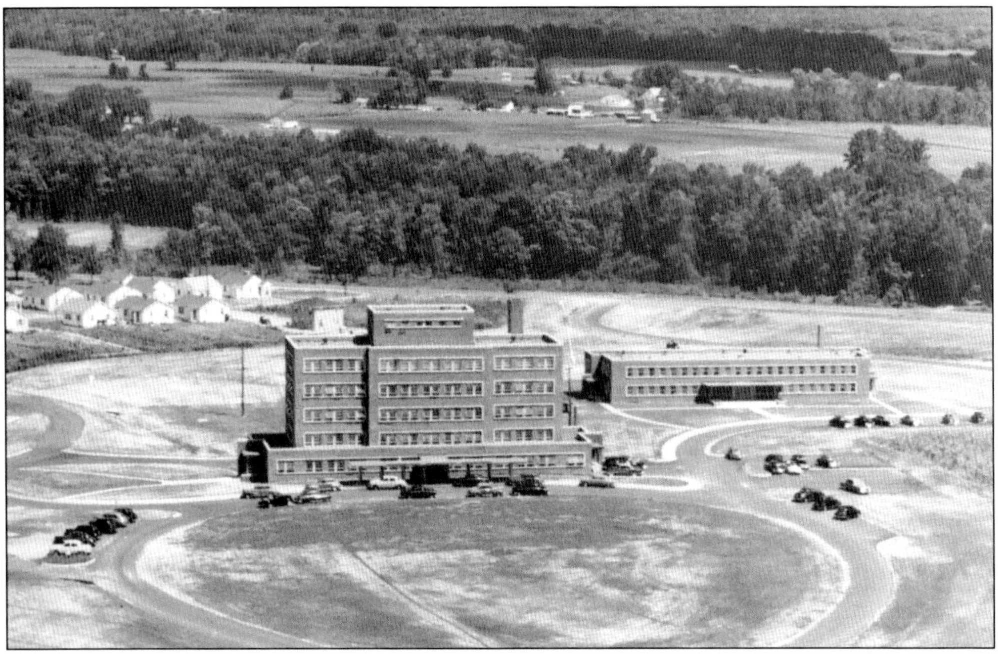

Johnston Memorial Hospital was built between 1949 and 1951 in Smithfield. It replaced the existing hospital that was only blocks away. Looking at this photograph, it is hard today to imagine so much undeveloped space surrounding the initial building.

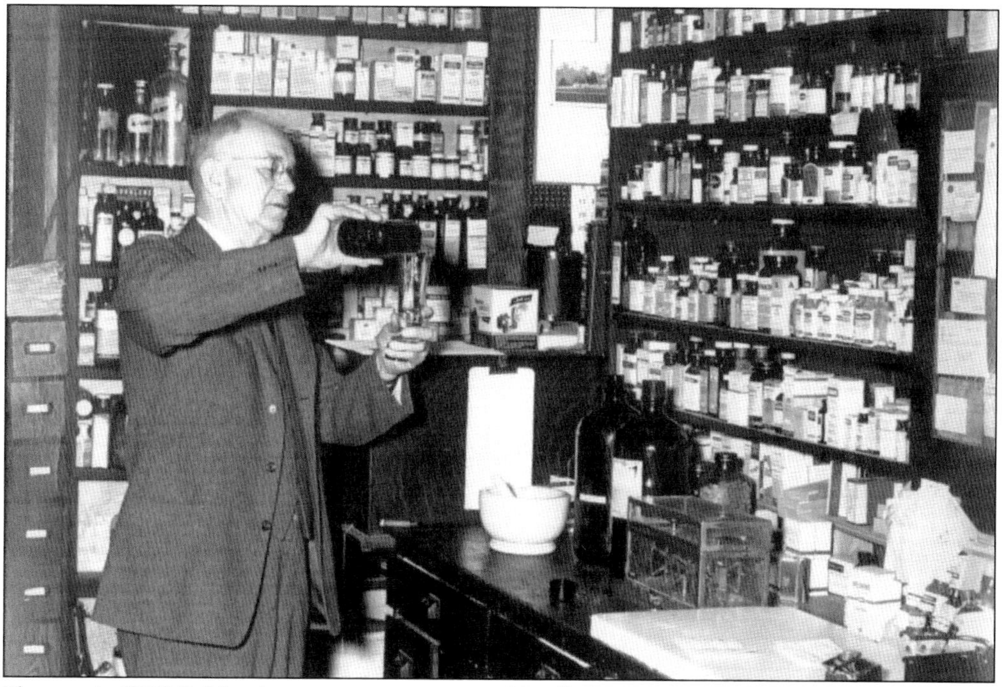

Pharmacist Will D. Hood mixes a concoction in Hood's Drug Store, at the corner of Market and Third Streets, sometime in the 1940s. He and brother Hal took over this family business when their father, Thomas R. Hood, took the reins of First and Citizens National Bank (later First Citizens) across the street in 1922. The Hoods' grandfather J.C. Hood moved from Bentonville to Smithfield and started the firm in 1873, and it stayed in the family until 1963, finally closing almost 100 years after its founding.

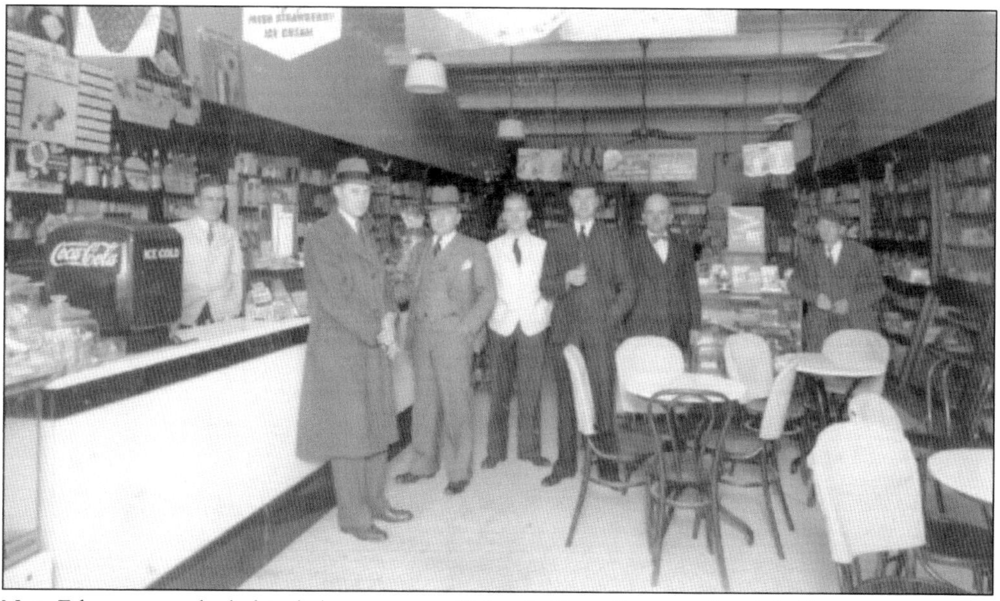

Nuit Edgerton works behind the counter of Hood's Drug Store in Smithfield sometime in the 1930s. For some reason, there was great emphasis on promoting strawberry ice cream. (Courtesy of Kirk Edgerton.)

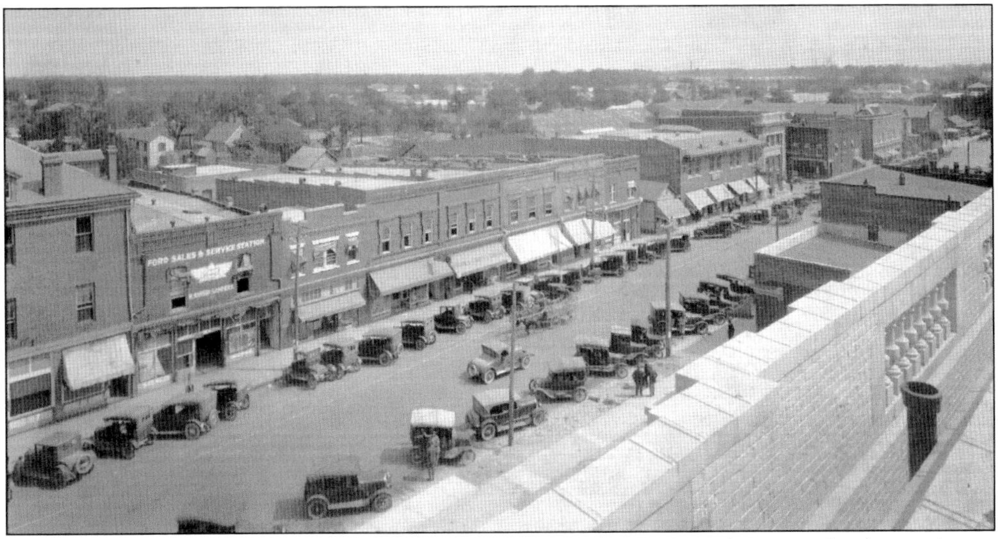

Looking northeast from the top of the new Johnston County Courthouse, a few horse-drawn wagons can be seen moving through the streets in this 1922 photograph, but it is obvious the Sanders Ford dealership across the street and other automobile dealers were doing a brisk business. The northeast corner of Third and Market Streets at right gives a rare view of the Ashley Smith Building, constructed by a former slave who was one of the wealthiest men in Smithfield in the early 20th century. Quite a number of lawyers had second-floor offices in these store buildings, conveniently located near the courthouse. Downtown supporters today would welcome the angled parking configuration that made this busy thoroughfare more pedestrian friendly.

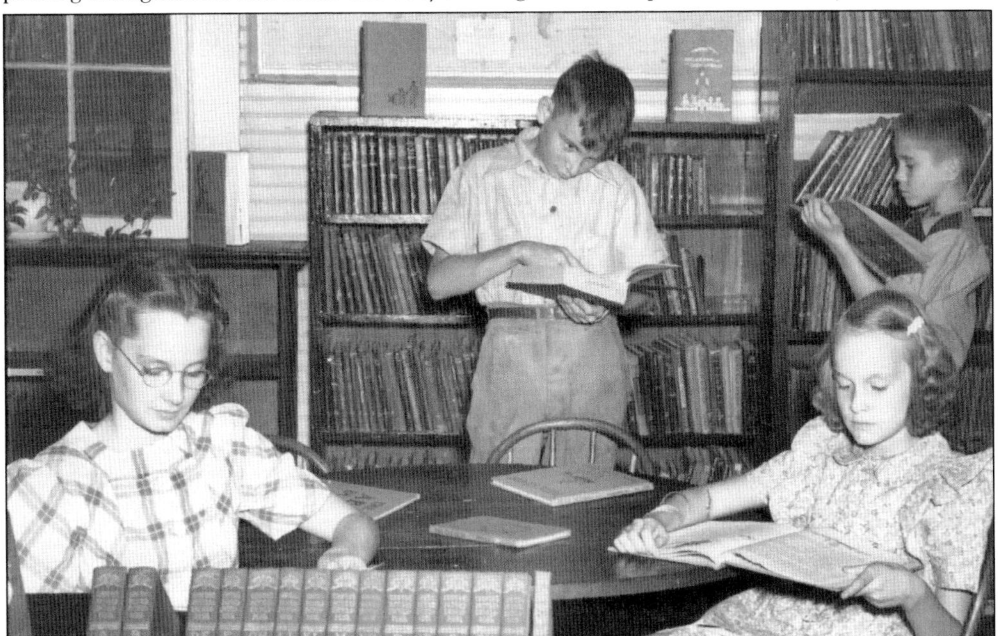

These kids are hitting the books hard in the children's section of the Smithfield Public Library in 1945. The Smithfield Public Library and the Johnston County Public Library were in adjacent buildings on Johnston Street. White citizens of Smithfield could check out books from either library, and black and non-Smithfield residents were served by the county library.

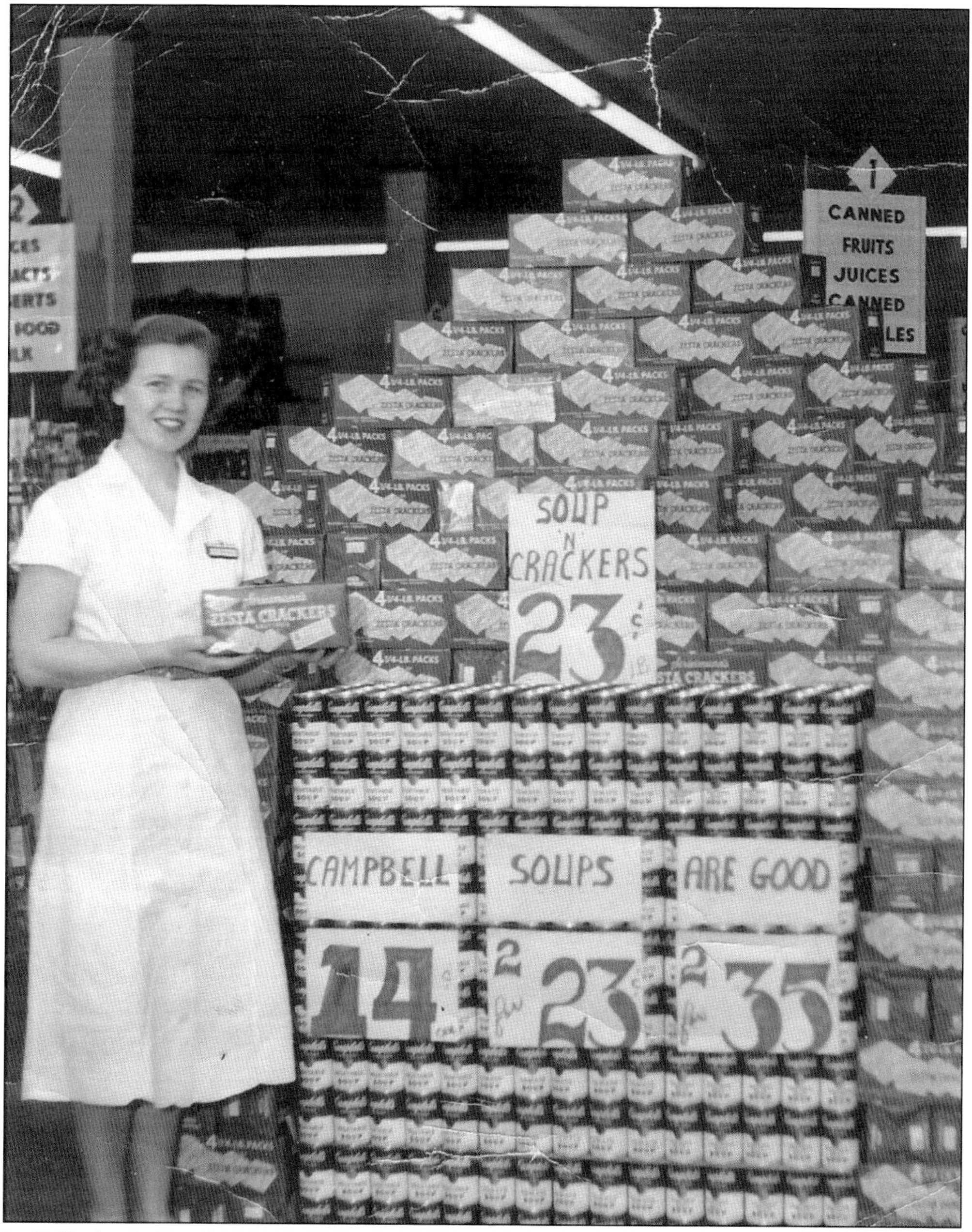

In 1952, the Colonial Store opened its doors in Smithfield. Earlier grocery stores had most of their goods behind counters, and clerks gathered items for customers. The Colonial Store ushered in an era of groceries arranged in aisles where customers could shop for themselves. Joyce W. Thompson is shown with a display of soup and crackers marking the opening of the new store.

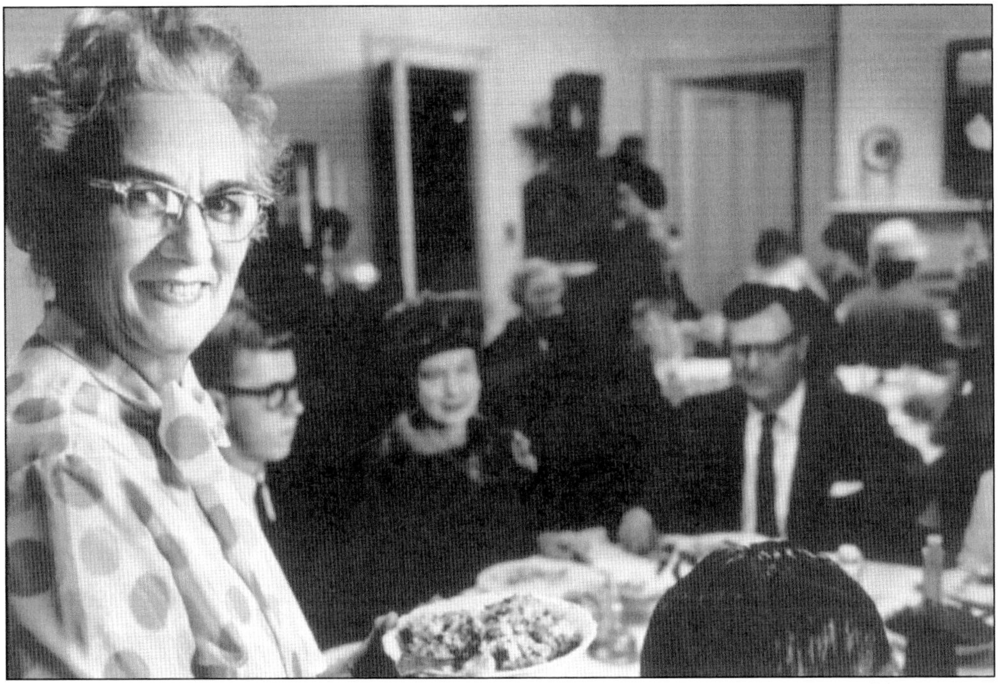

Ellena Talton Fleming, pictured here in 1964, serves one of many sumptuous and bounteous family-style meals enjoyed in the large dining room of her Smithfield boardinghouse between 1935 and 1976. In 1957, Rena Bingham Lassiter wrote in her *Smithfield Herald* column "Personal Slants" that Fleming and all the boardinghouse operators who preceded her were remembered not simply for "good eats" but also for offering a venue for "the gentle art of conversation."

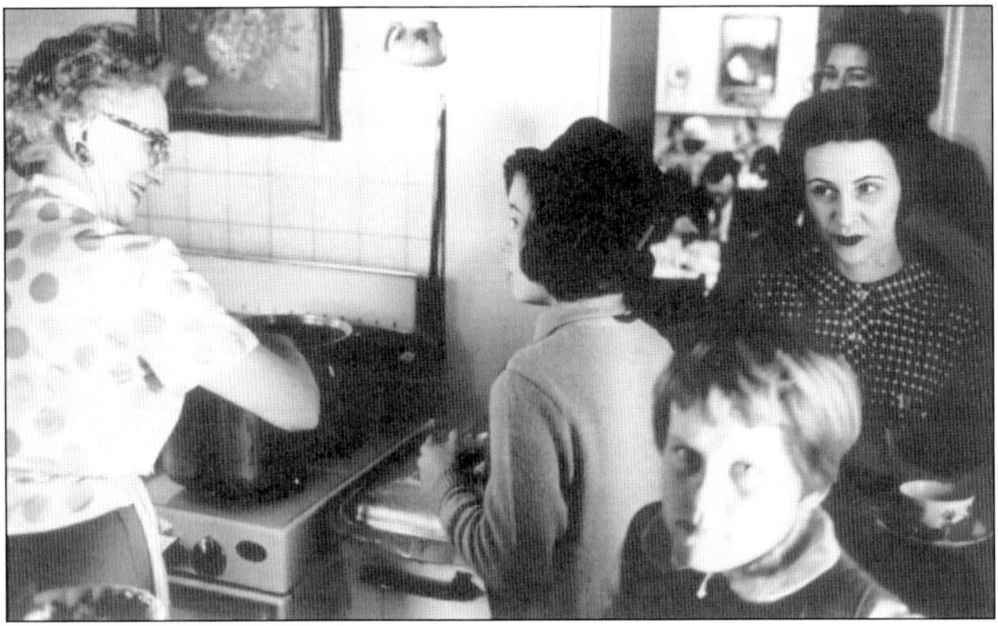

Fleming takes time to converse with diner Jane Cunningham during the lunch rush. Also shown are Dell Cunningham (front) and boardinghouse employee Annie Lee Creech (at right). Courtesy of the *Raleigh Times*.)

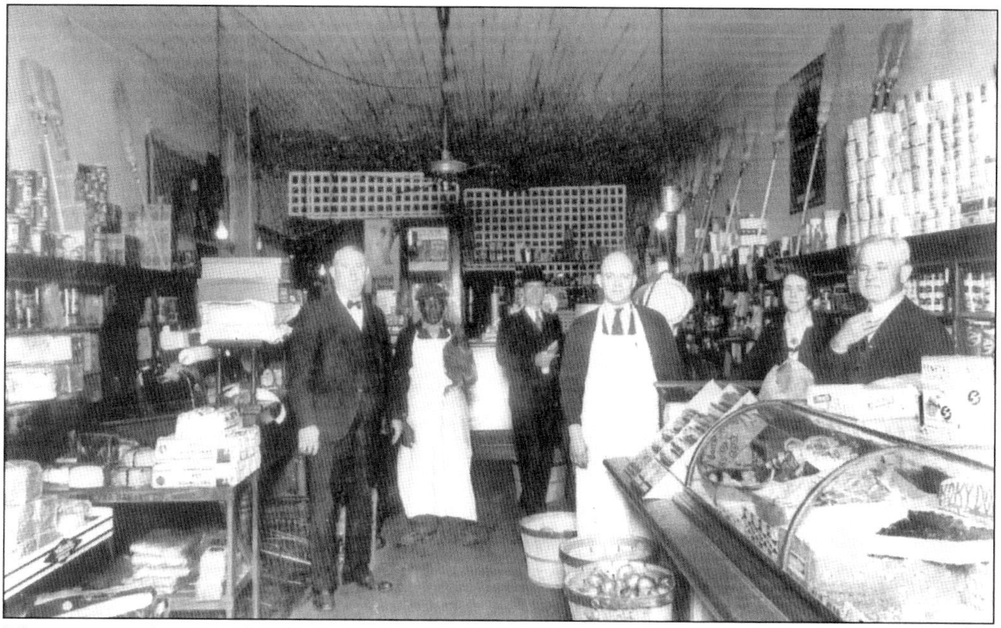

This interior photograph of Smithfield's Turnage and Talton Grocery Store on Third Street dates from the 1930s. Pictured here are, from left to right, Ralph R. Talton, Cub Watson, possibly Luby F. Royall Sr., R.S. Fleming, Laura Turnage Talton, and possibly Charles A. Creech. Next to the bread displays are cages for live chickens, which customers brought in to barter for store items.

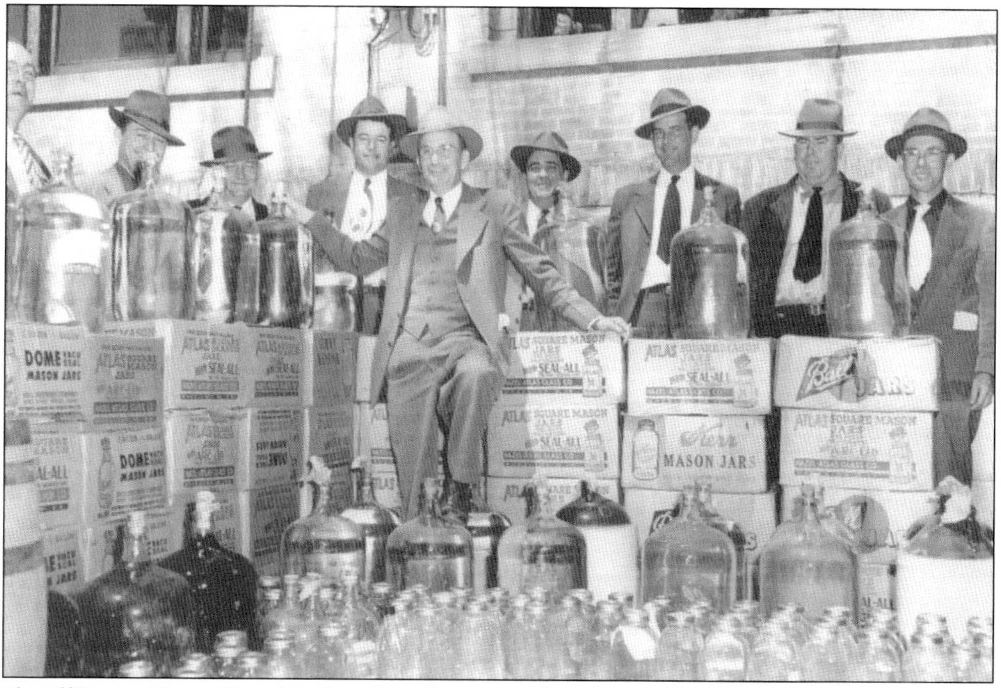

Sheriff Barney Henry (front) is all smiles as he shows off confiscated liquor from his latest moonshine still raid in 1954. Joining the revelry are, from left to right, jailor Roy Hinton, deputy J.T. Smith, assistant jailor Carl Narron, and deputies Hughes Lamm, Alvin Narron, Woodrow Massengill, Ernie Beasley, and Ira Ford. (Courtesy of North Carolina State Archives.)

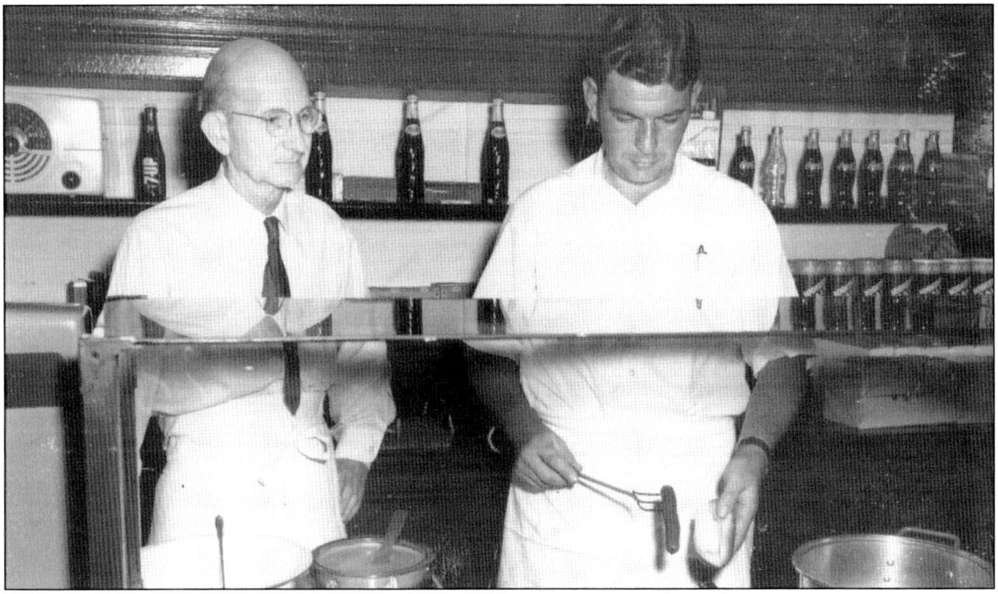

Many people in Johnston County ate a hot dog and drank a Coca-Cola from Fred's Place on Third Street in Smithfield from the 1920s to the 1980s. Fred Adams (left) is shown in 1971 when he turned over the business to Eldridge Penny (right). As a young man in his early 20s in 1924, Adams purchased the business from D.H. "Sonny" Warren, who in turn had bought it from two Greeks. Fred's famous chili recipe, brought over from Greece, was passed on to Penny, whose widow later sold it to Johnston County Industries.

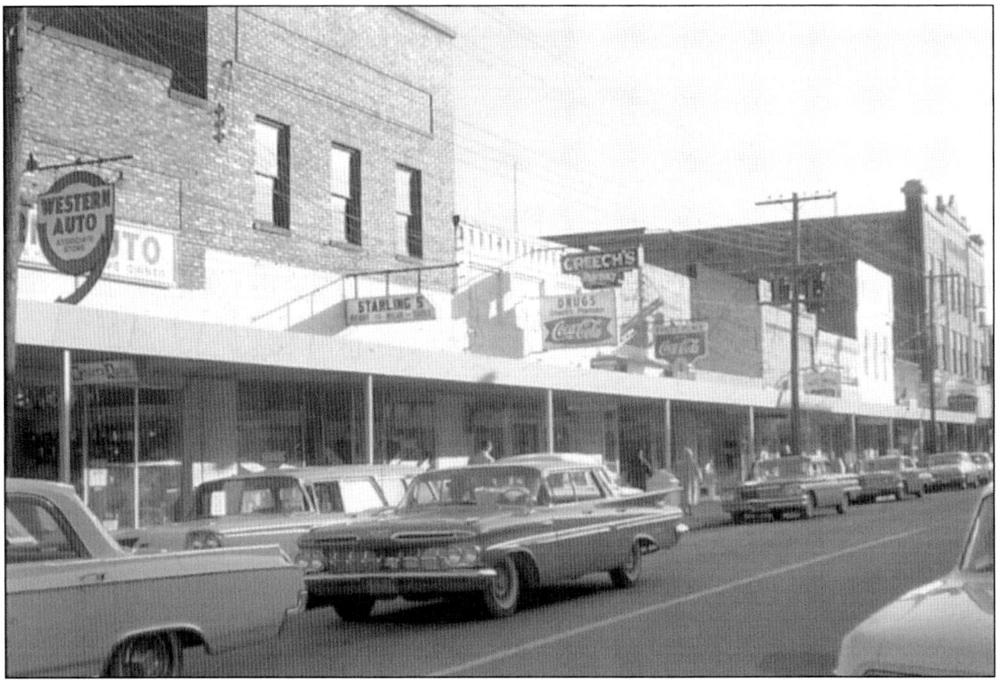

Smithfield's Third Street commercial row, shown here in the 1960s, featured an array of retail establishments. Of course, the greatest draw was Fred's Place, where bottles of cola and hot dogs covered with Fred's famous chili were always a big hit.

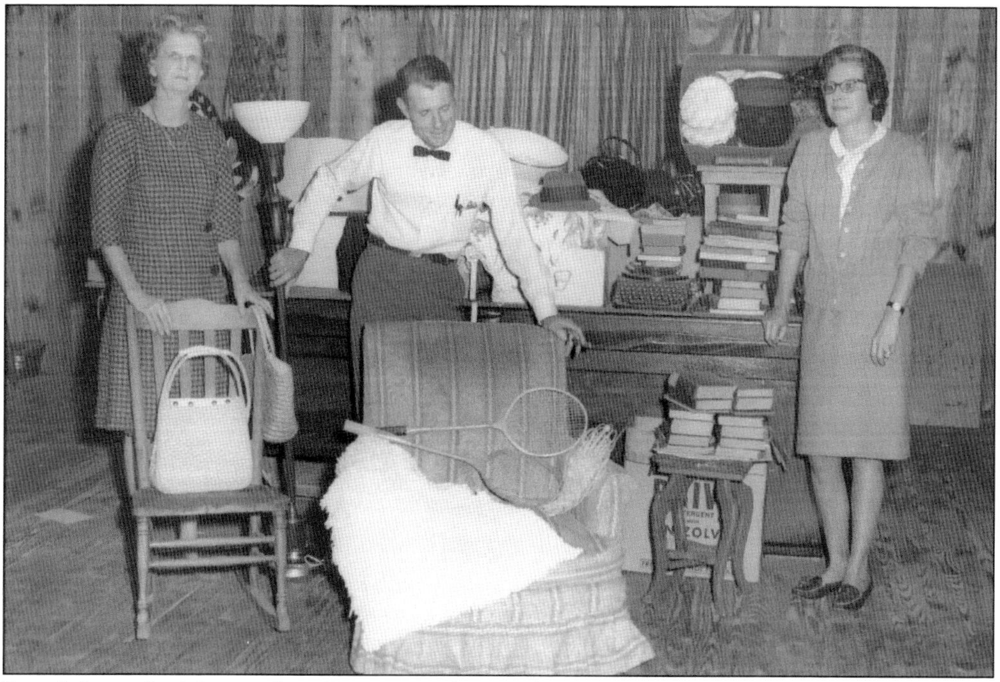

From left to right, Margaret Lee, Dixon Hamilton, and Pat Story worked at a rummage sale in 1964 to raise funds for the Hastings House preservation project. Lee often recalled the sale was so successful that her apron was sold while she was out on a lunch break. (Photograph by Reuben Johnson.)

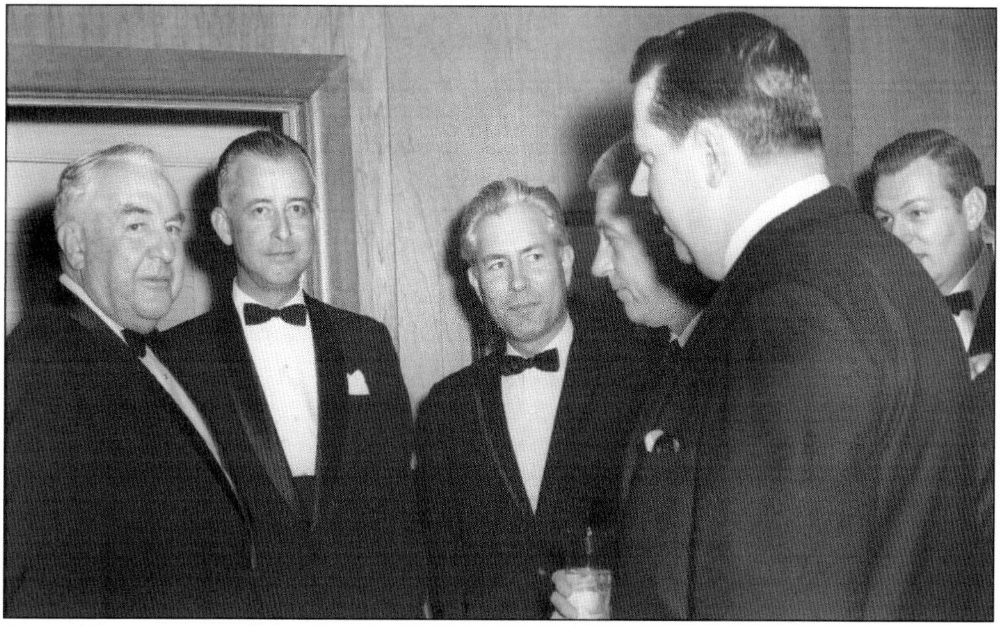

Pictured here are, from left to right, US senator Sam Ervin, John W. Wells, Robert P. Holding Jr., unidentified, and Dr. John L. Ryberg, longtime pastor of the town's First Baptist Church, at the Hastings House Ball, an event held in the National Guard Armory during the centennial of the Battle of Bentonville in 1965 to raise funds for moving and restoring Smithfield's historic Hastings House. (Photograph by Reuben Johnson.)

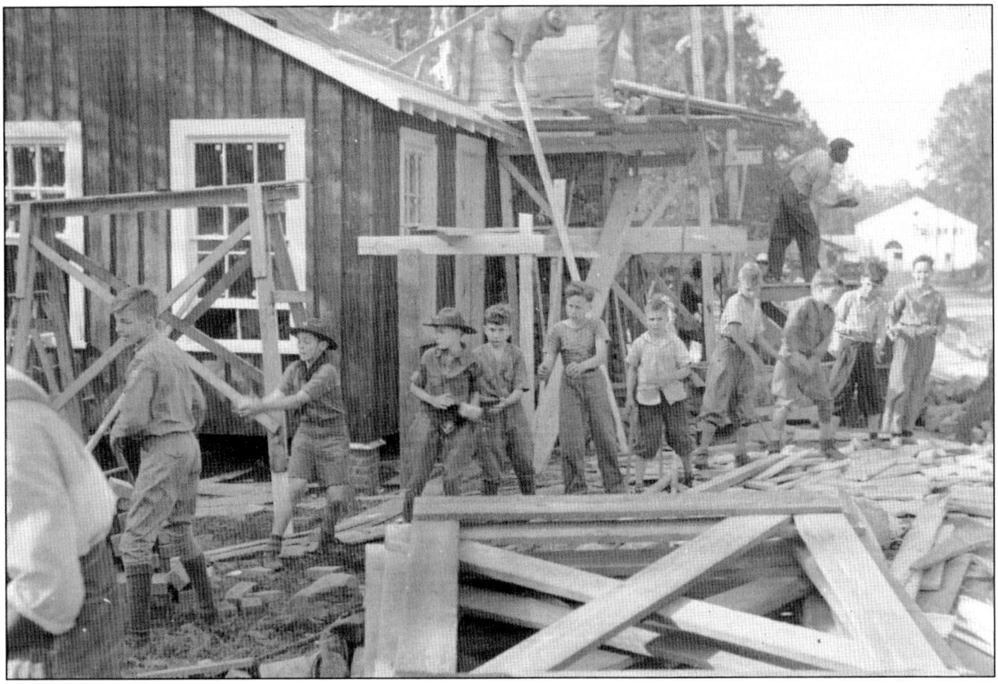

In a single day, May 15, 1940, Smithfield Boy Scouts from Troop 22 and an army of adult volunteers built a Scout Hut on Front Street between Market and Bridge Streets.

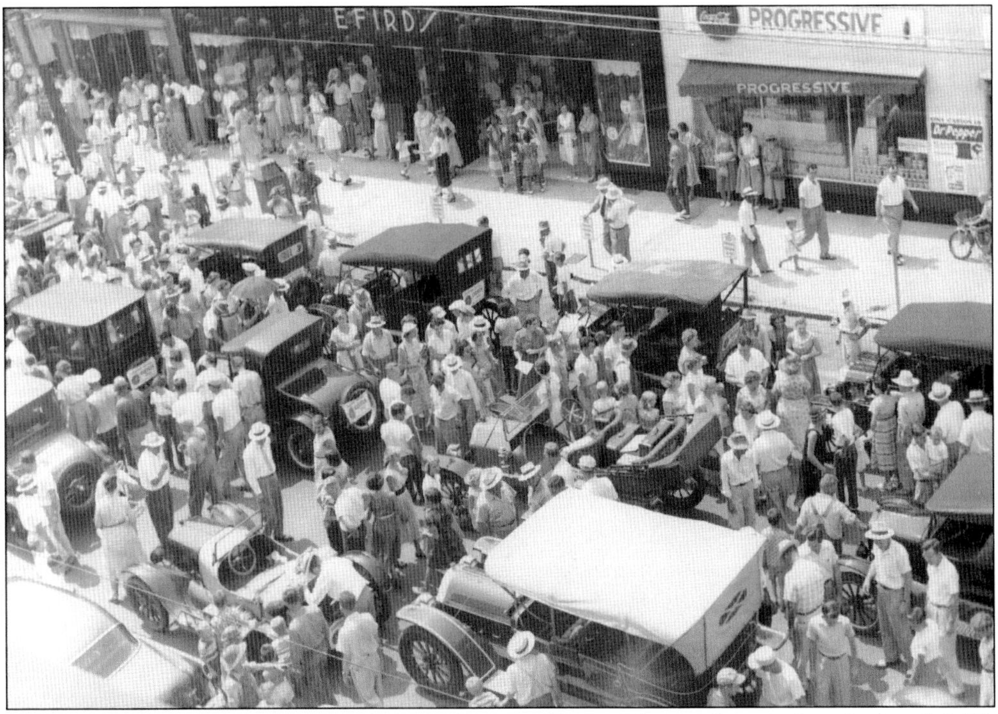

Farmers dressed in suits and town folk dressed in overalls turned out in big numbers for Smithfield's Farmer's Day celebrations. In this 1950s photograph, antique cars are on display on Market Street near the Efird's Department Store and the Progressive grocery store.

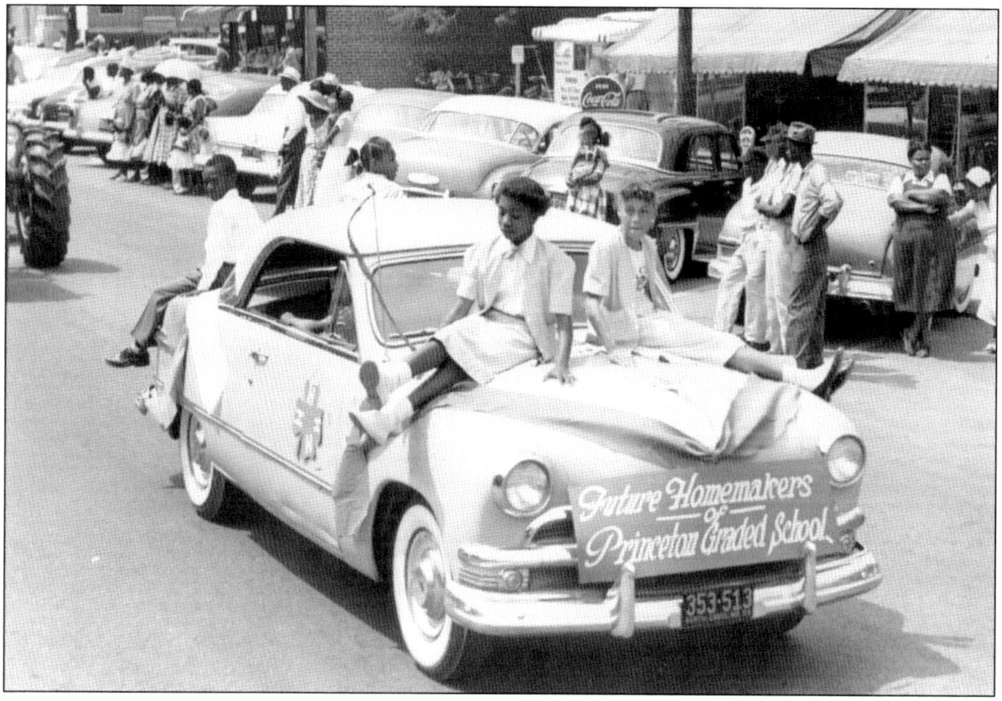

The Future Homemakers of Princeton Graded School ride in Johnston County Training School's annual homecoming parade in Smithfield in 1955. Princeton Graded is one of two black schools left in Johnston County that were built with assistance from the Julius Rosenwald Fund.

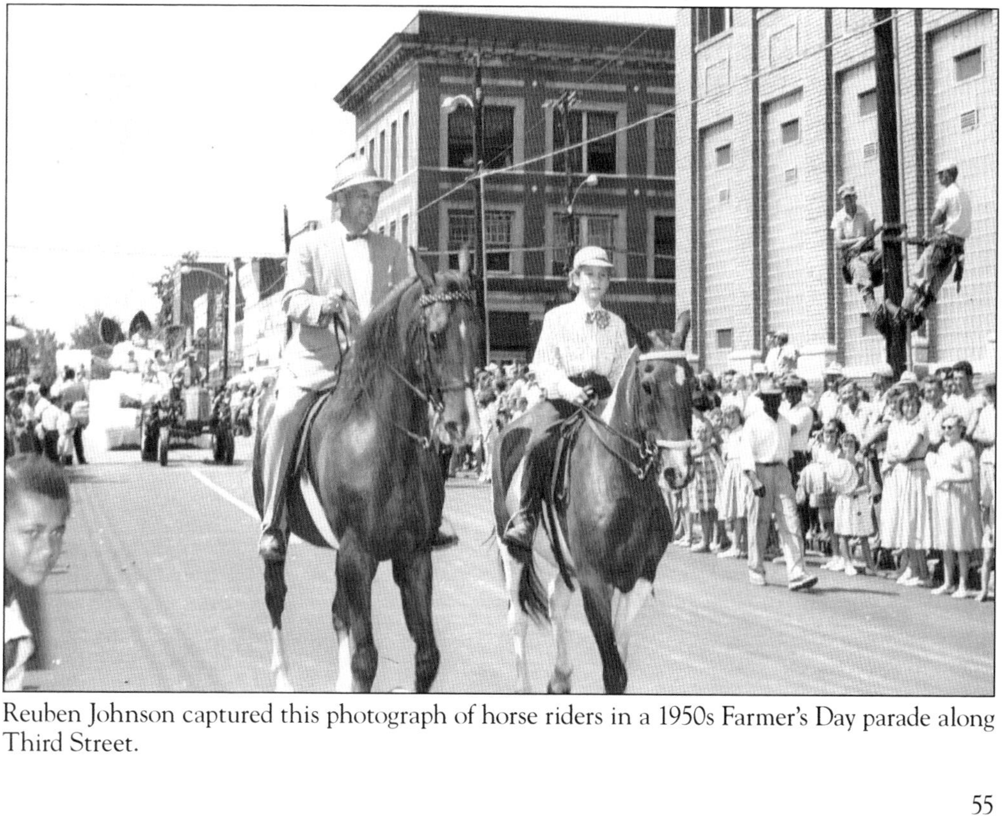

Reuben Johnson captured this photograph of horse riders in a 1950s Farmer's Day parade along Third Street.

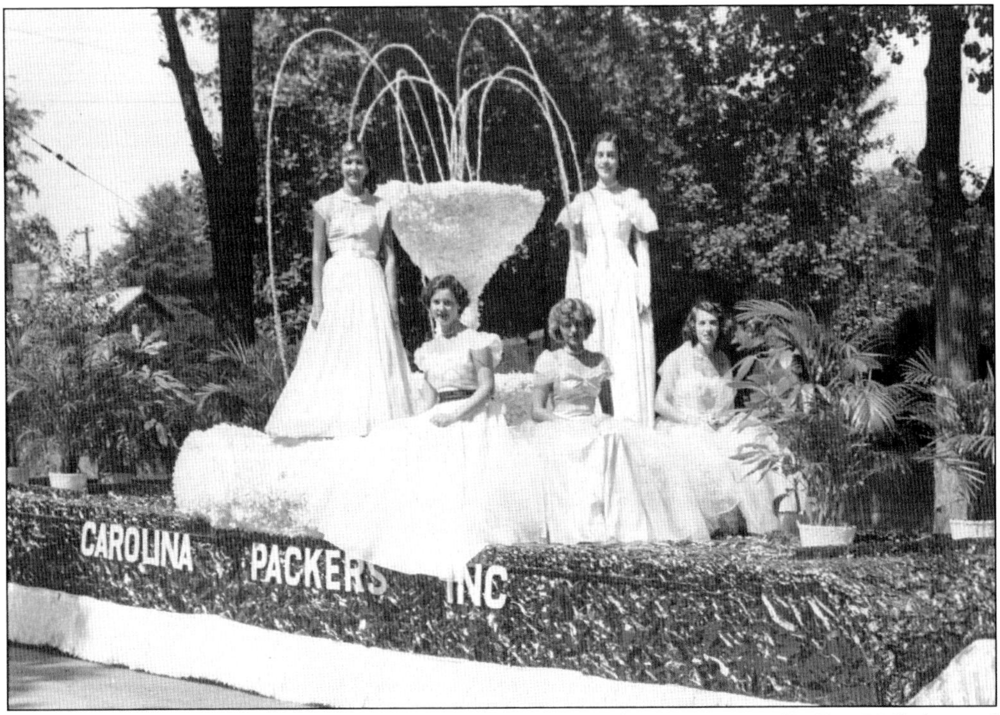

From left to right are (first row) Mary Jane Warrick, Mary Edna Grimes, and LaRue Hill; (second row) Cathryn Cheek and Doris Allen. They grace this Carolina Packers float in a Farmer's Day parade in the early 1950s.

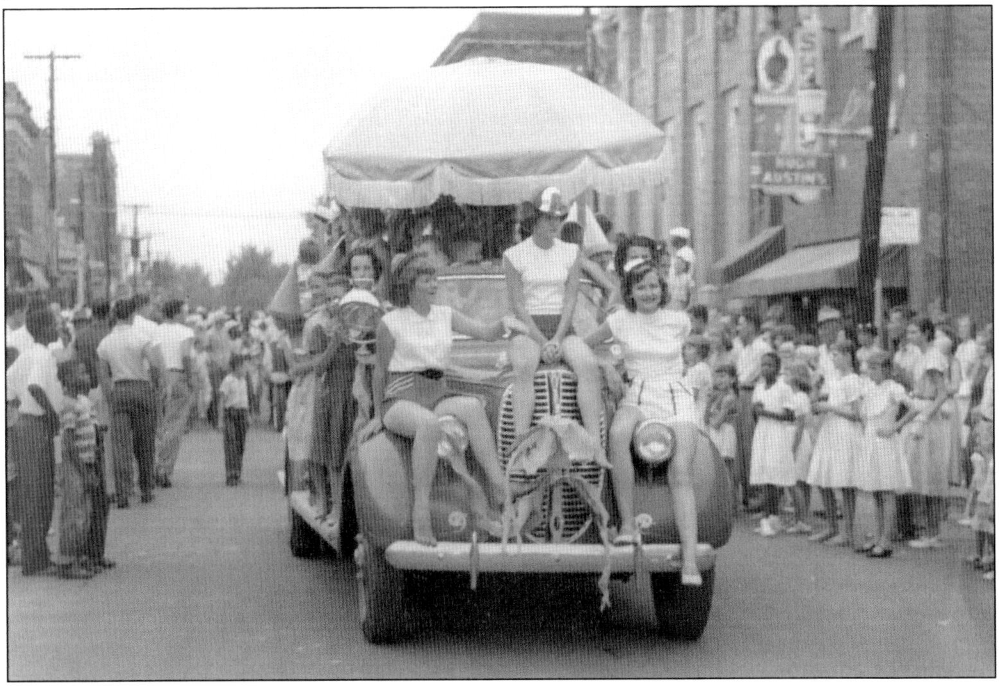

One must wonder how well the driver of this classic car was able to see his way along Third Street in this Farmer's Day parade photograph from 1951. (Photograph by Larry Wallace.)

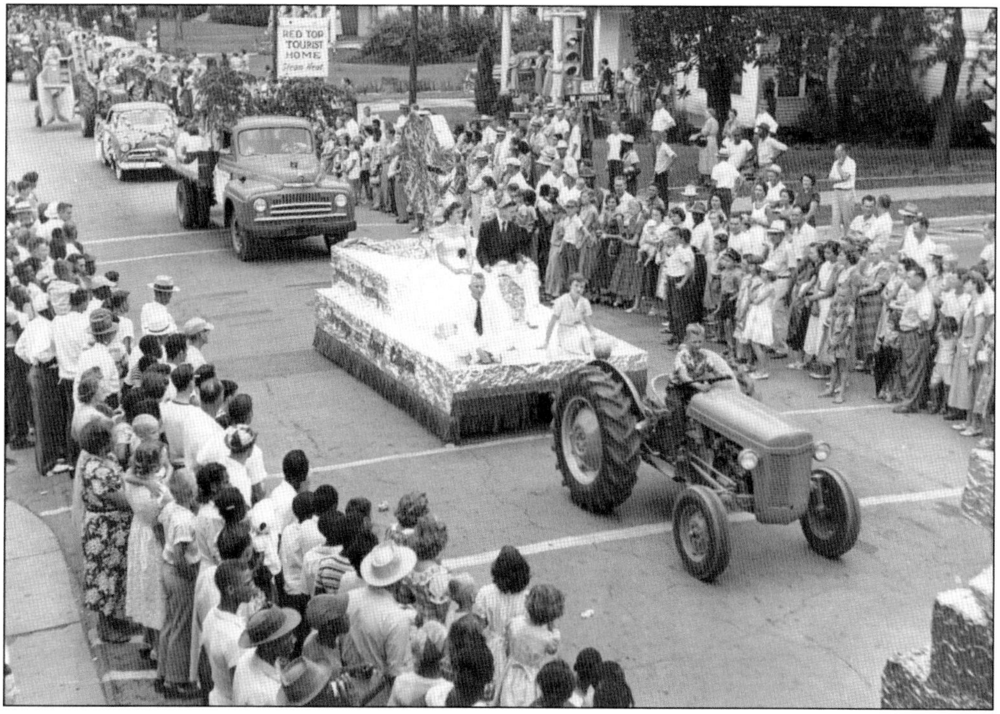

This float in the 1955 Farmer's Day parade was sponsored by Johnston County's 4-H Clubs. (Photograph by Larry Wallace.)

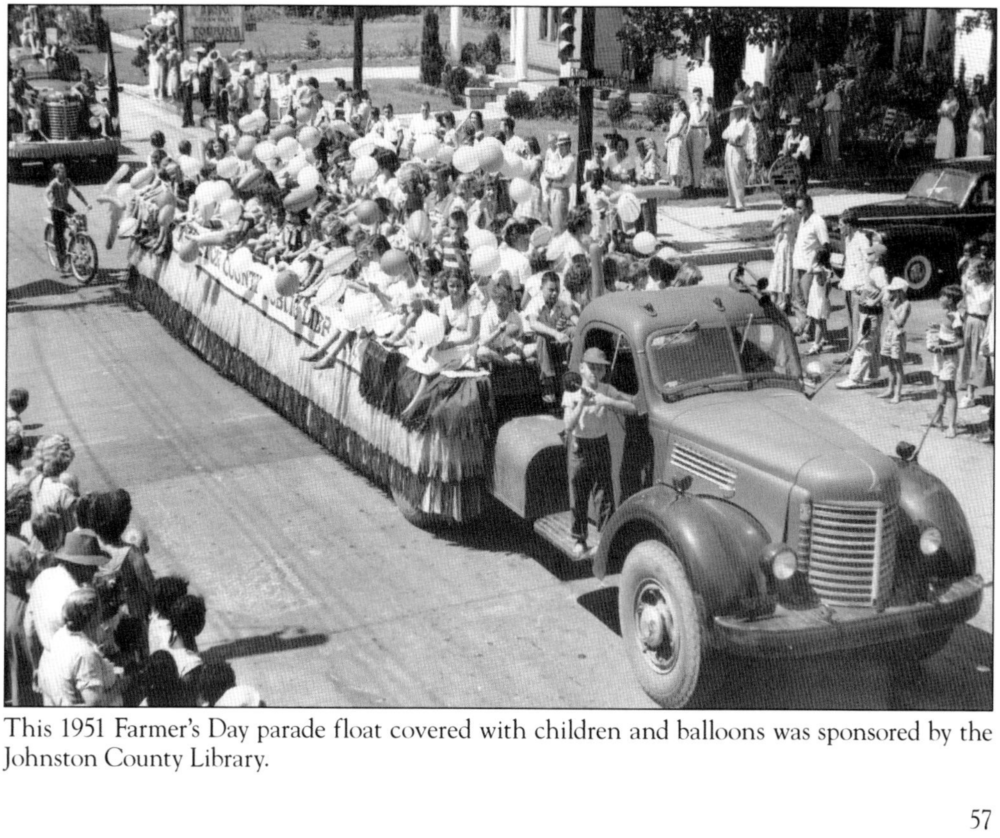

This 1951 Farmer's Day parade float covered with children and balloons was sponsored by the Johnston County Library.

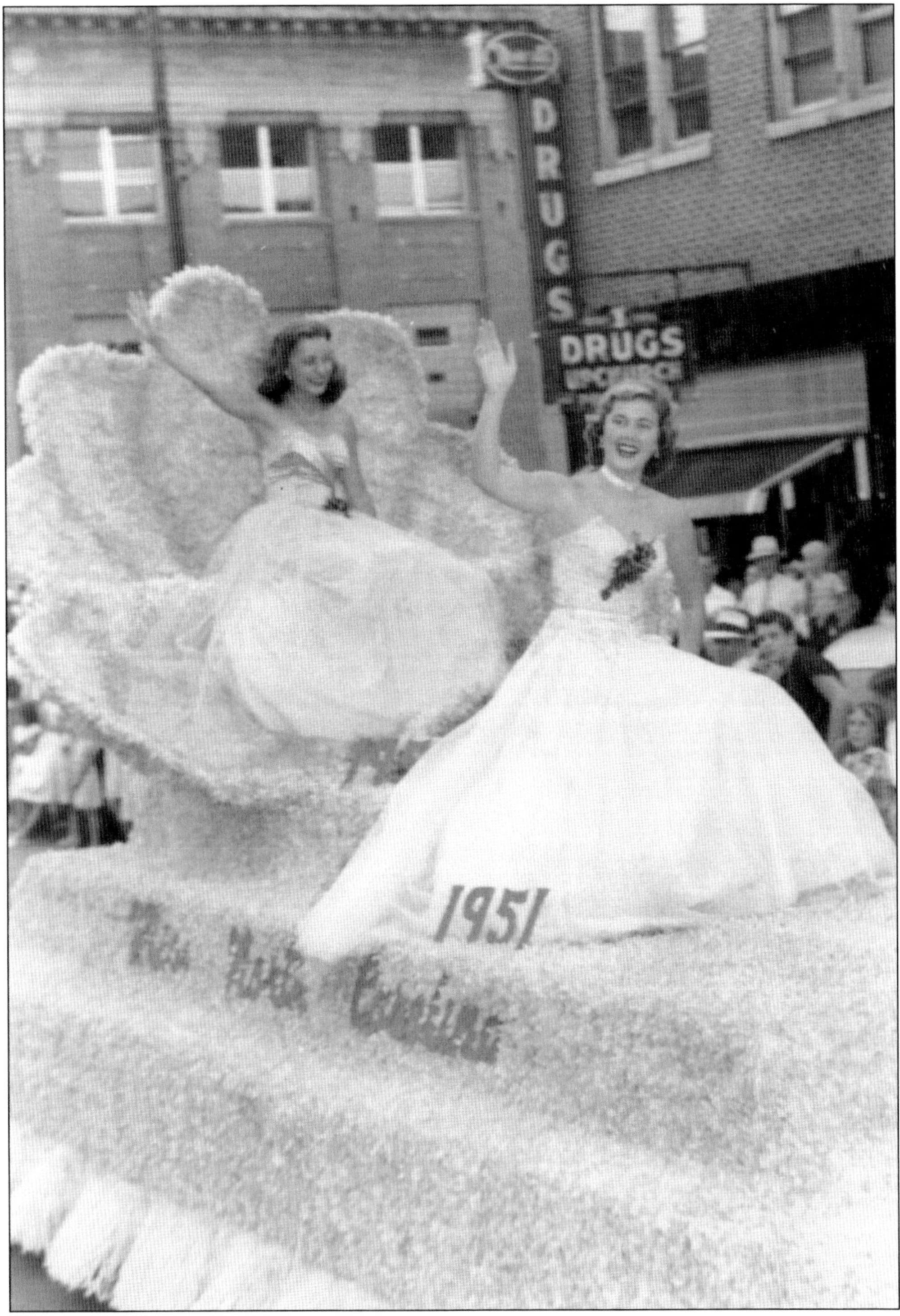

Lu Long Ogburn (in front), Smithfield's own Miss North Carolina, turns heads in the 1951 Farmer's Day parade. She would go on to be a runner-up in the Miss America pageant that year. (Photograph by Larry Wallace.)

Four

CHURCHES AND SCHOOLS

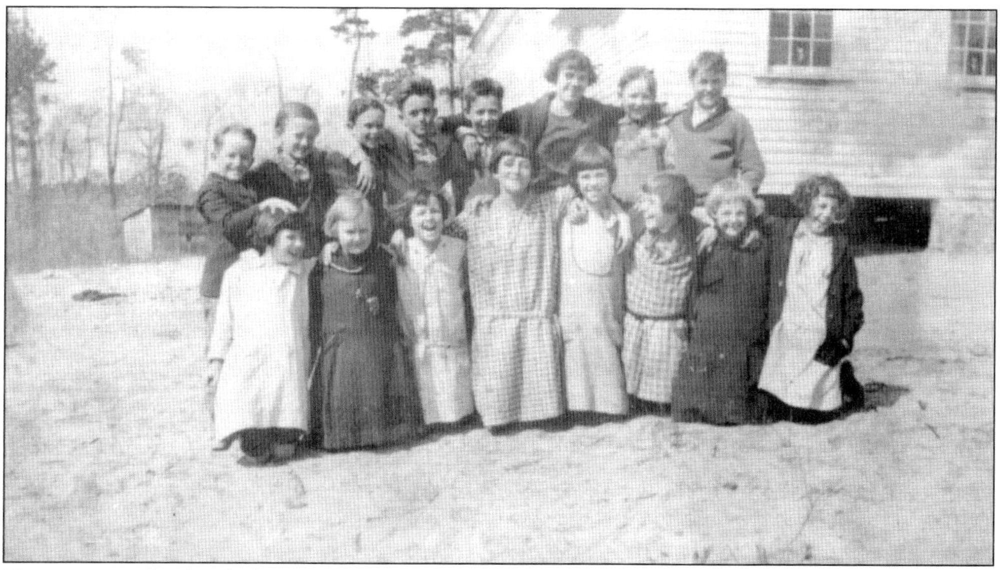

No image in this book shows a happier group of children than these students at Sandy Springs School in O'Neals Township in 1925. Little did they know that one of them would play baseball with the St. Louis Cardinals just 10 years later. Sam Narron (second row, fifth from left) played with the Cardinals in 1935 and from 1942 to 1943. He later served as bullpen coach for the Pittsburgh Pirates when they won the 1960 World Series.

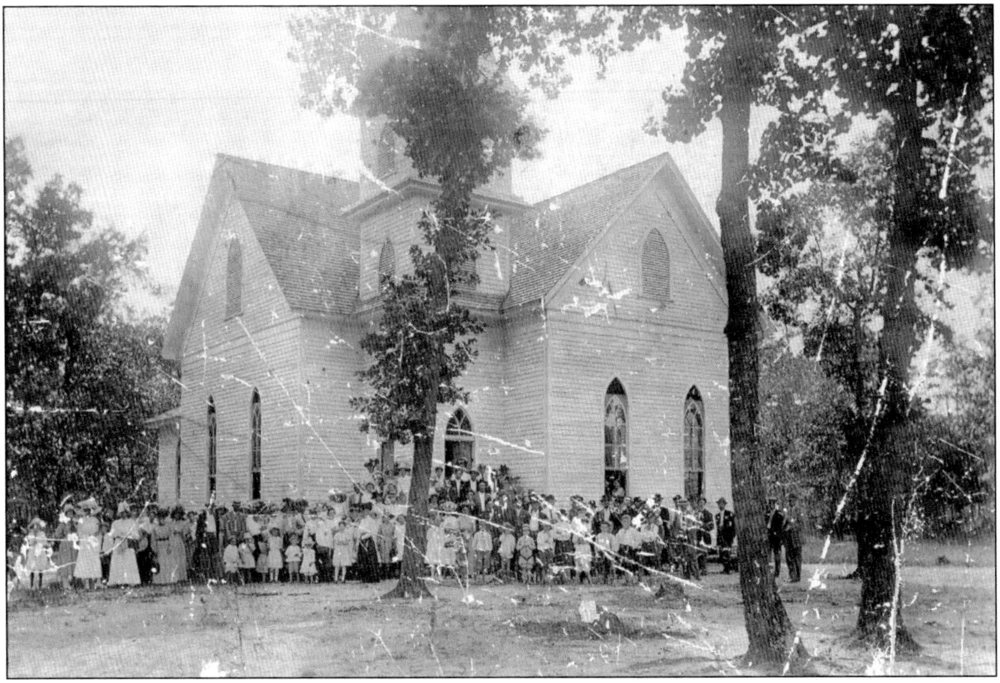

The congregation of White Oak Baptist Church in Archer Lodge gathered in front of their picturesque sanctuary for this photograph in 1910. Note the typically barren churchyard, kept free of grass and swept regularly for a smooth surface. (Courtesy of Carlton Vinson.)

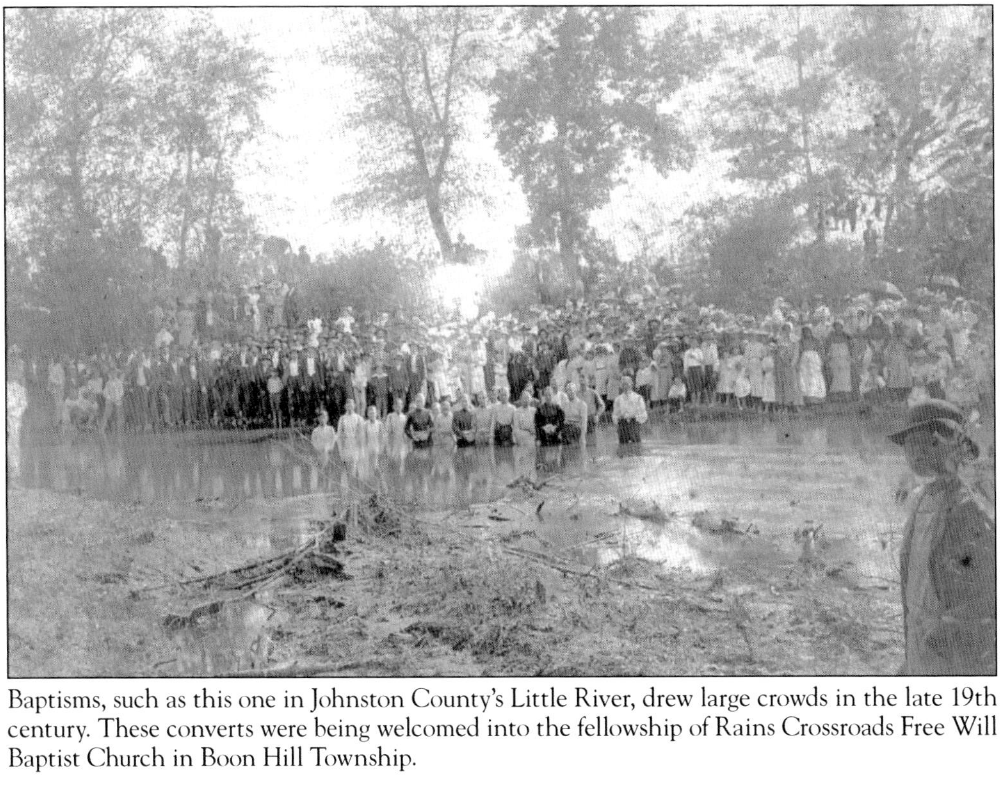

Baptisms, such as this one in Johnston County's Little River, drew large crowds in the late 19th century. These converts were being welcomed into the fellowship of Rains Crossroads Free Will Baptist Church in Boon Hill Township.

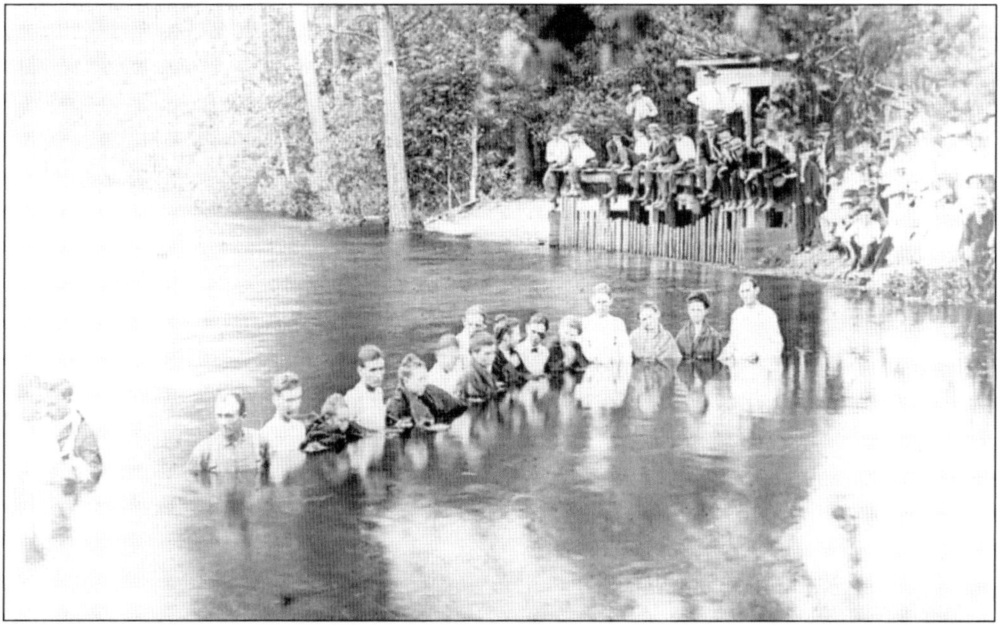

Rev. J.W. Tyndall of Mill Creek Christian Church in Bentonville Township baptizes Frank Weaver in Dick Blackmon's millpond in 1908. Waiting their turns are, from left to right, a Mr. Holder, John Rose, Venie Tart, Joe Rose, Bertha Boyette, Clarence Massengill, Bud Massengill, Cora Blackmon, Betty Massengill, Walter Barfield, Dora Weaver, unidentified, Vonnie Grant, Ophelia Weaver, and Rube Weaver.

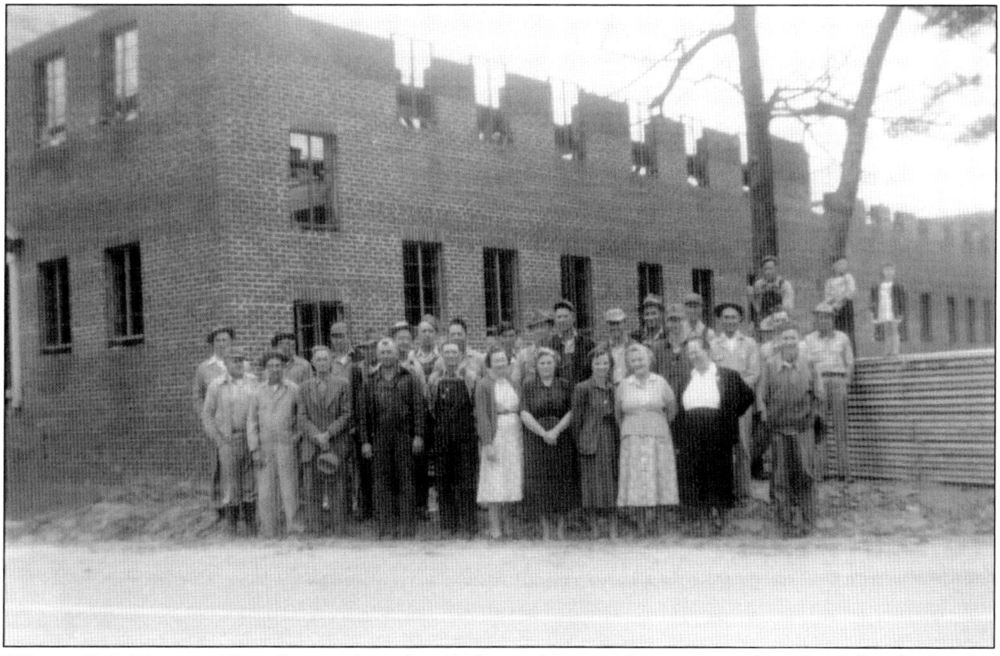

White Oak Baptist Church members break from their work on a new Sunday school wing in the late 1940s to pose for this photograph. After World War II, country churches were urged to expand and update their facilities in order to remain vital in their communities and compete with churches in towns and cities. (Courtesy of Carlton Vinson.)

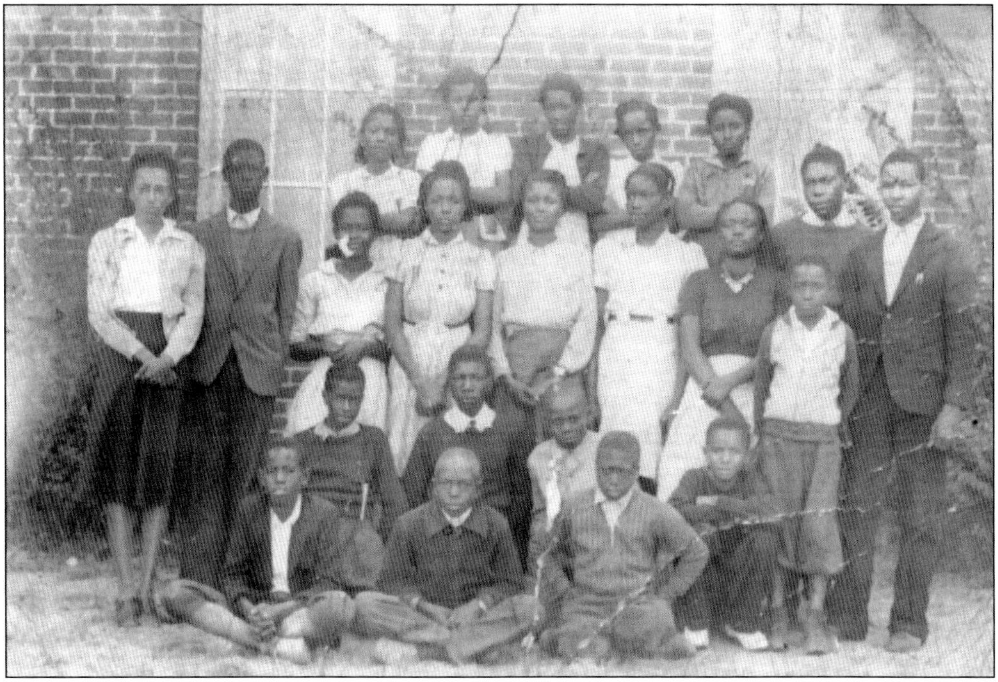

Sixth graders at Wilson's Mills School pose for this photograph in 1940.

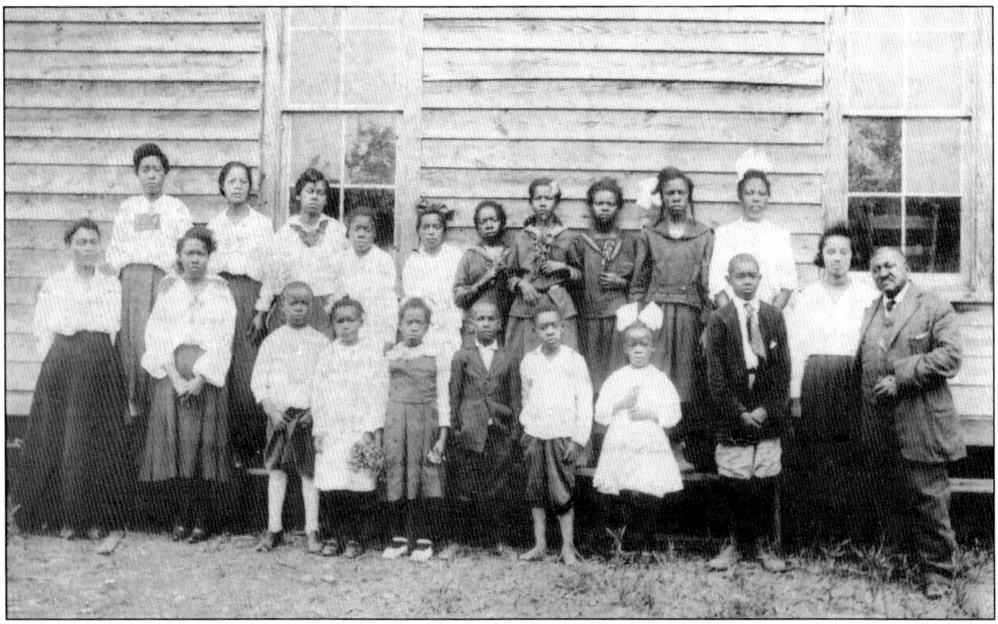

Black Free Will Baptists established what was known as "Skinner's College" in a neighborhood called Macedonia, near Kenly, in 1914. Shown here are students and teachers around 1923. From left to right are (first row) teacher named Florence, unidentified, David Williams, Mary Manning, Luvenia Williams, student named Scott, Hallie Purvis, Helen Squall, Buddy Scott, teacher Annie Pearl Pearsall, and Prof. J. H. Skinner; (second row) Pollie Simms, Ester Price, Mae Carter Sutton, unidentified, Thelma Jenkins, two unidentified, Adeline Jones, Lillian Horton, and Naomi Turner.

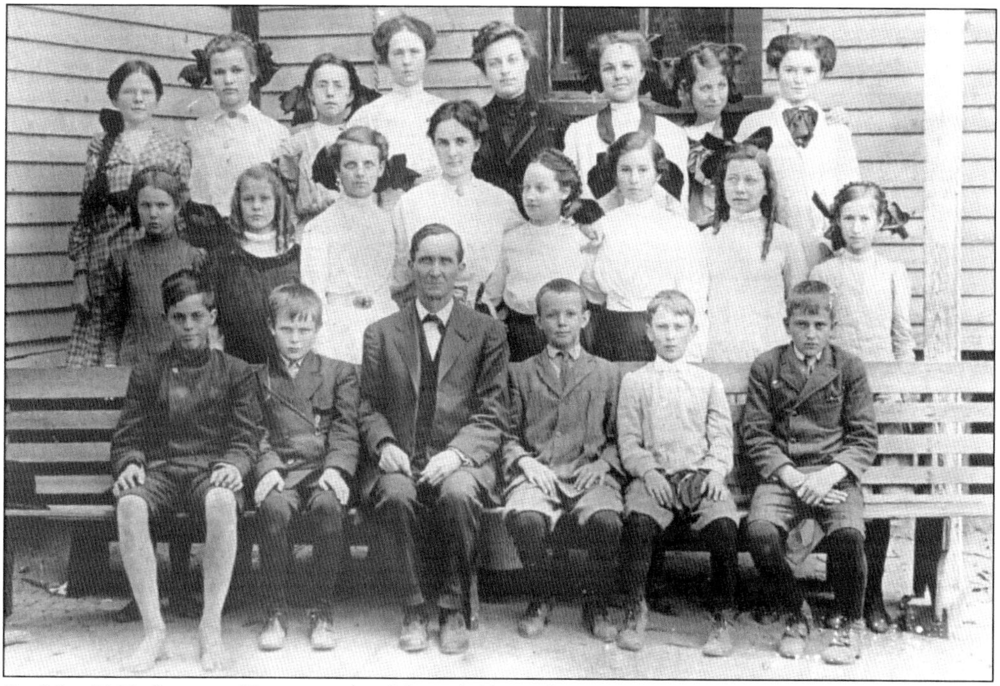

Prof. Ira T. Turlington (first row, third from left) sat down for a pose with students at Turlington Graded School in Smithfield about 1912. To Turlington's left is Edwin Smith Pou, who in a few short years would lose his life fighting in Europe during World War I. John Avera is the shoeless boy. Pioneer female attorney Rhetta Martin is the girl with long curls (second row, second from right).

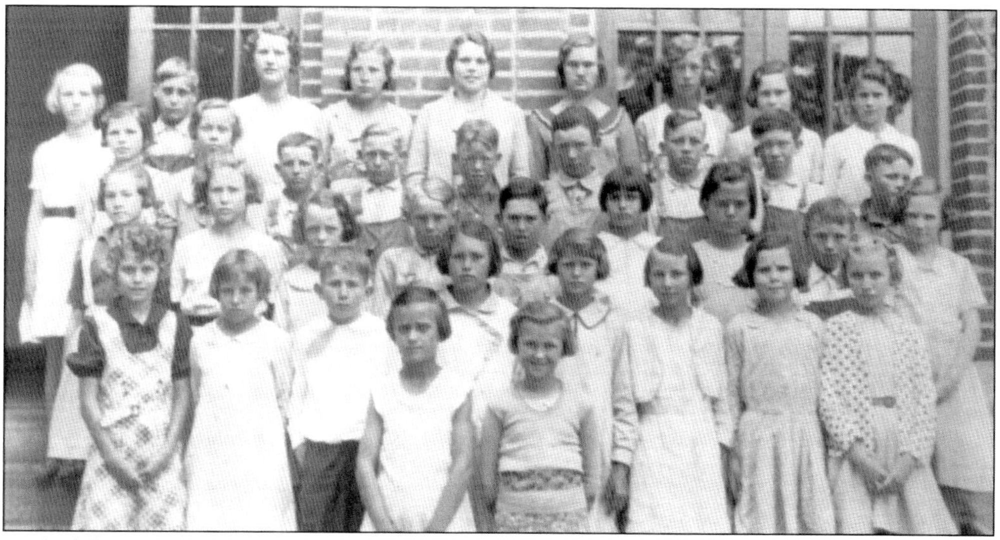

Little did anyone in this Brogden School fifth grade class know when this photograph was taken in 1932 that one of their classmates would become a famous Hollywood movie star. Ava Gardner is the curly-haired girl at far left in the second row. Gardner lived next door in the Brogden Teacherage, where her mother was matron and cook for boarding female teachers. Two years later, the county school system closed the boardinghouse, and Ava moved with her parents to Newport News, Virginia.

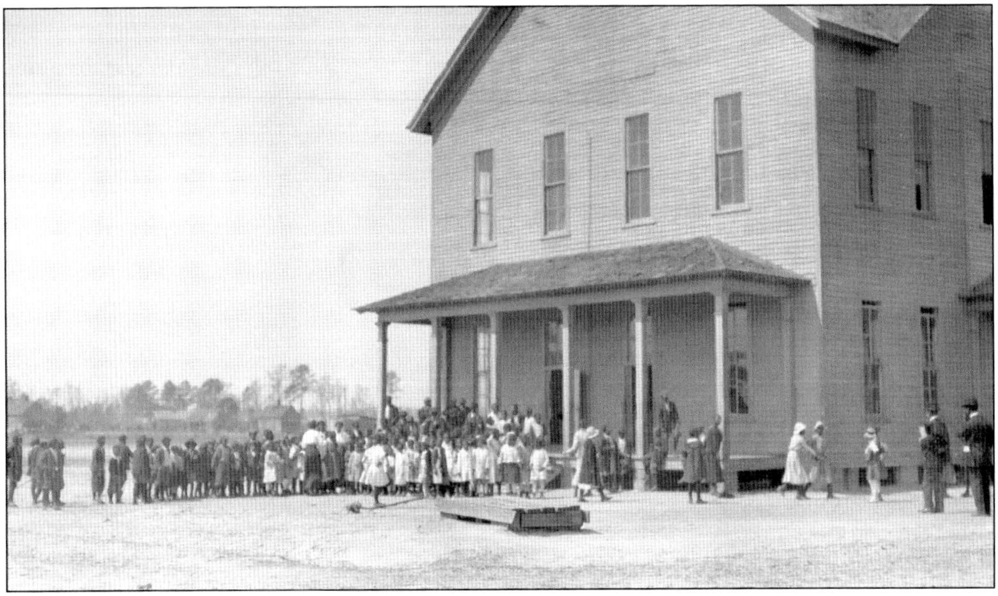

The former Turlington Institute structure was moved from its Third Street location to the Belmont section of Smithfield in 1914 to be used as the first classroom building for Johnston County Training School, the county's first public high school for African Americans. Jackson Davis, supervisor of the general education board in New York, took this photograph on one of at least two visits to the school in its beginning years, 1915–1916. The board worked with the Slater Fund and later the Rosenwald Fund to start training schools that placed an emphasis on industrial and vocational education. (Courtesy of the Albert and Shirley Small Special Collections Library, University of Virginia, Charlottesville.)

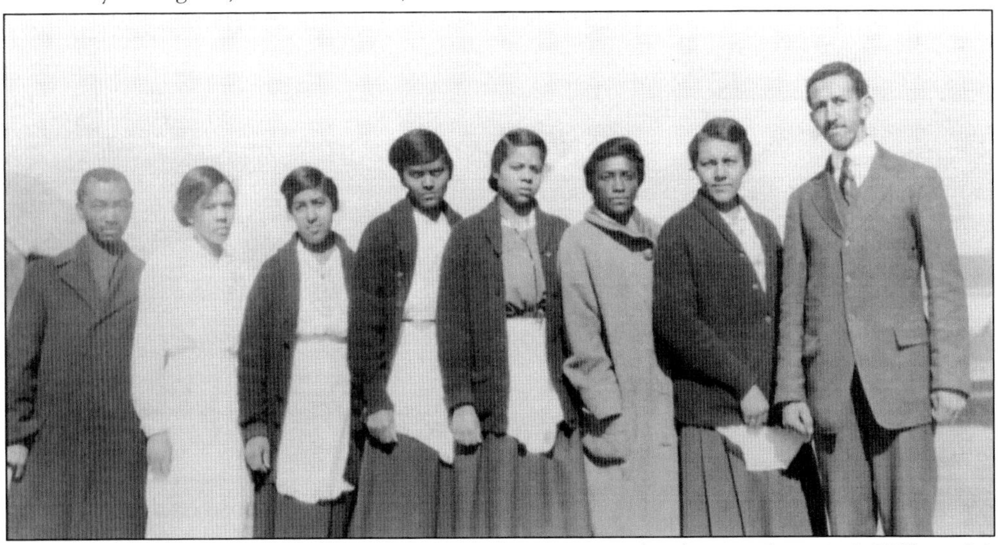

Pictured here is the faculty of Johnston County Training School in 1915 or 1916. William M. Cooper from Hampton, Virginia, was principal, and the following teachers were listed in a 1917 report: Mrs. W.M. Cooper, Lillian D. Pearce, Susie G. Weeden, Amanda B. Rhone, Ellen F. Blow, Mildred Freeman, and Louise Bryan. All these teachers except Mrs. Cooper were unmarried and brought in from Hampton, Raleigh, and other places outside Johnston County. (Courtesy of Albert and Shirley Small Special Collections Library, University of Virginia, Charlottesville)

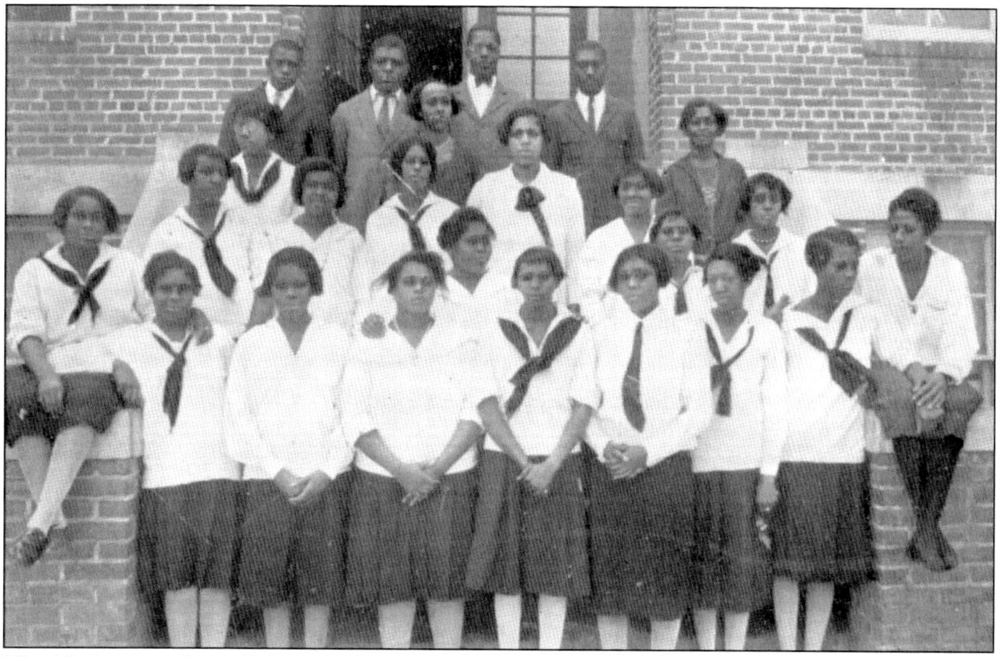

The 1926 senior class of Johnston County Training School included (in no particular order) Cora Avera, Lucile Allen, Neppie Barbour, Lucilla Barbour, Ned Barbour, Velma Campbell, Rachel Holden, Luella Hood, Magnolia Judkins, Alexander Judkins, Percy Mitchener, Lugenia Mitchener, Elmer Mitchener, Eddie Dora Mitchener, Flossie Raiford, Dora Smith, Ellen Sanders, Leasie Ann Smith, Castella Vinson, Gussie Sanders, Mollie White, Estella Williams, and Pearl Williams.

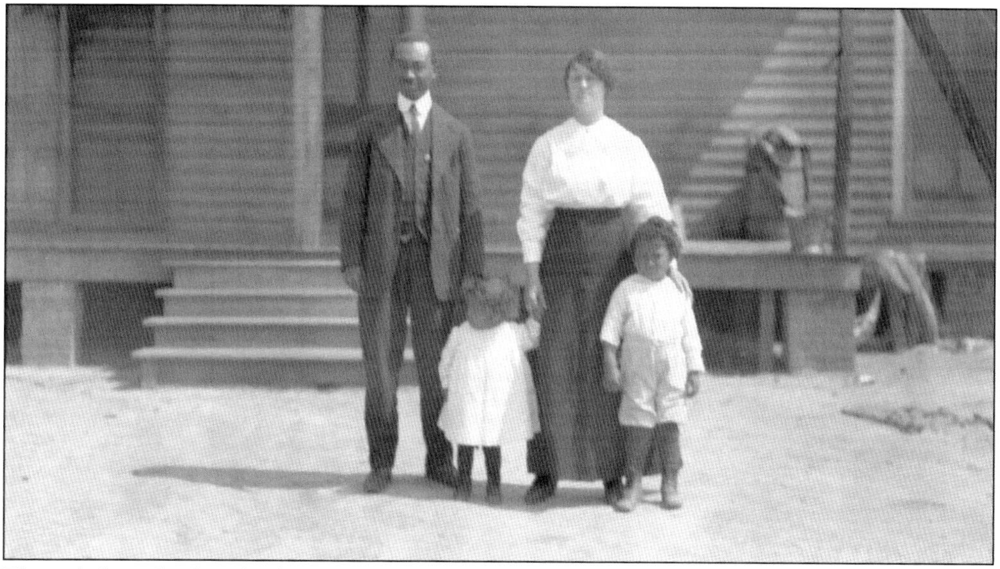

This is believed to be Charles L.W. Smith; his wife, Ella; and their two children. Smith, the son of wealthy businessman Ashley Smith, was a teacher who held the title of Johnston County Negro School supervisor and was principal of the Smithfield public school for blacks (on Fourth Street) when it was replaced by the County Training School in 1914. He served as the first principal of Johnston County Training School. (Courtesy of the Albert and Shirley Small Special Collections Library, University of Virginia, Charlottesville.)

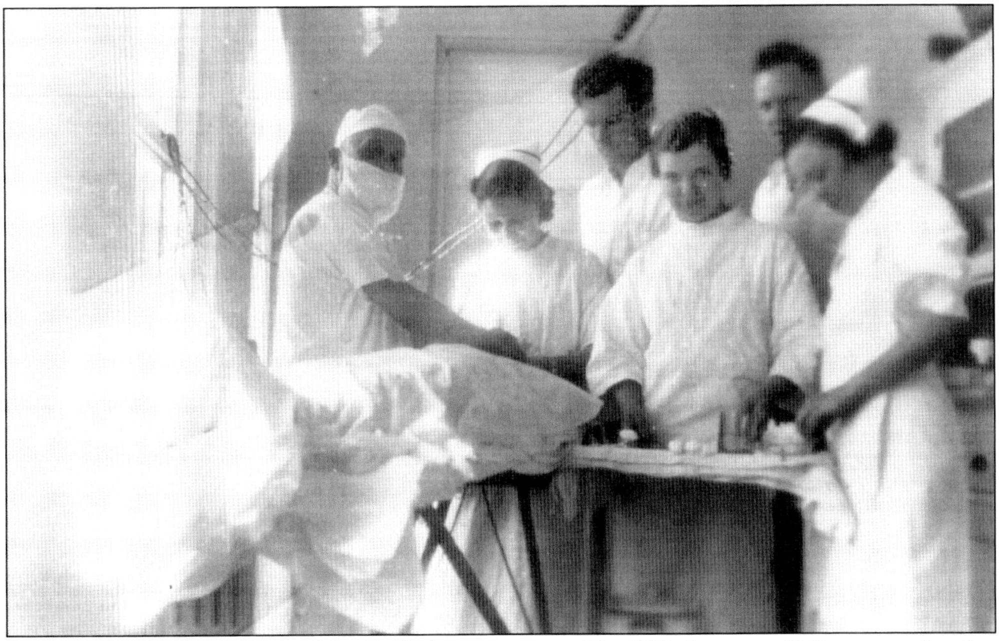

In the 1920s, Dr. Wade H. Atkinson (left, wearing mask) of Washington, DC, returned to his native Johnston County to perform free tonsillectomies on local schoolchildren whose parents were struggling in the midst of an agricultural depression. Here, he is shown with nurses and interns during a procedure in the Corbett-Hatcher School in O'Neals Township.

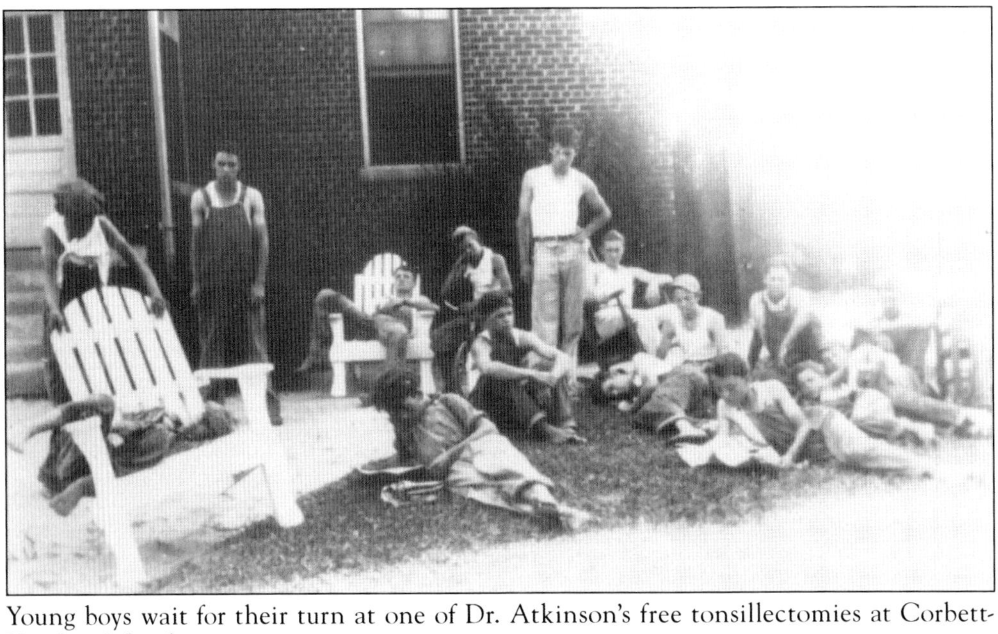

Young boys wait for their turn at one of Dr. Atkinson's free tonsillectomies at Corbett-Hatcher School.

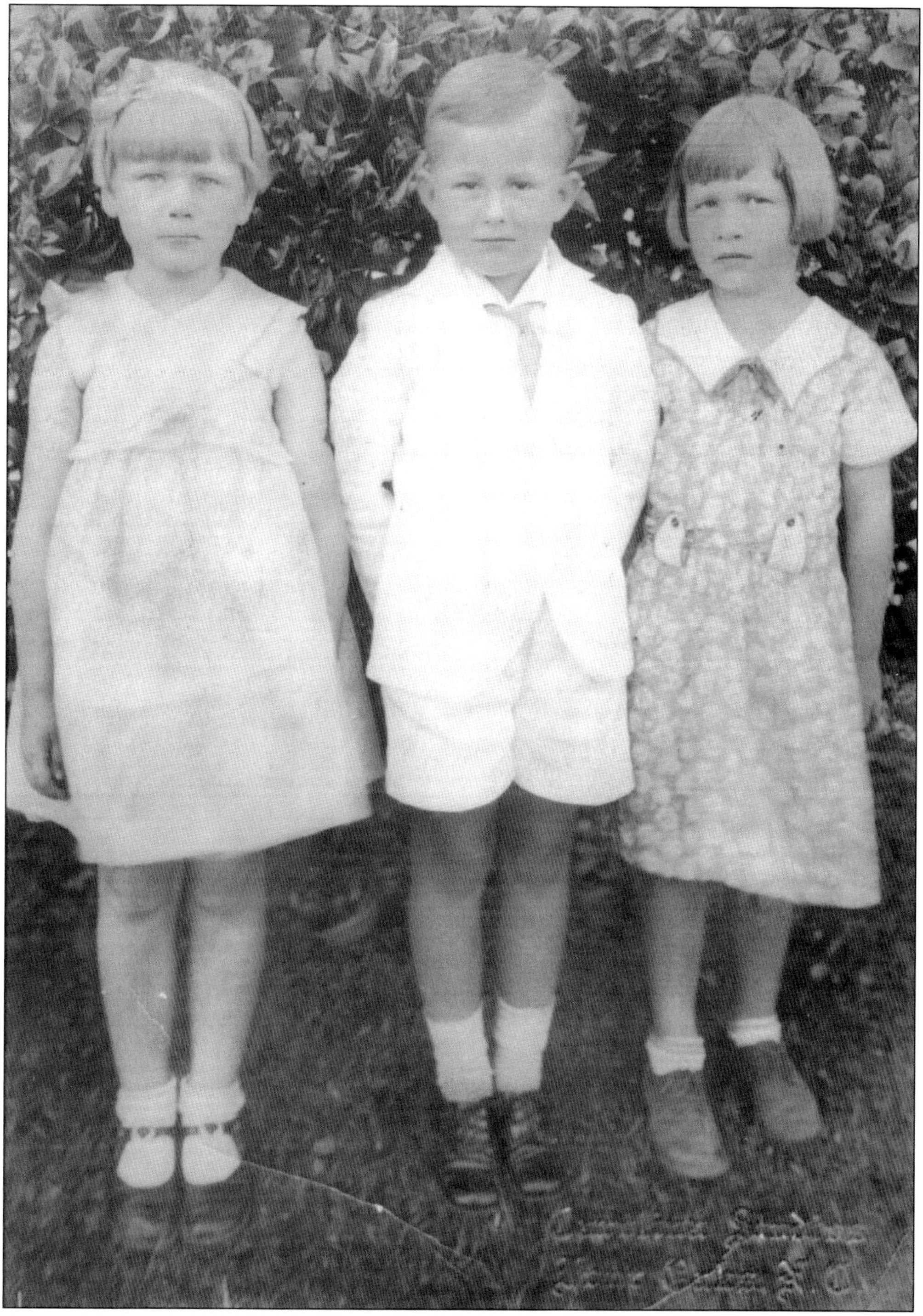

"Three Children Physically Perfect" is the headline from the front page of the *Smithfield Herald* on May 26, 1933. They are, from left to right, Joyce Williams, Jack Hamilton Jr., and Dorothy Mae Toler. In 1933, it was very rare to have local images published in the paper due to the expense of making printing plates from photographs.

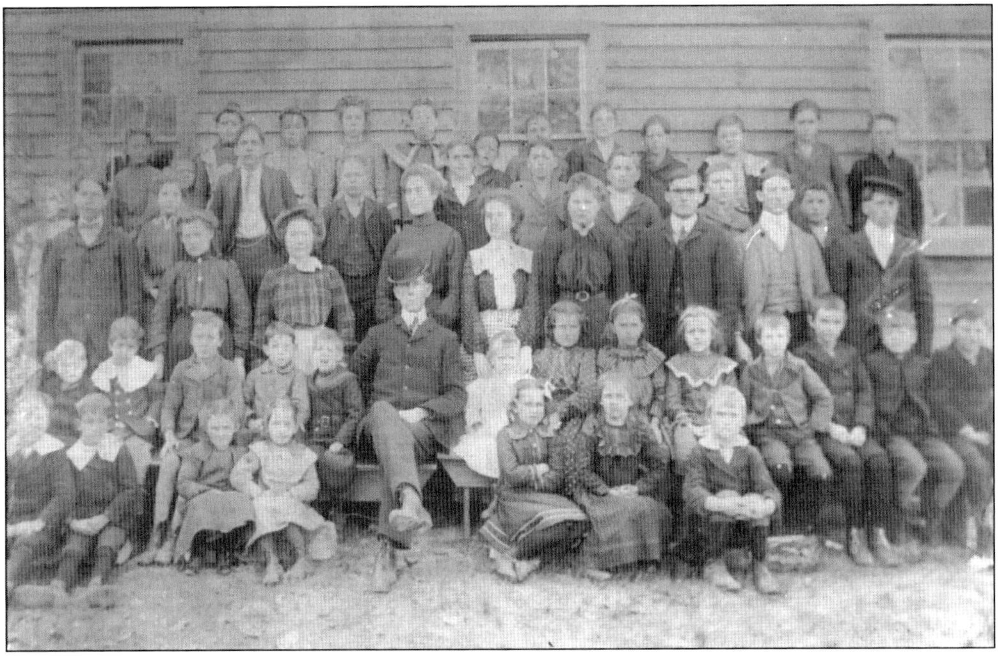

Students from about six years old to early adulthood pose with their dapper teacher in front of the one-room Elevation School around 1900. (Courtesy of Benson Museum of Local History.)

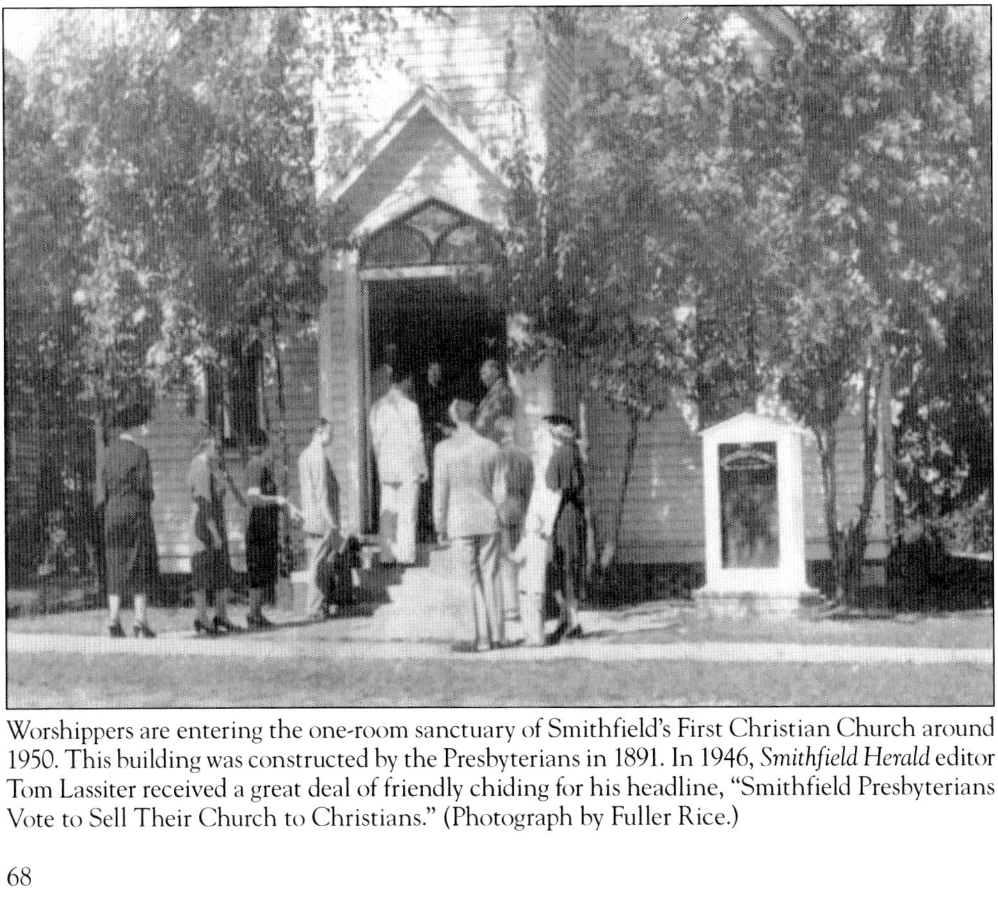

Worshippers are entering the one-room sanctuary of Smithfield's First Christian Church around 1950. This building was constructed by the Presbyterians in 1891. In 1946, *Smithfield Herald* editor Tom Lassiter received a great deal of friendly chiding for his headline, "Smithfield Presbyterians Vote to Sell Their Church to Christians." (Photograph by Fuller Rice.)

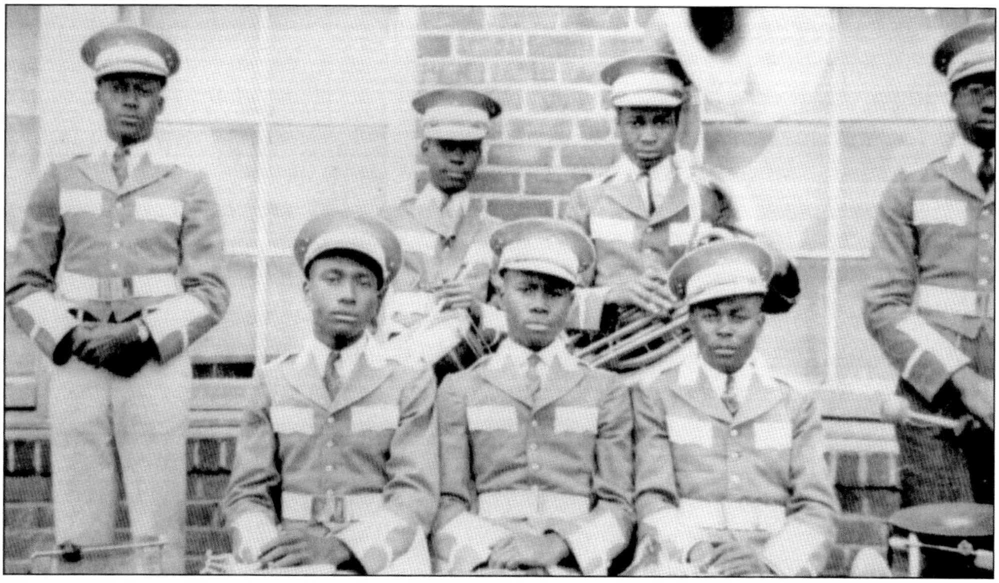

These well-dressed band members from William M. Cooper High School in Clayton are captured on camera sometime around 1946. (Courtesy of Hocutt-Ellington Memorial Library.)

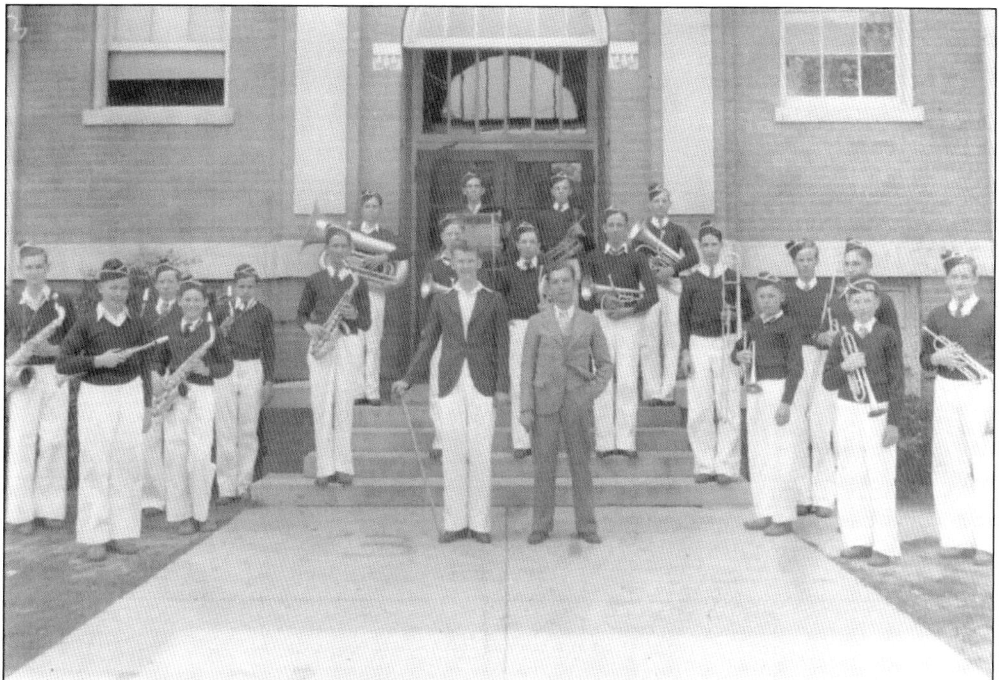

Band teacher Shorty Groves (in front wearing non-matching suit) stands proudly with his all-male Smithfield High School Band about 1930. Band members are, from left to right, (on ground level) William Norman Holt, Glen Grier, Charlie Parrish, Eddie Perkins, Pope Lyon, Lemuel Creech, Rudolph Howell, Nuit Edgerton, Nathan Lassiter, Hubert Woodall Jr., and Edwin Broadhurst; (on first step) Paul Johnston and Charlie Royall; (second step) two unidentified and James Smith; (third step) Jeff Wallace, Raymond Talton, Richard Noble, and Ben Grimes.

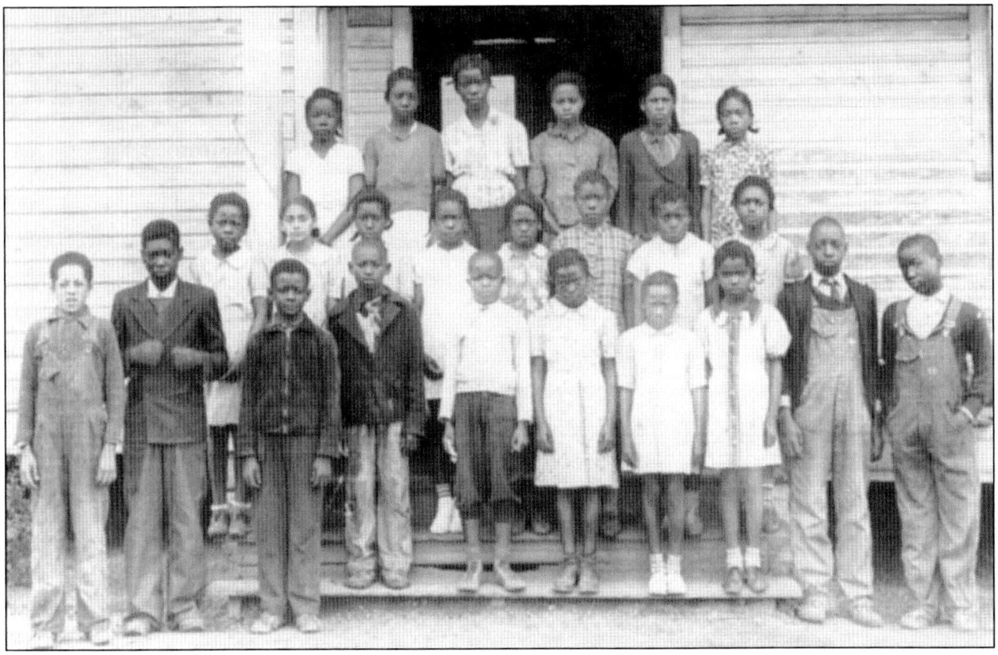

This group of students in Kenly in 1938 appear none too happy about having their photograph taken.

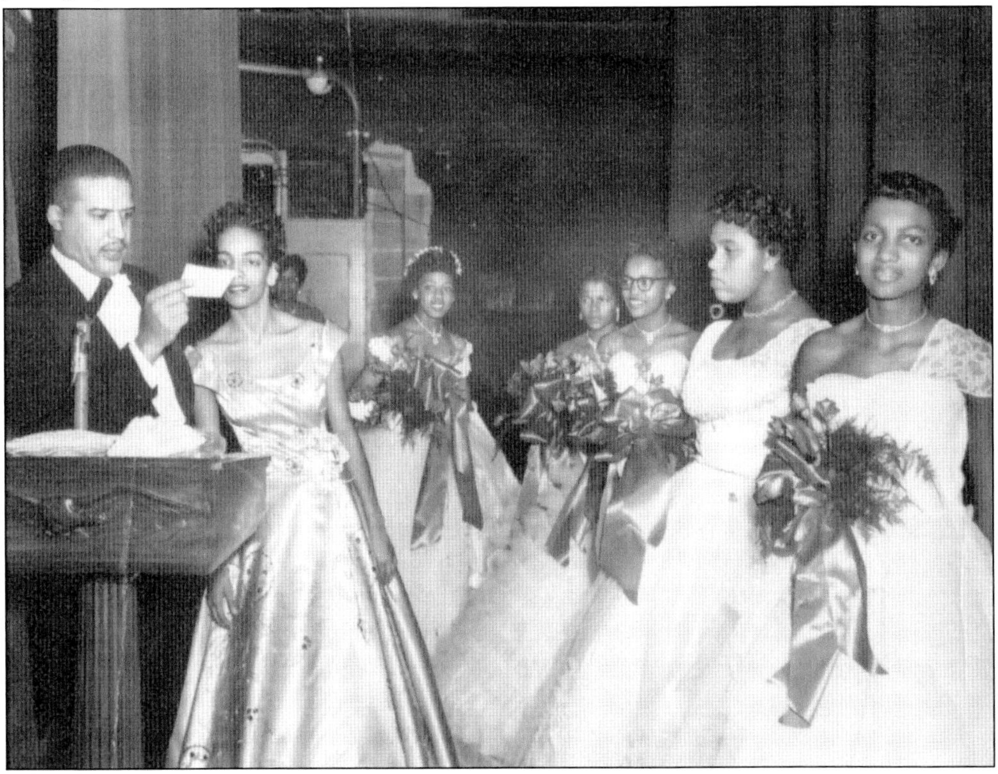

WRAL radio personality J.D. Lewis is master of ceremonies for the Miss Cooper High School pageant in Clayton in the mid-1950s. (Courtesy of Hocutt-Ellington Memorial Library.)

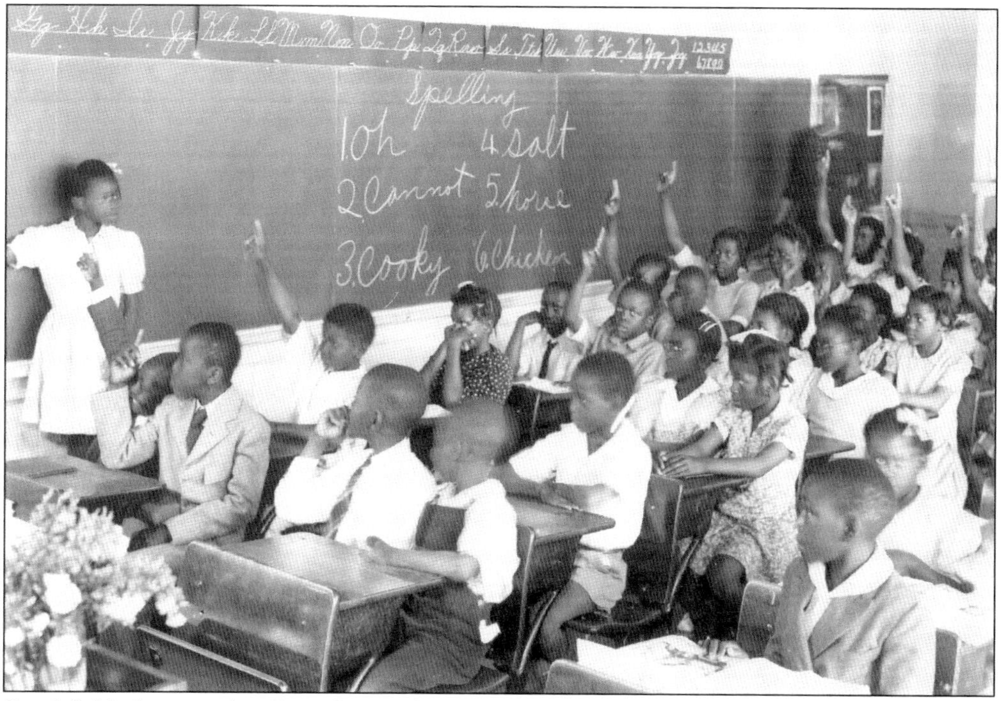

Smithfield photographer Dorothy Hooks caught these students at Short Journey School near Smithfield on camera about 1946. The teacher stood in the back as a student led the class.

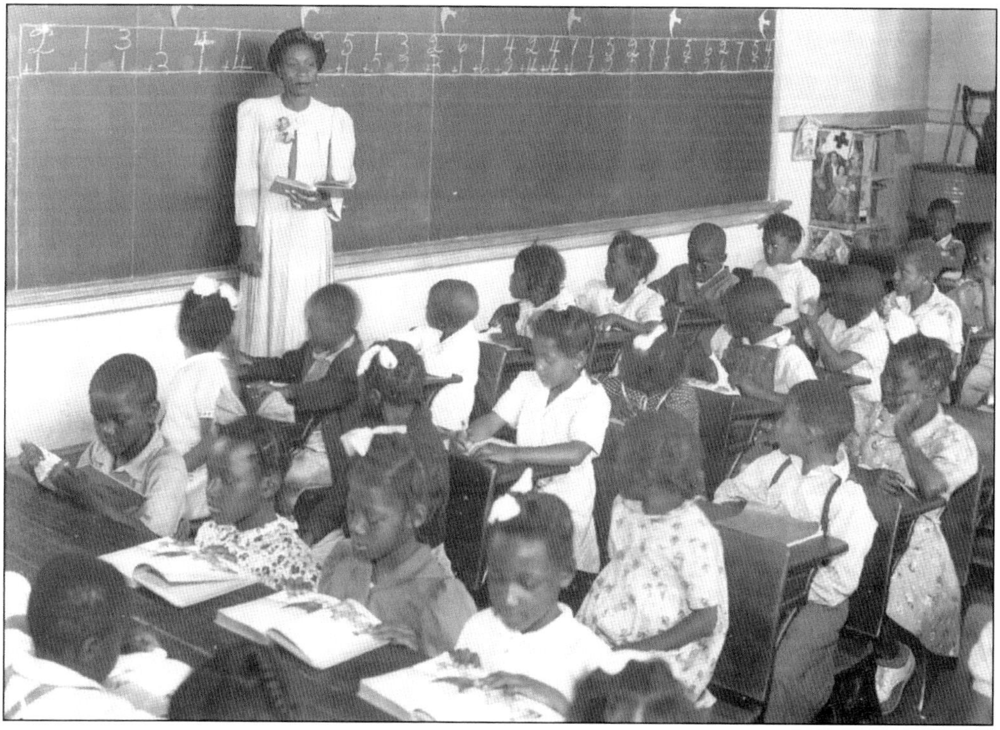

Math teacher Cora Tolar leads her class at Short Journey School around 1946. The American Red Cross poster in the back signifies the war effort was still ongoing.

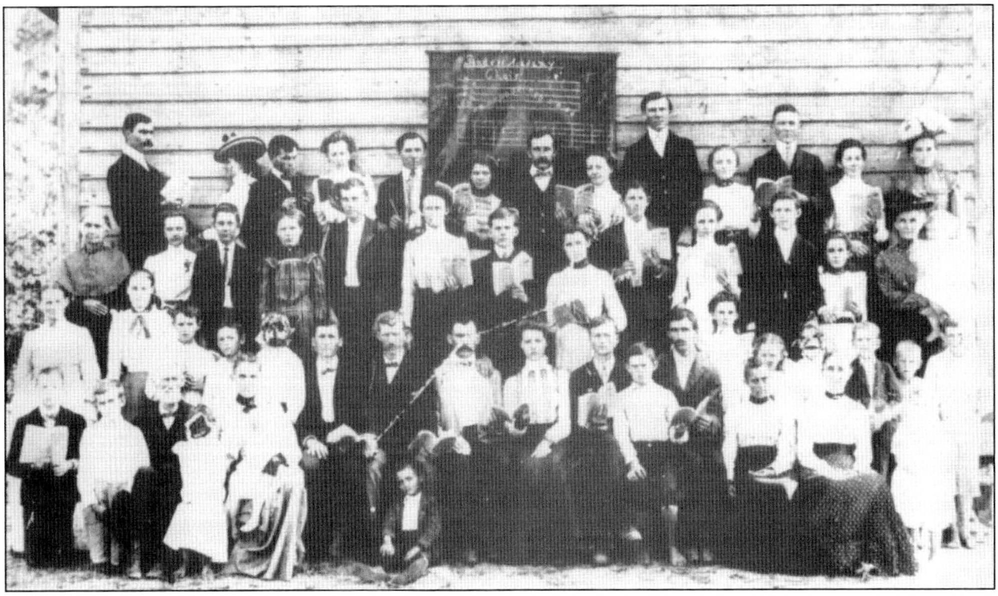

When cotton was laid by in late summer prior to the picking season, farm families enjoyed activities such as this singing school held at the Lizzard Hill School in Ingrams Township. Teacher Neil Eason is the mustached gentleman in front with dark coat, and Jimmy Rhodes is at his feet. This photograph was taken on graduation day, August 19, 1903. The blackboard reads, "Sanders Academy Choir."

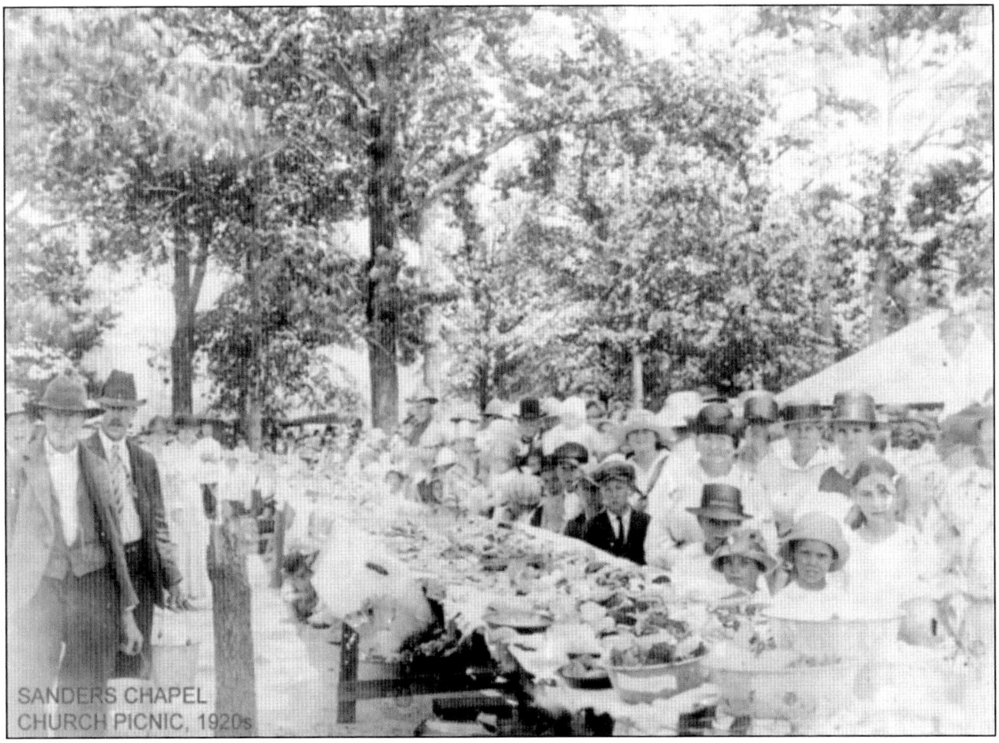

This church picnic at Sanders Chapel Methodist Church near Smithfield in the 1920s shows a spread of country cooking almost as far as the eye can see.

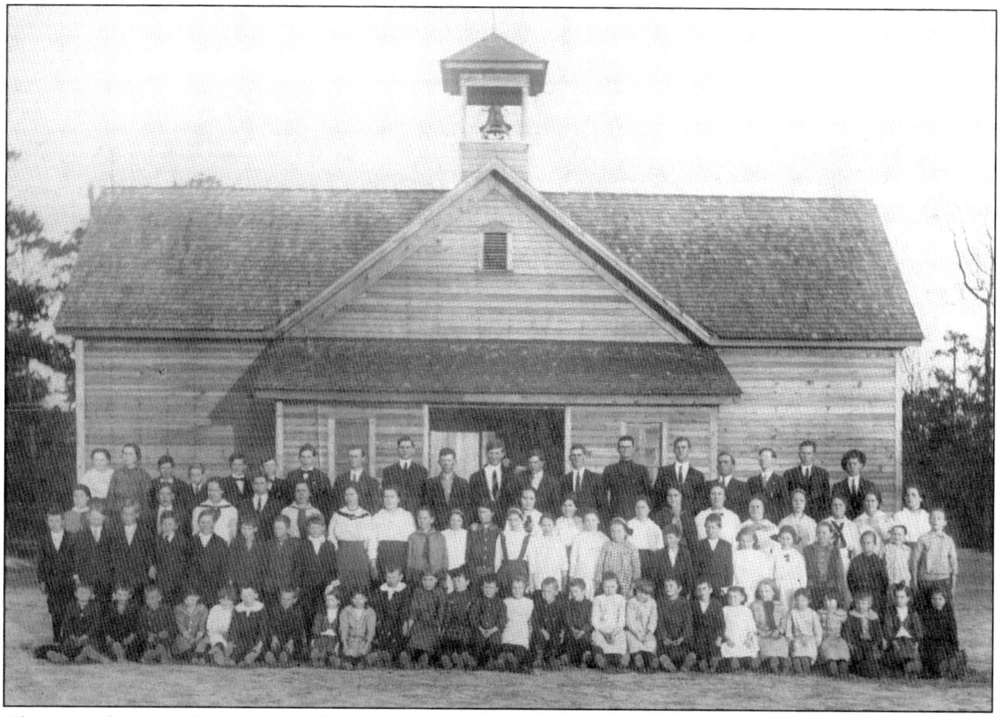

These students and teachers at the Allen School near Blackman's Crossroads in Ingrams Township are dressed in their finest for this photograph in the mid-1910s. This typical two-room school featured a prominent bell tower in the center. (Courtesy of Stanton Massengill.)

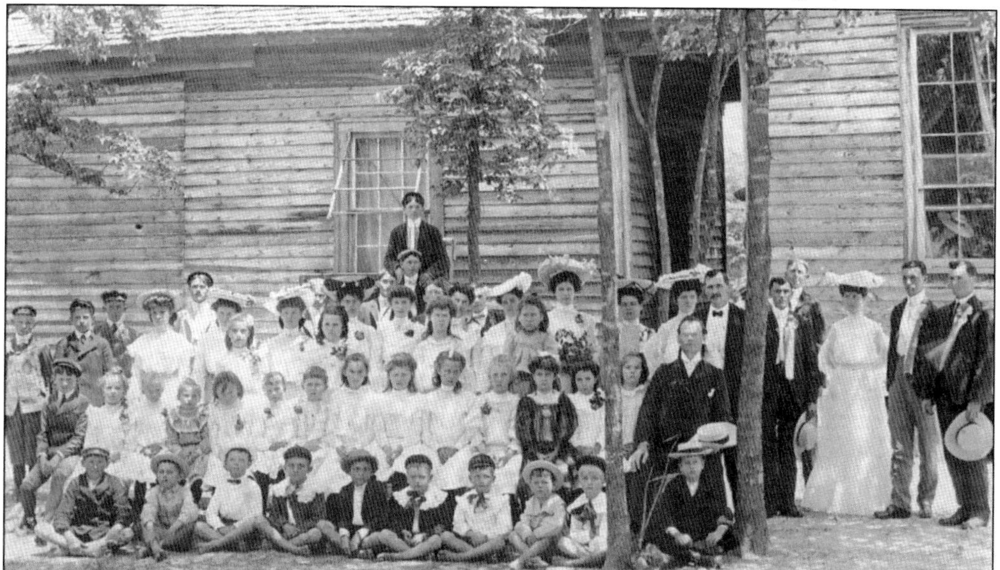

The spring school closing program was one of the biggest events in rural communities in the early 20th century and an occasion to dress in one's Sunday finest. This rare image is from the Royall School in Elevation Township around 1910. The beribboned judges at the right probably decided who received prizes for best song, poem, or speech. Perhaps the little girl peeping through the window was camera shy. (Courtesy of Benson Museum of Local History.)

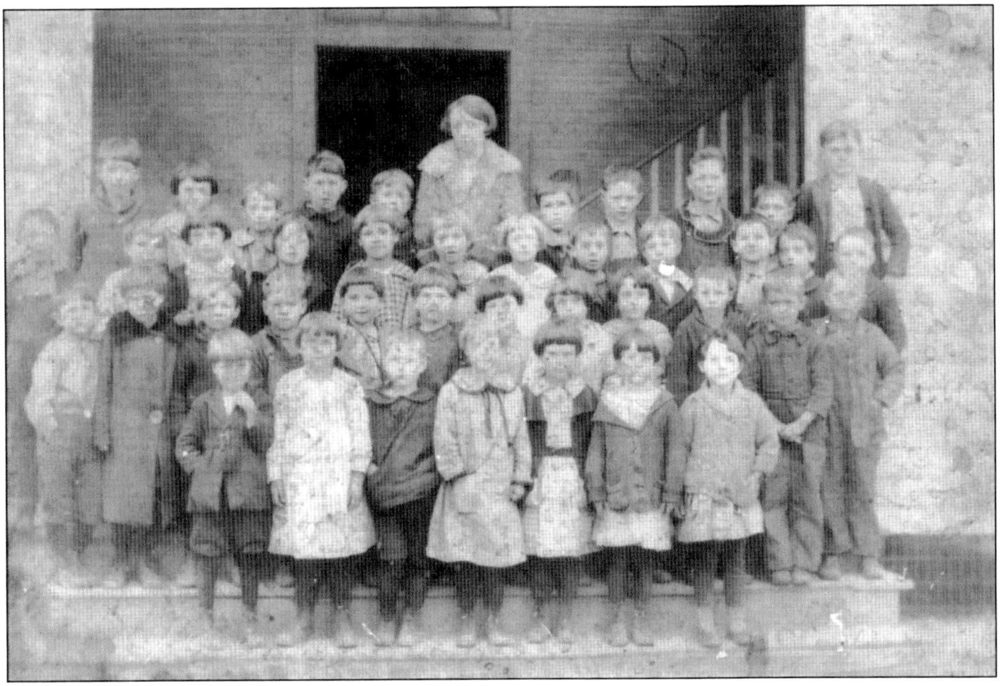

This image of a Meadow School group dates from 1924, the year before a new brick school was completed. (Courtesy of Michael Wheeler.)

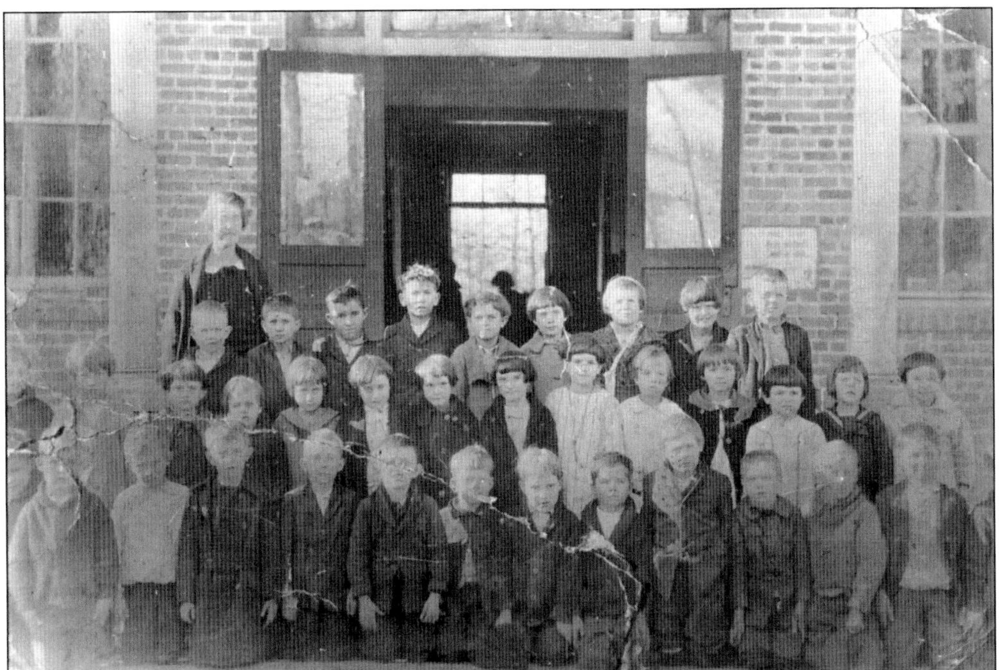

This photograph shows the Pine Level School's first grade class in 1923. Apparently some of these students were not thrilled to have their photograph taken or else were told to keep mouths closed to hide all the missing teeth.

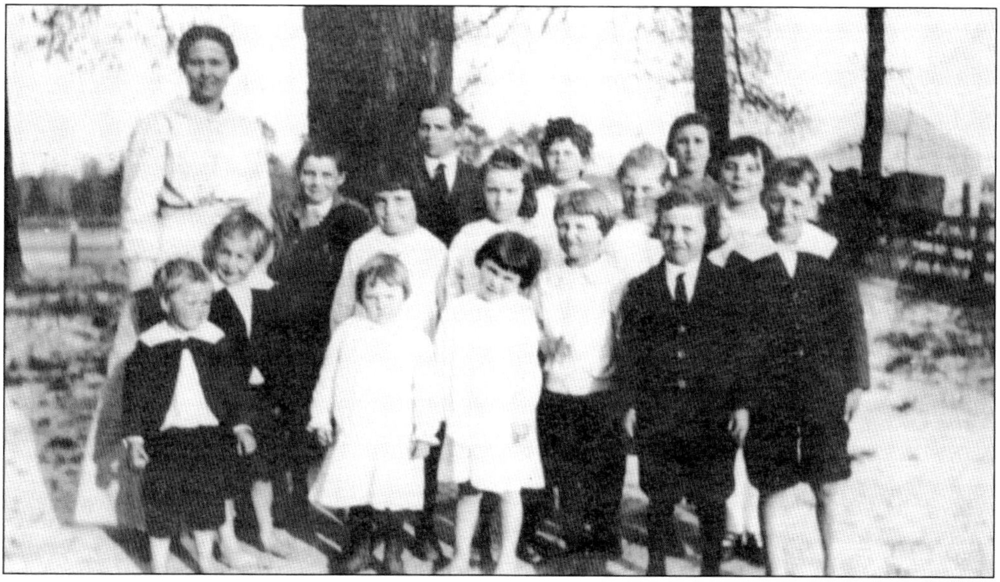

Elizabeth Holt Johnson (back row, left) is pictured with her Sunday school pupils at Oakland Presbyterian Church in Cleveland Township around 1910. Page Taylor and Elsie Barber, who later married, are spotted in the back row (third and fourth from left).

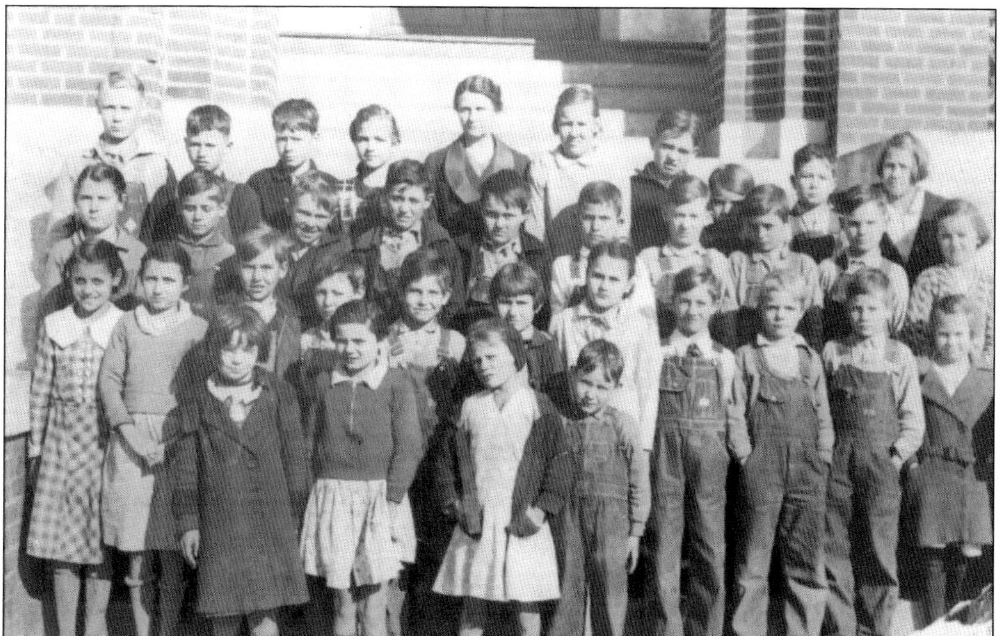

This group of students, who appear to be in third or fourth grade, are posing in front of Cleveland School sometime in the 1930s. Most all the boys are wearing overalls.

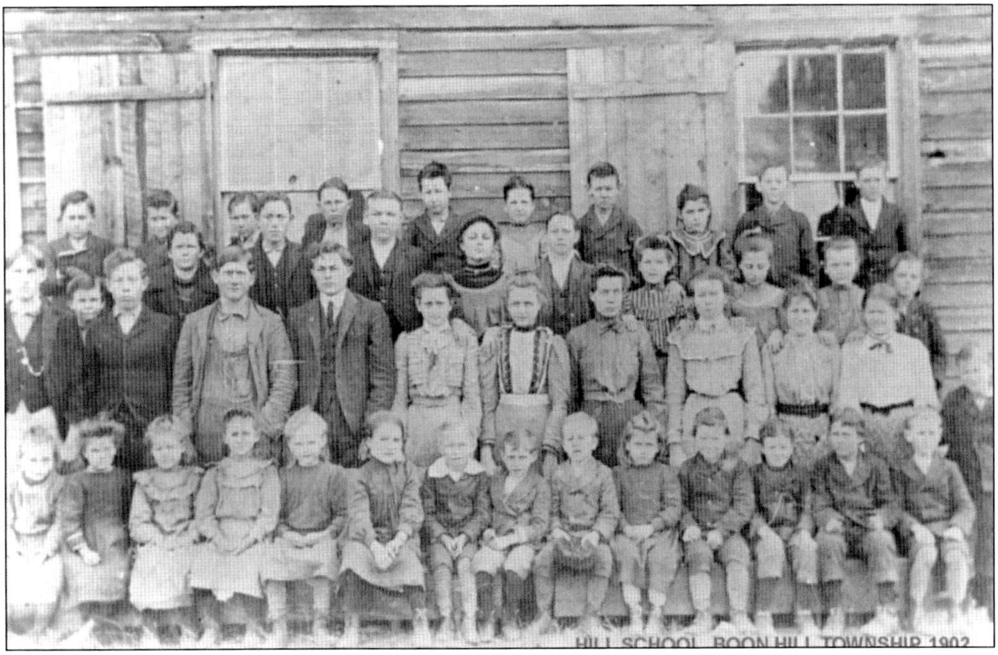

These Boon Hill Township children are dressed up for picture day at the Hill School in 1902. Teachers normally stood to the side, but the only person in this faded photograph who appears old enough for a teacher is fourth from right in the second row.

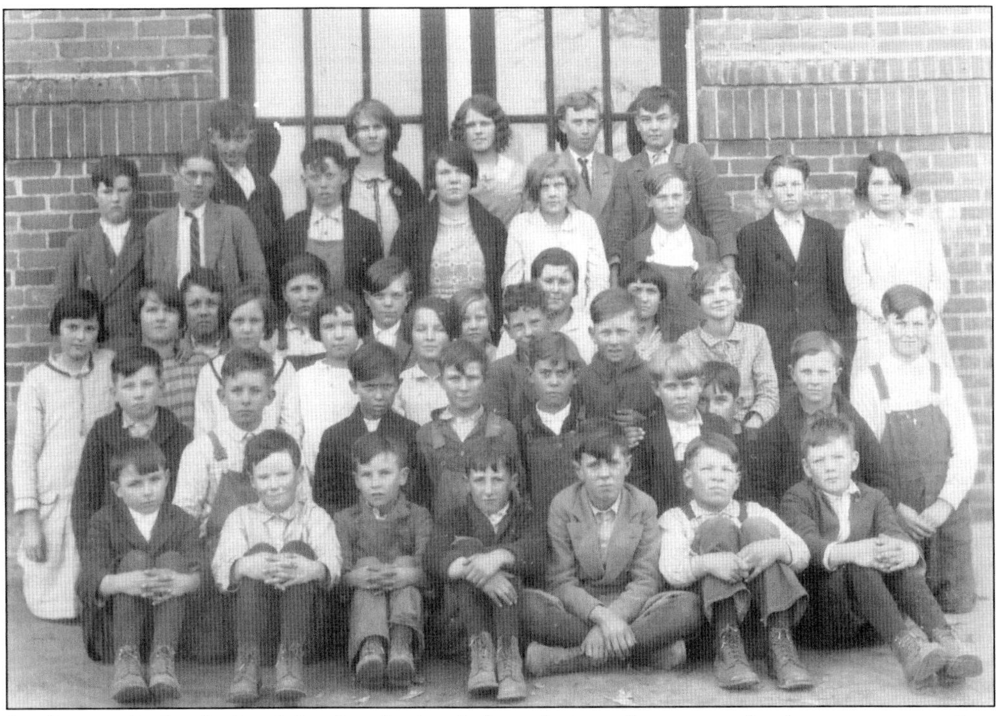

Students at Archer Lodge School took a break from their studies to pose for the camera sometime in the 1930s. (Courtesy of Carlton Vinson.)

Five

Making a Living

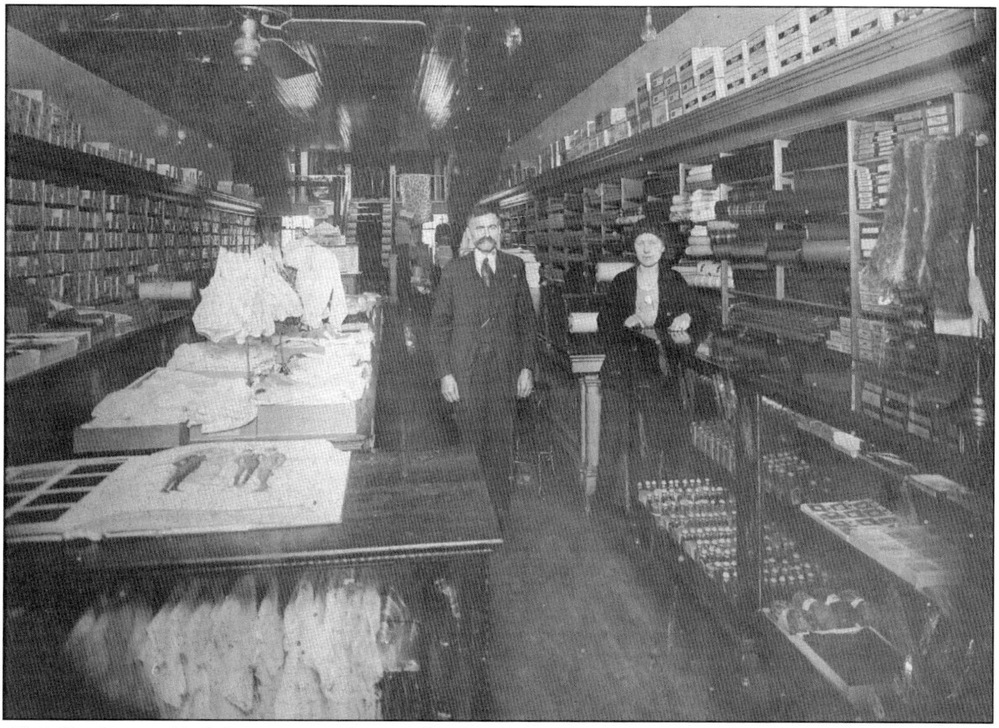

Abdalla George Rabil was one of several Lebanese immigrants who came to Smithfield in the early 20th century to escape persecution of Christians by Muslim Turks. He worked hard and saved money to open this dry goods store prior to 1920. Customers could buy ready-made clothing or an assortment of cloth to make their own. He also carried shoes, boots, ties, and other apparel. The lady pictured here with Rabil in this 1920s photograph may be Annie Peacock, who is listed as a dry goods saleslady in the 1920 census. She lived in the historic Hastings House when it sat at the corner of Second and Johnston Streets. When Rabil died at age 42 in 1932, the *Smithfield Herald* reported that all the local "Syrian" businesses closed the day of his funeral.

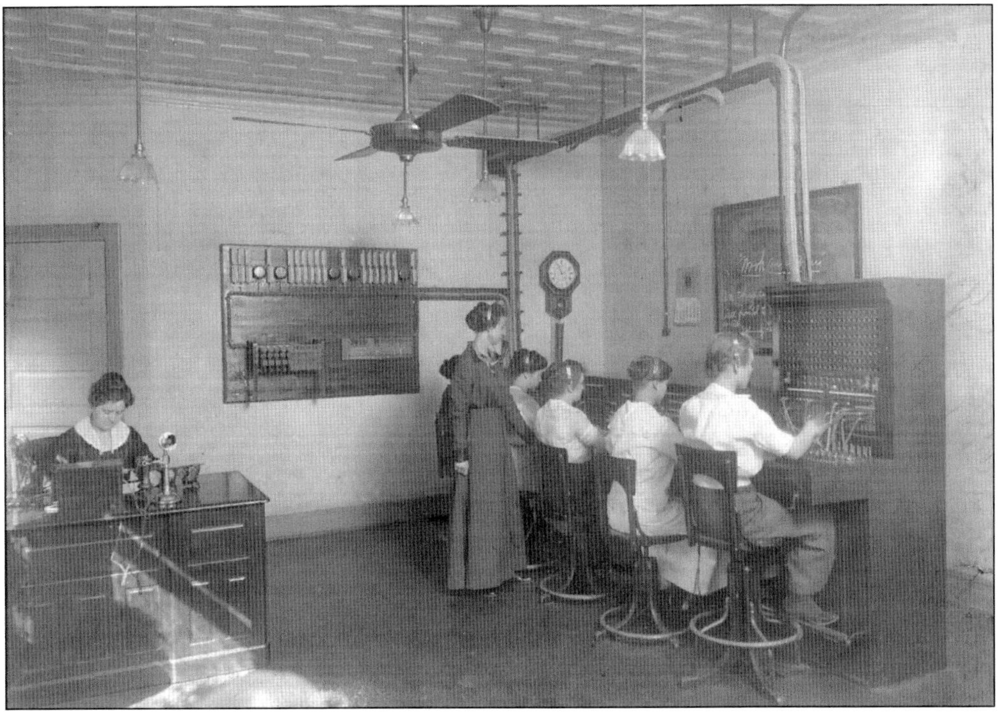

Operators in the Selma telephone office are shown busy at work in November 1915 (the date on the calendar). AT&T officials moved their crew and equipment to Selma in 1910 and made the town their toll switching station from New York to Atlanta. When the Bank of Selma was completed at 100 West Anderson Street in 1912, the AT&T office was located there on an upper floor. The supervisor is believed to be either Blanche Mitchener or Nannie Bailey. (Courtesy of Norwood Thompson, Cattail Mill.)

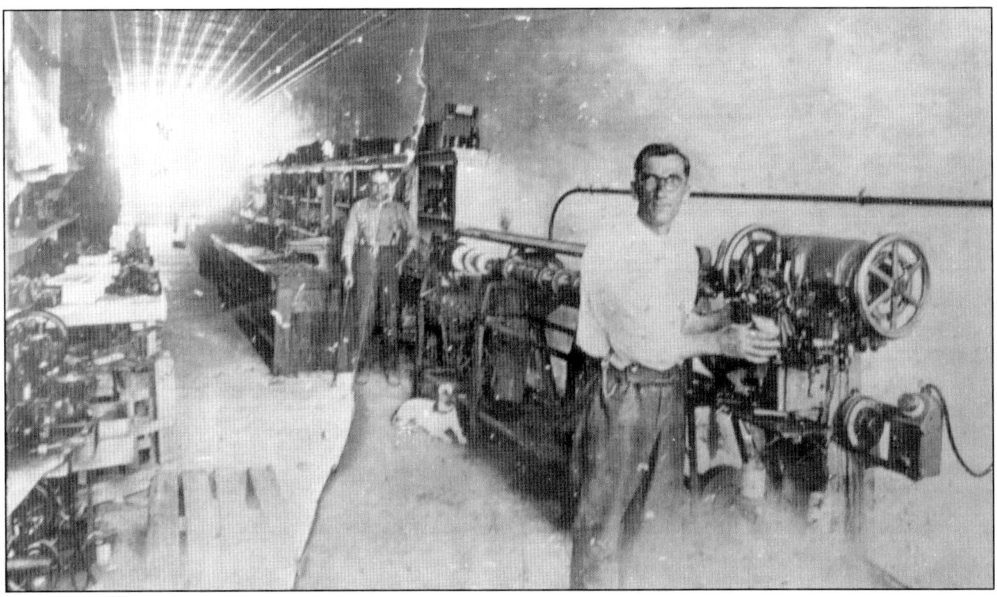

Eppie N. Clifton (foreground) is operating a shoe-sewing machine in his Benson shoe shop around 1925. Addison Ryals is working in the back.

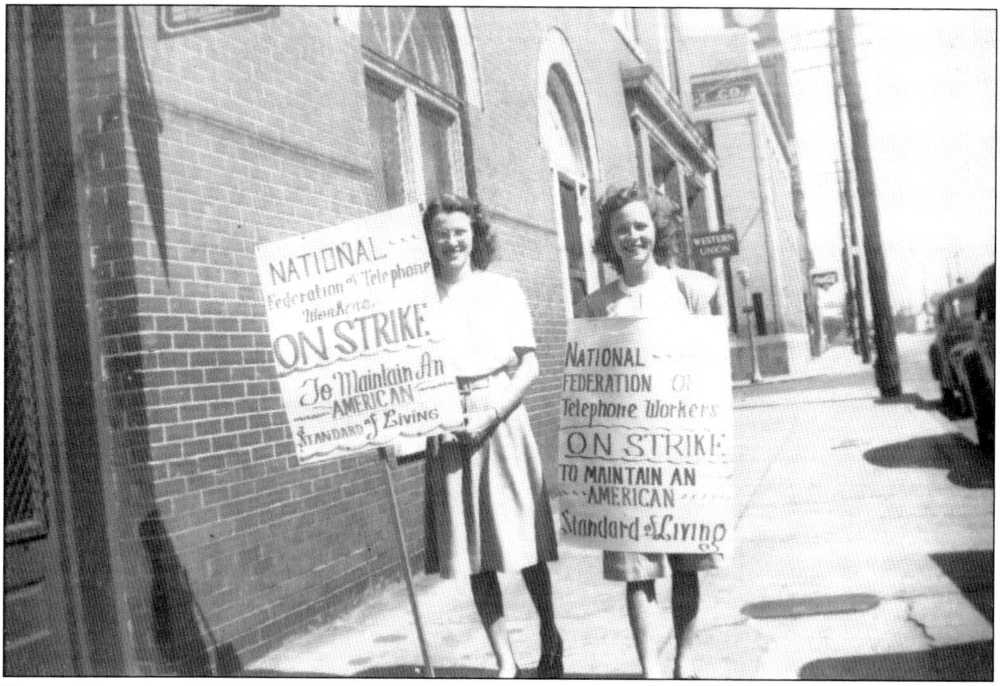

Pictured here in 1947, Josephine "Jo" Flowers (left) and Dorothy "Dot" Walters (right) are among several Southern Bell belles picketing at the corner of Raiford and Anderson Streets in Selma in hopes of a pay raise.

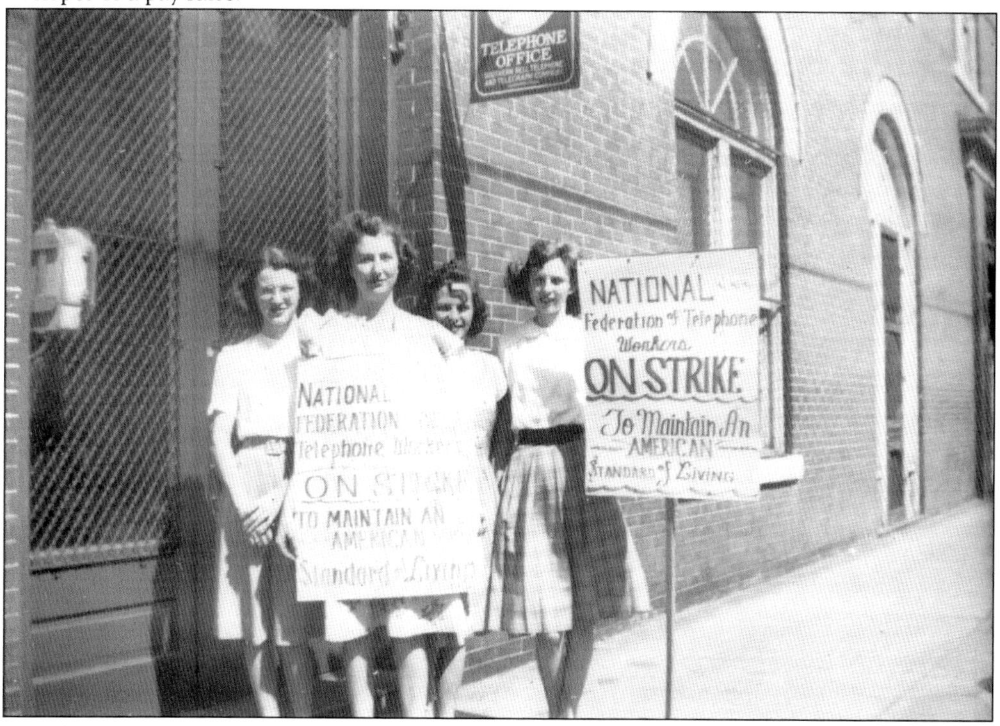

Jo and Dot are joined by Margie Brown (second from left) and Mable Broadwell (far right) during the Southern Bell strike.

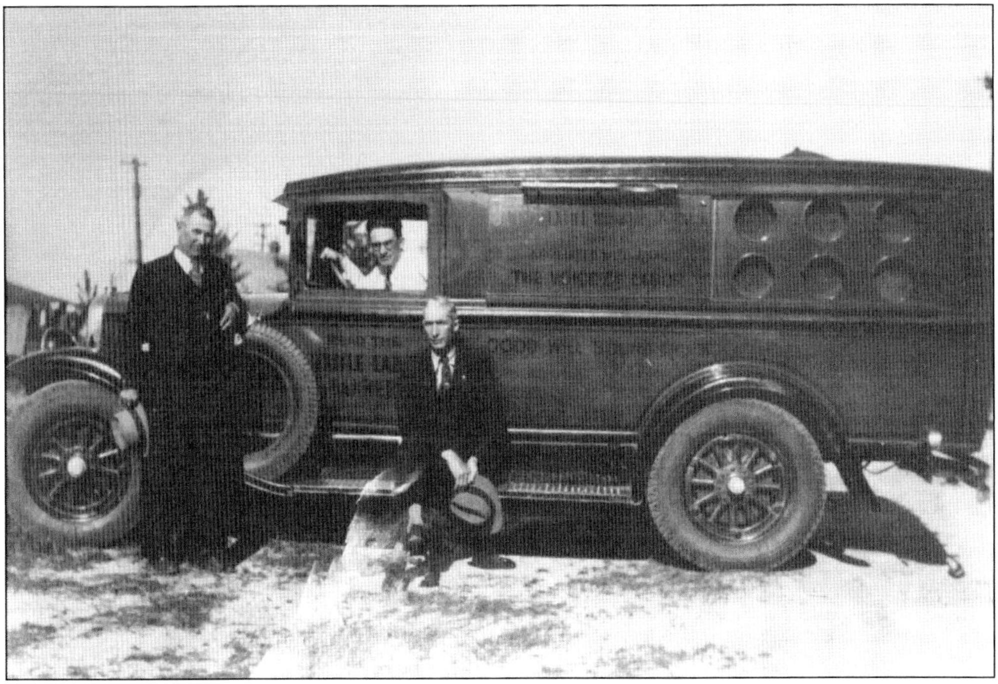

Richard Furman Strickland, a Selma cotton mill employee, is seen driving a vehicle used by labor organizers in the 1930s. His granddaughter recalled that local merchants and townspeople shunned him after he organized a union in Selma. The other two men are unidentified.

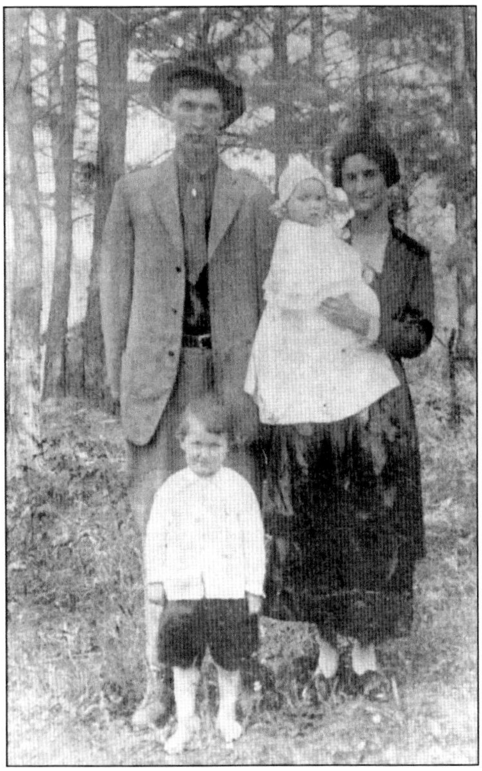

R.F. Strickland is shown with his family in the Selma cotton mill village about 1919.

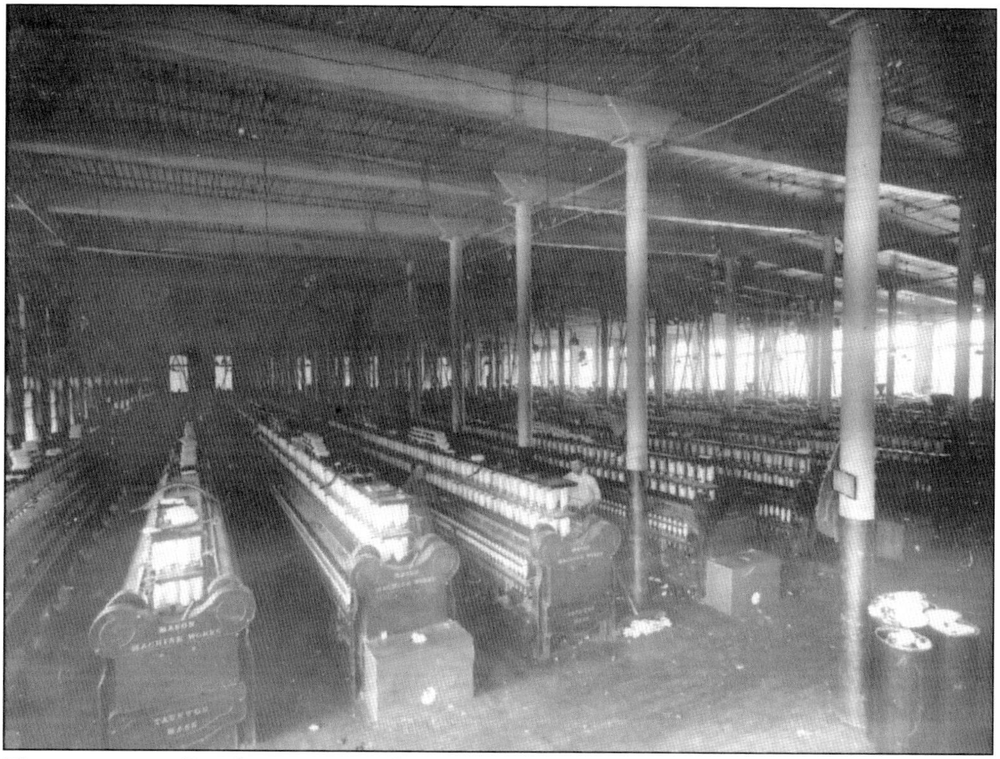

This rare image of Ivanhoe Cotton Mill's interior is taken from a lantern slide shown in the Victory Theater in the early 1920s. The mill closed briefly in the mid-1920s when officers filed bankruptcy, but it soon reopened and resumed its place as one of Smithfield's leading employers.

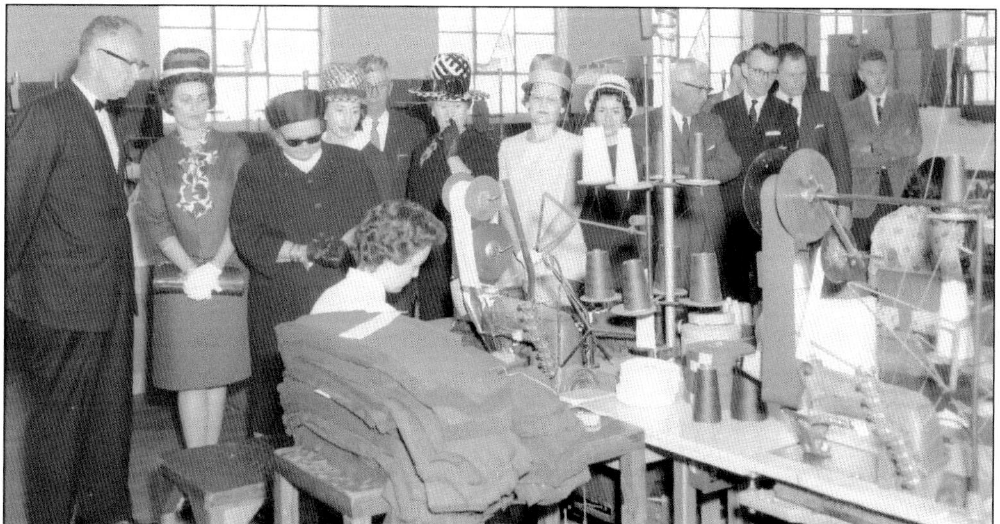

School superintendent Evander S. Simpson (second from right) and other county leaders tour the plant at Norwich Mills in Clayton in 1966. Much attention was placed on industrial recruitment, especially in manufacturing, during those days to reverse the county's declining population. Fancy hats and horn-rimmed glasses were still in style with the ladies. (Photograph by Charles Barden; courtesy of Hocutt-Ellington Memorial Library.)

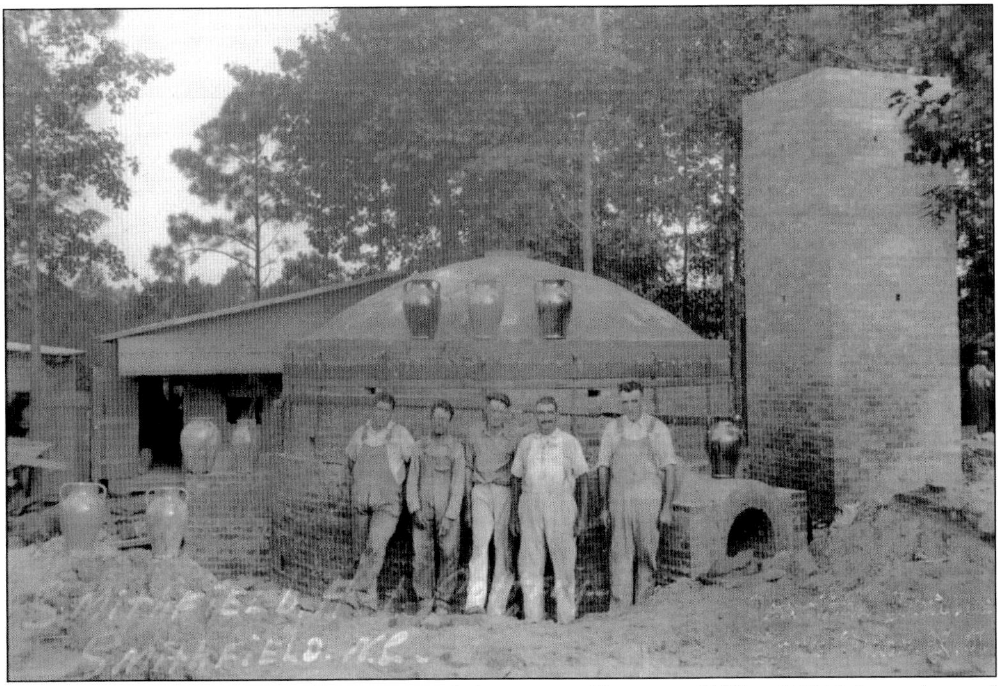

Smithfield Art Pottery, owned by Herman Cole, operated between 1927 and 1940. It was located on Highway 301 south of Smithfield by the Neuse River. Neuse River mud made for some fine clay pots, many of which were fired in a kiln fueled by coal. The pots often lined the bridge over the Neuse River and were sold to tourists who carried them up and down the Eastern Seaboard.

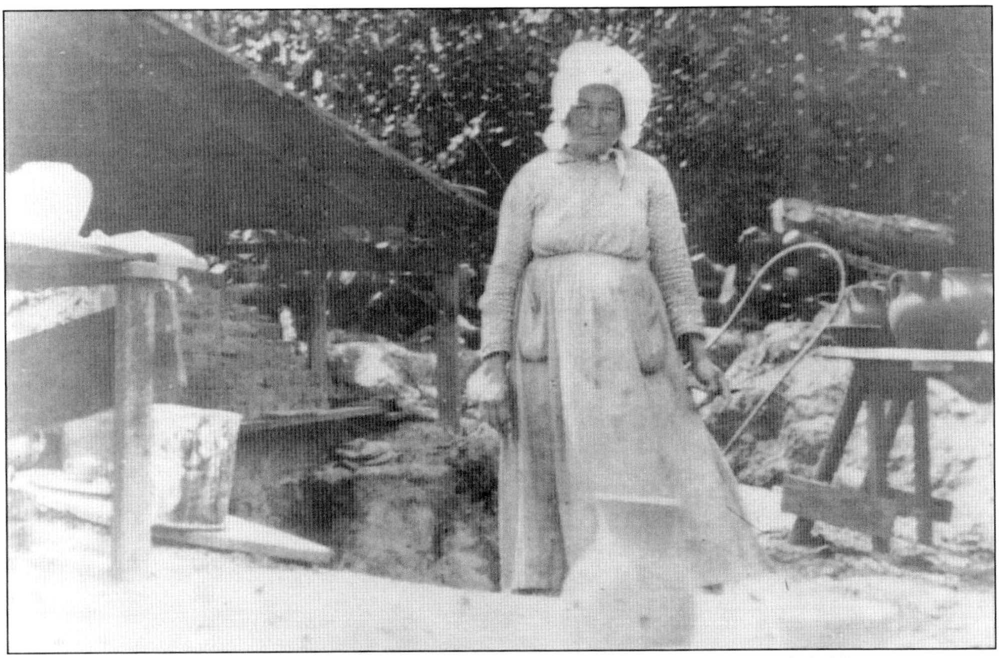

Leacy Baker Strickland, donning the traditional farm bonnet, worked at Smithfield Art Pottery in the 1930s when this photograph was taken. Children worked at the pottery loading and unloading the kilns for 5¢ or 10¢ per hour.

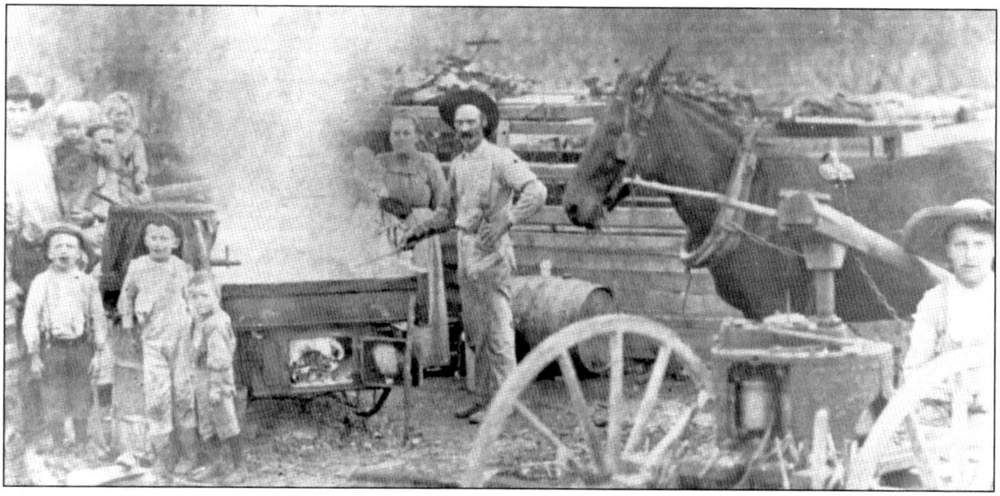

Thomas Cockrell is making syrup with sorghum cane ground up in the mule-powered mill he had on his Beulah Township farm in the early 20th century. Those children and babies certainly are mighty close to the heat.

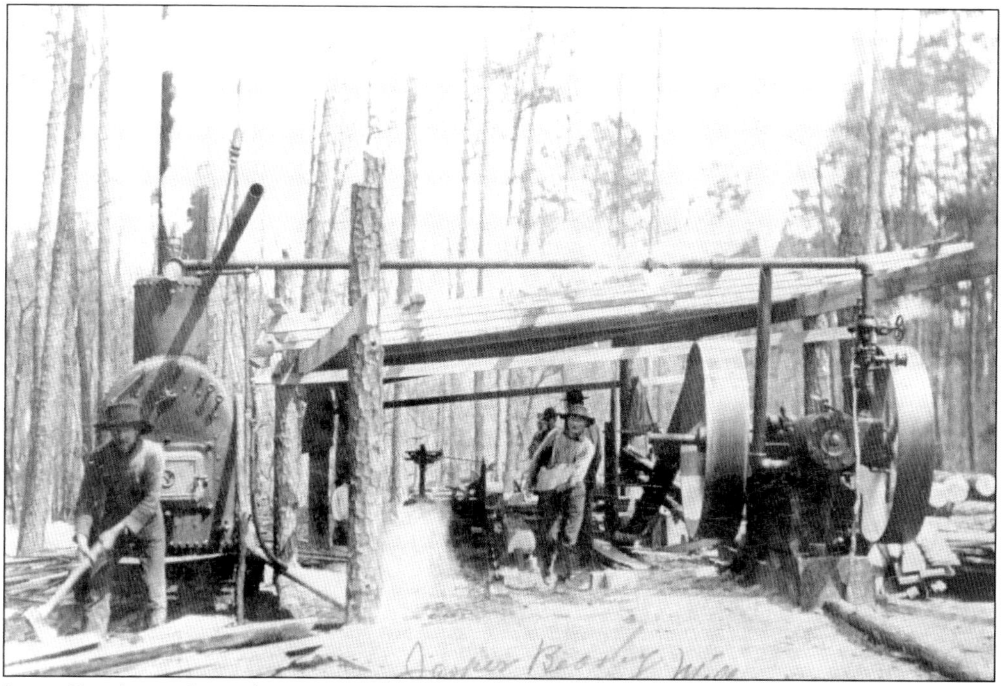

Jasper Beasley is shown here operating a sawmill deep in the pine forests of Meadow Township about 1910. Only a few years earlier, Johnston's plentiful pines were used primarily to harvest resin for turpentine. (Courtesy of Benson Museum of Local History.)

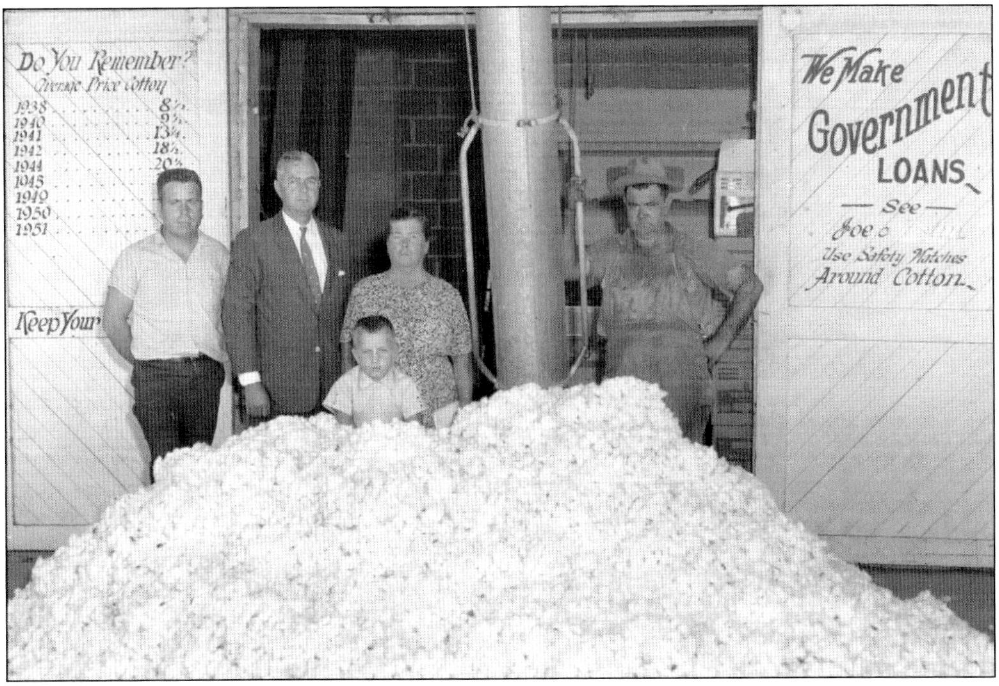

J. Marvin Johnson (second from left) poses with customers at his Smithfield Oil and Gin Company in the early 1950s for photographer Reuben Johnson. Tobacco had dethroned "King Cotton" by this time, but a few local farmers continued growing their white fleecy crop in the postwar years.

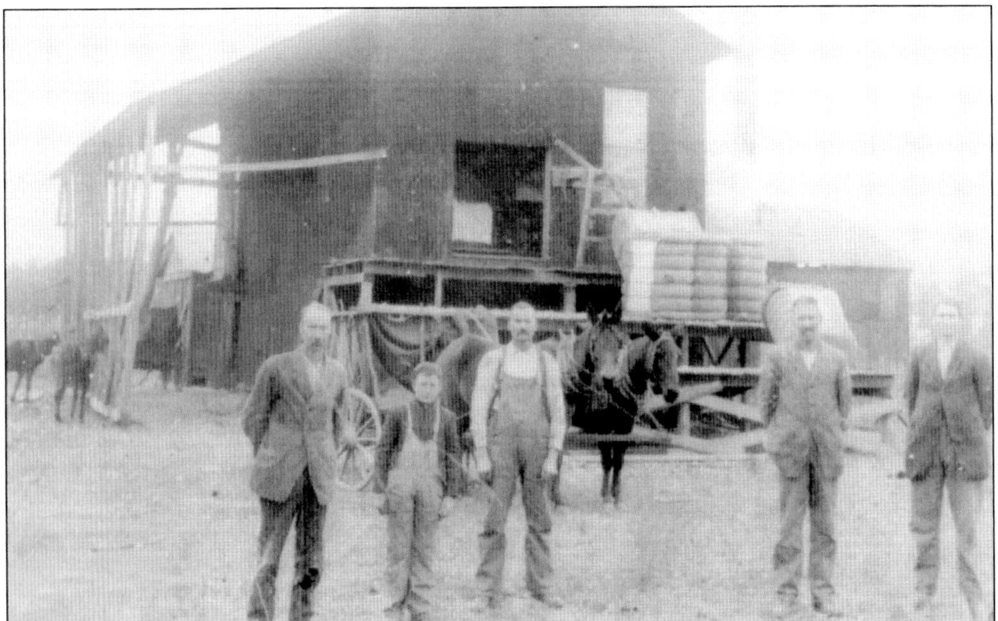

Cotton was still king in Johnston County when this photograph was taken at the Creech Brothers' Gin at Emit Crossroads about 1915. Stephen Worley Creech and brothers Clem and Aaron were the owners. Shown here are, from left to right, Jimmy Price, Sevella Price, Stephen Worley Creech, Clem Creech, and Brantley Richardson. (Courtesy of Charles and Carmen Creech.)

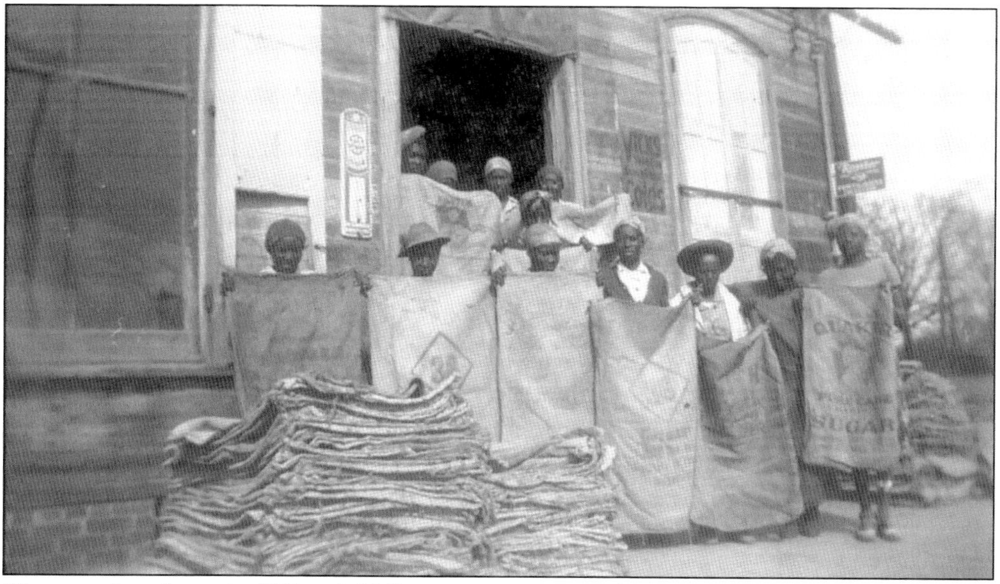

These workers from the Wilson's Mills area were among the 18 employees of Meyer Mackler's Smithfield Bagging Company, which was west of the county seat in 1941. Mackler opened a distribution warehouse in Smithfield for jute bags his Philadelphia-based company recycled, and local cotton gin owner Howard Mitchiner convinced him to add a manufacturing operation in Wilson's Mills in the late 1930s. Not only were bags cleaned and recycled, but the residue material left in the bags (including tapioca starch, sugar, sulfate of potash, and dried blood) was also saved and reused. Bags were turned inside out to hide decals and lettering. Local production was estimated at $100,000 in the early 1940s.

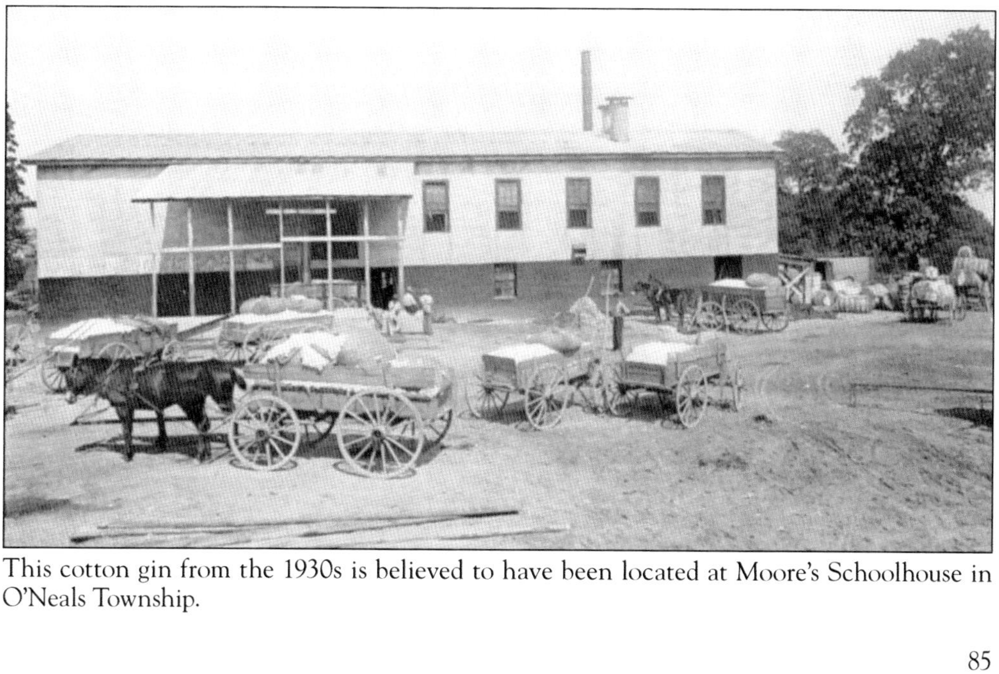

This cotton gin from the 1930s is believed to have been located at Moore's Schoolhouse in O'Neals Township.

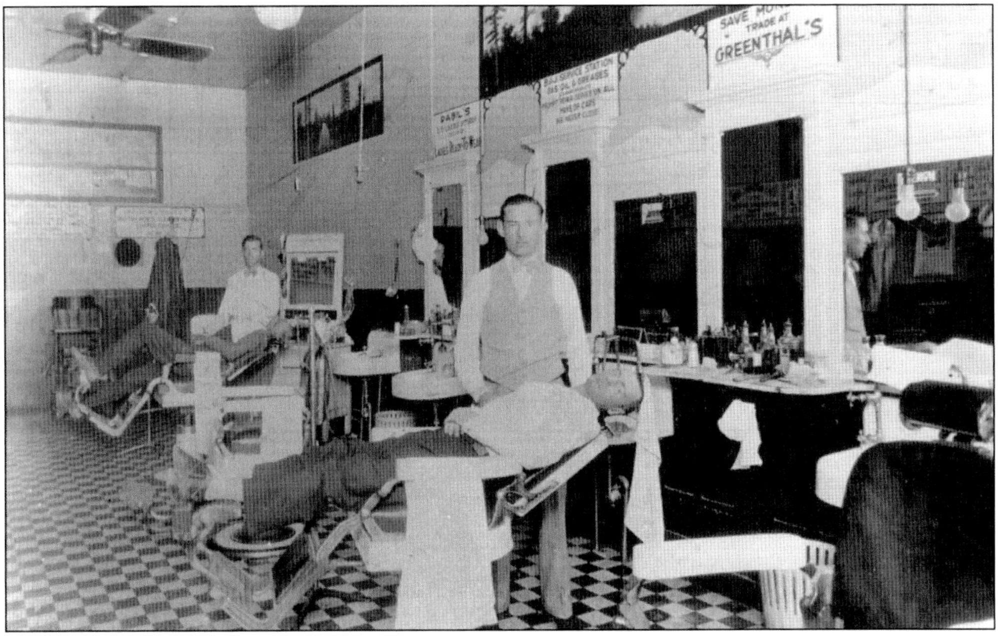

Donning vest and bow tie, Charlie Gilbert and his partner Otis Porter pose in their immaculate barber shop on Benson's Main Street in 1928. In addition to providing a shave and a haircut, Gilbert also advertised local businesses such as Jake Greenthal's clothing store, Rabil's Ladies Store, and the always-open B & J Service Station, which offered "gas, oil, and greases." (Courtesy of Benson Museum of Local History.)

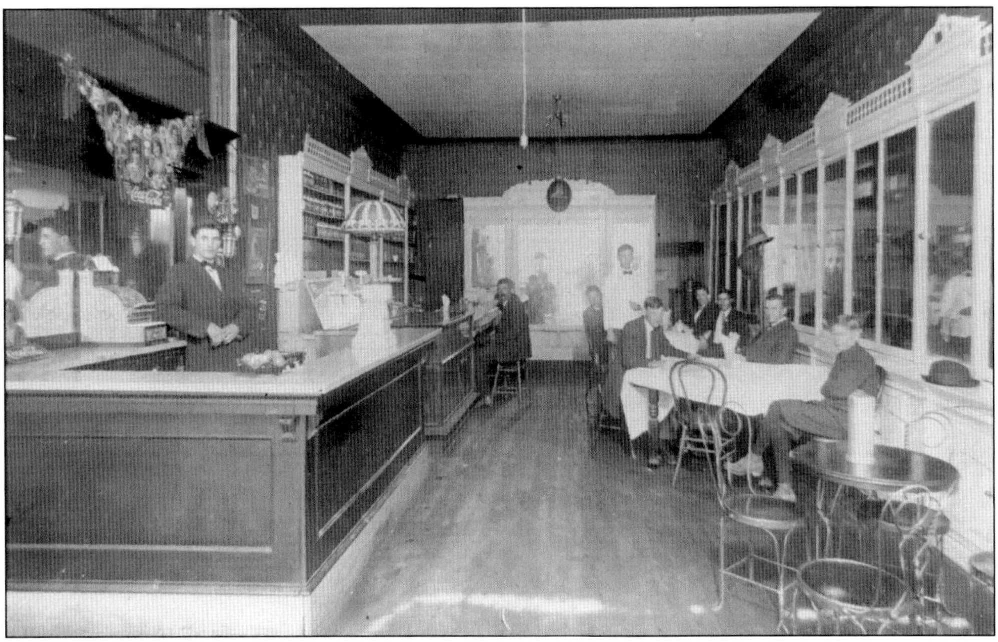

This drugstore scene, believed to be from the Johnston and Stephenson Drug Store in the Tuscarora Inn across from the courthouse, dates from the early 1920s and appears on a lantern slide shown in Smithfield's Victory Theater. The slides included scenes around Smithfield, including many images of children, and were shown between movies to draw larger audiences.

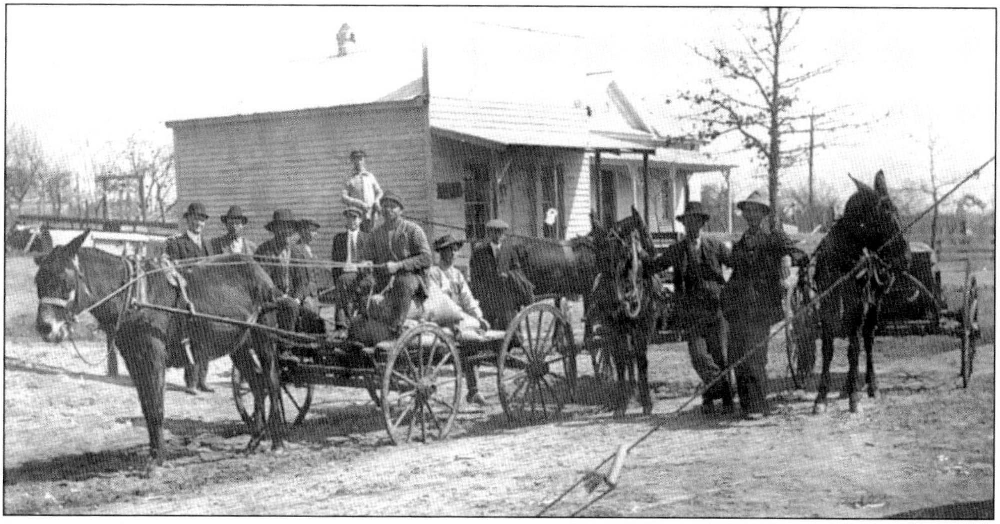

Rural merchant Victor Stephenson is shown with several customers hauling fertilizer from his store in Elevation Township about 1910. The store was on the site of present-day Benson Grove Baptist Church on Highway 50 (or as natives say, "50 Highway") north of Benson. (Courtesy of Steve Parrish.)

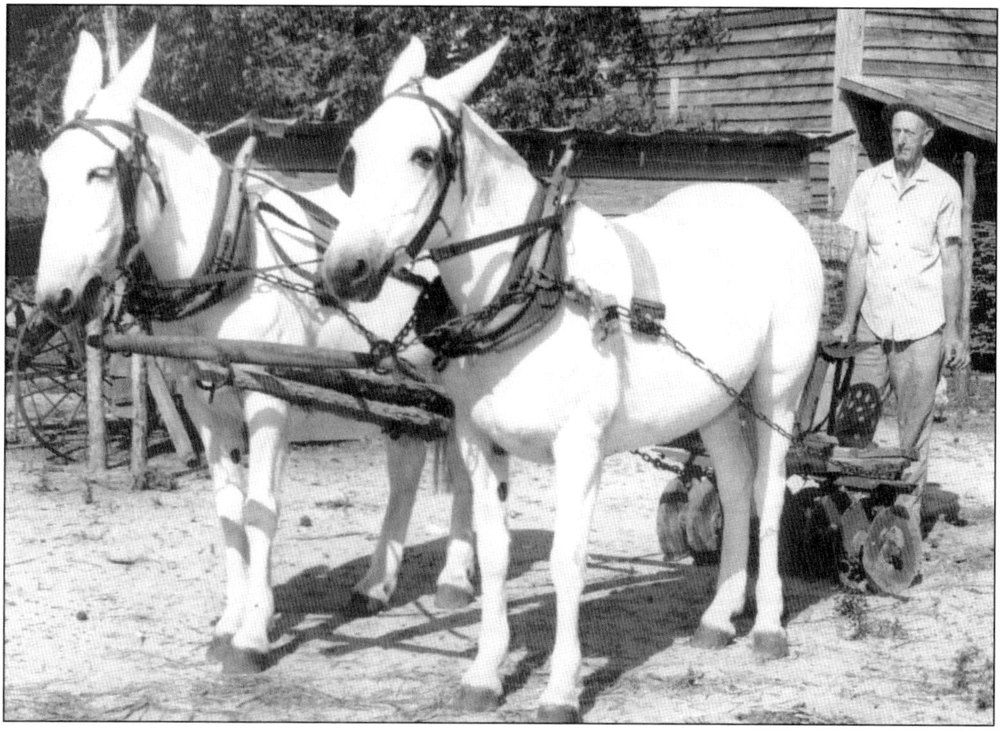

One might presume this photograph of Pine Level Township tenant farmer Earl Worley and his mules Hattie and Big Mule predates the farm mechanization of the 1950s. However, it is from the 1960s, long after most farmers had graduated from mules to tractors. *Smithfield Herald* managing editor Herman Lawson found Worley while scouring the county for interesting people to write about. Worley explained he still used mules to tend the 33 acres he farmed on halves (farmer kept half his proceeds, the other half went to the landlord) simply to avoid debt.

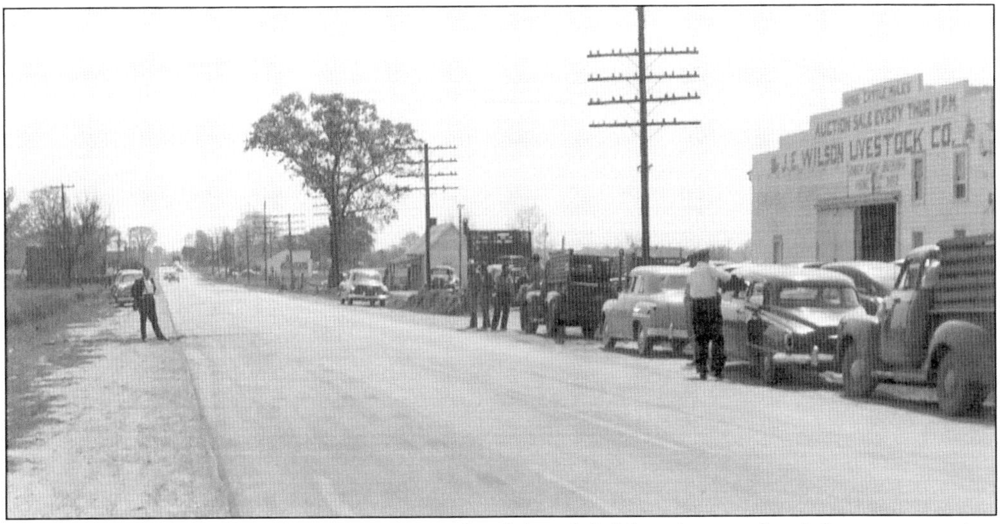

The J.E. Wilson Livestock Company south of Smithfield is doing a brisk business in this 1950s photograph.

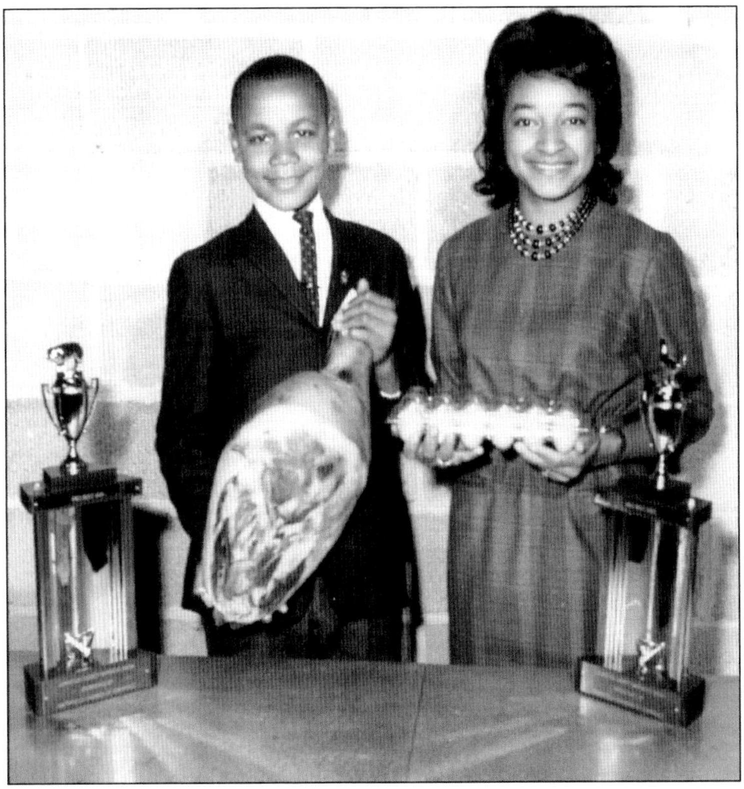

These 4-H members, Donald Williams of Clayton (left) and Gloria Cogdell of Newton Grove (right), show off their Best of Show prize-winning entries at the 1963 Ham and Egg Show, sponsored by the Johnston County Cooperative Extension Service.

Tobacco auctioneer Clarence "Snoxie" Stephenson (left) helps county agent L.R. Johnson (right) of the Agricultural Extension Service get top bid for a prize-winning country ham during this 1950s Ham and Egg Show. Johnson hatched the idea for this event after being hired by the Agricultural Extension Service in 1944. The show was carried on each April for over 20 years, beginning in 1948, to raise awareness among African American farmers about improved methods for raising and curing meat. One of the highlights of the show was in 1953, when a prize-winning ham sold for $55 a pound and was presented to President Eisenhower at the White House. (Photograph by Reuben Johnson.)

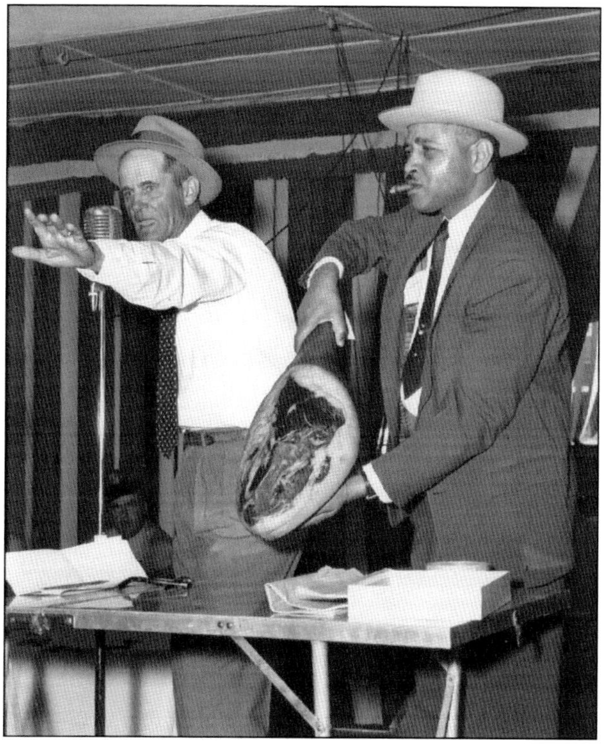

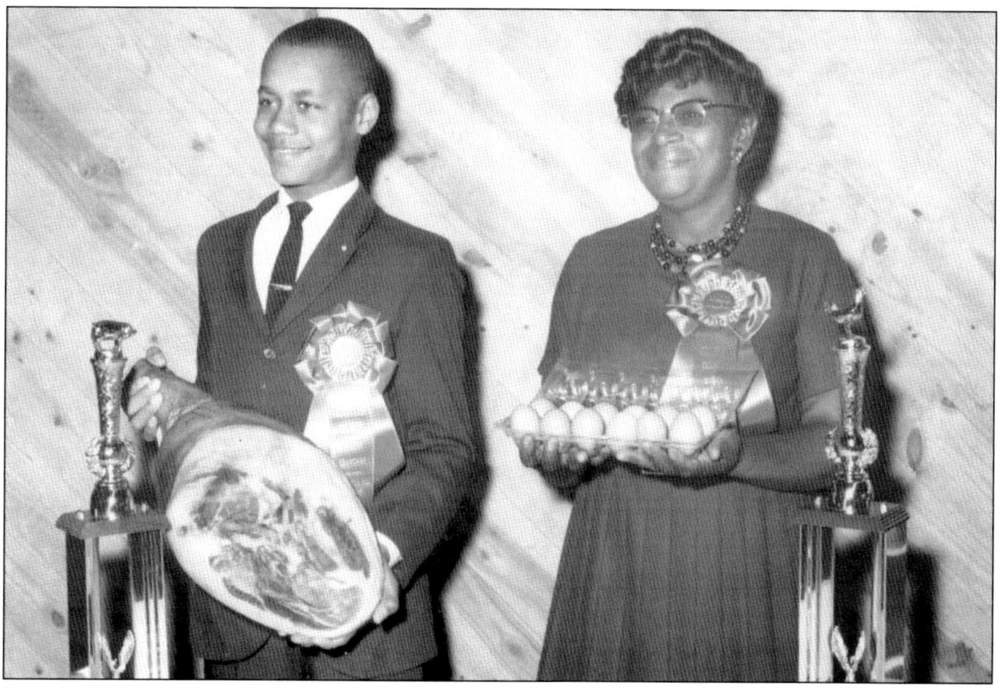

John Williams of the Clayton area is pictured with his prize-winning 15.5-pound ham from a Yorkshire hog, while Bettie Sims of Wilson's Mills shows off the grand champion dozen eggs she raised from a flock of 55 Rhode Island Red hens. They took top honors at the 1964 Ham and Egg Show. (Photograph by Herman Lawson.)

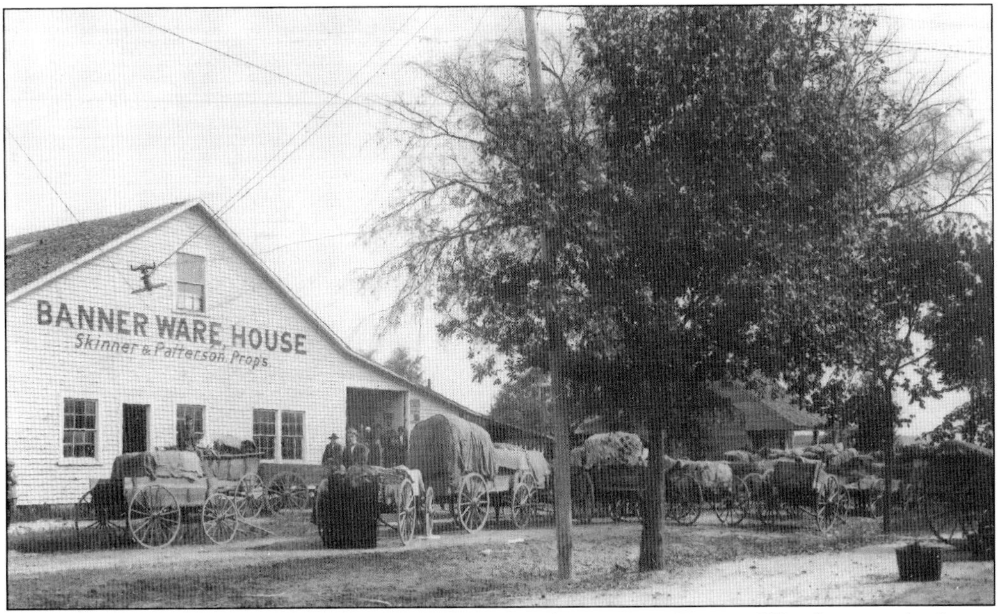

Wagons of bright leaf tobacco sit outside Skinner and Patterson's Banner Warehouse, which was built at the turn of the 20th century in Smithfield. This beautiful image came from one of the lantern slides used in the Victory Theater in the early 1920s.

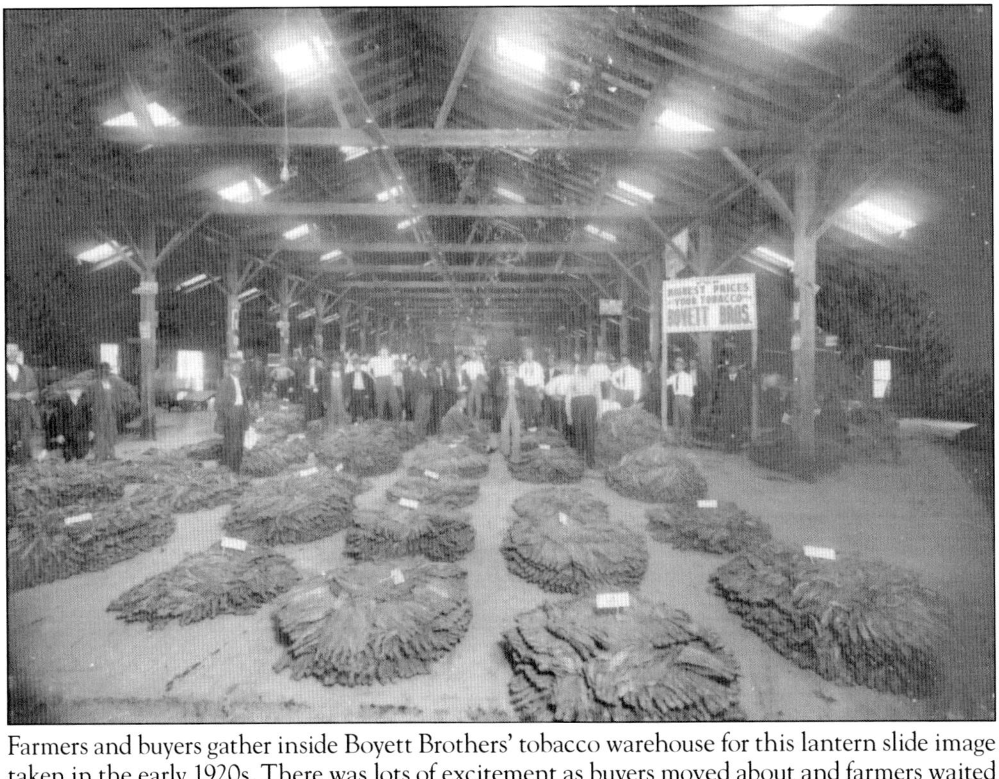

Farmers and buyers gather inside Boyett Brothers' tobacco warehouse for this lantern slide image taken in the early 1920s. There was lots of excitement as buyers moved about and farmers waited to see how much they would be paid for their crops. Local merchants looked forward to seeing all the farm families come to town to spend their earnings and pay off their accounts.

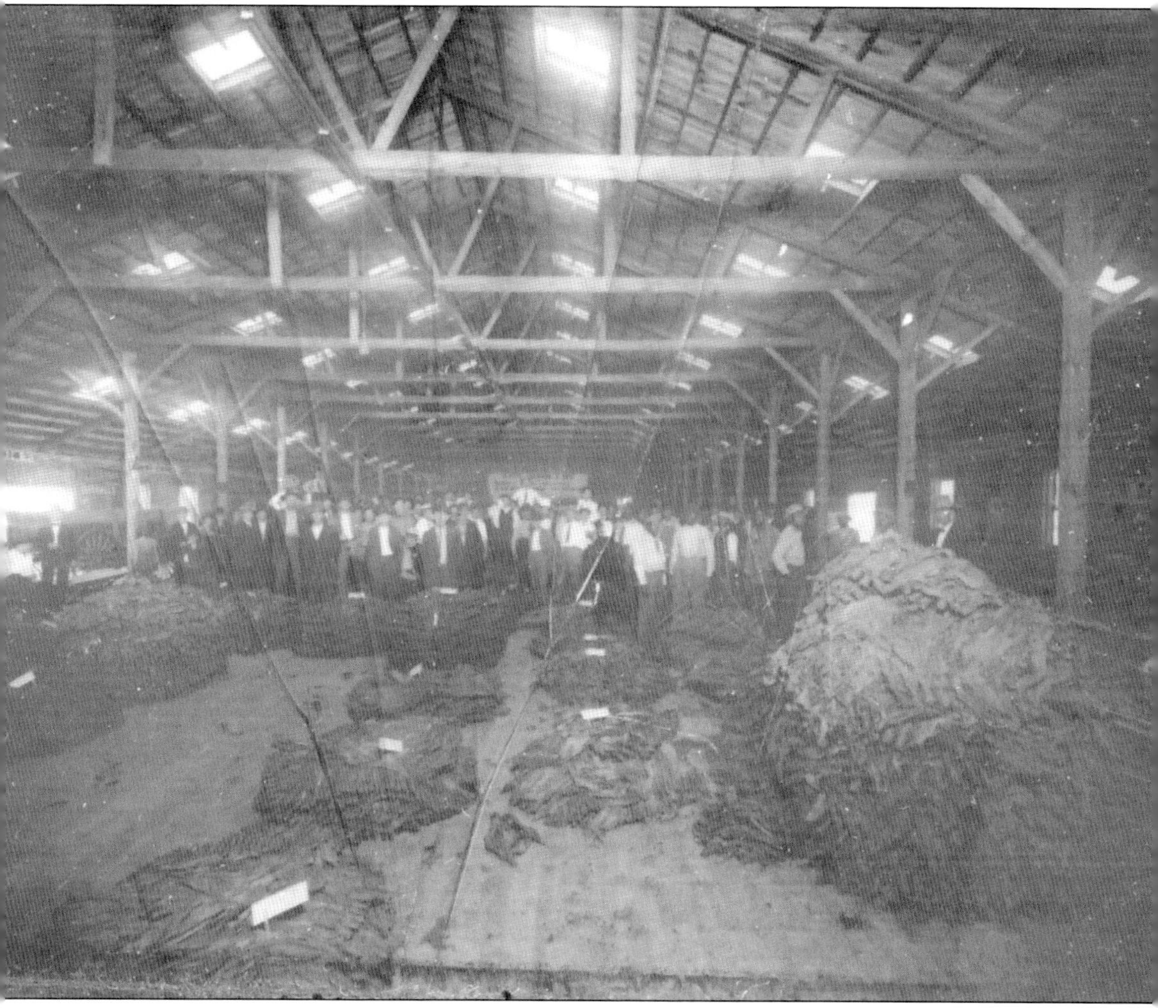

This Smithfield tobacco warehouse interior shot from about 1920, captured on a lantern slide, is believed to be from the Banner Warehouse.

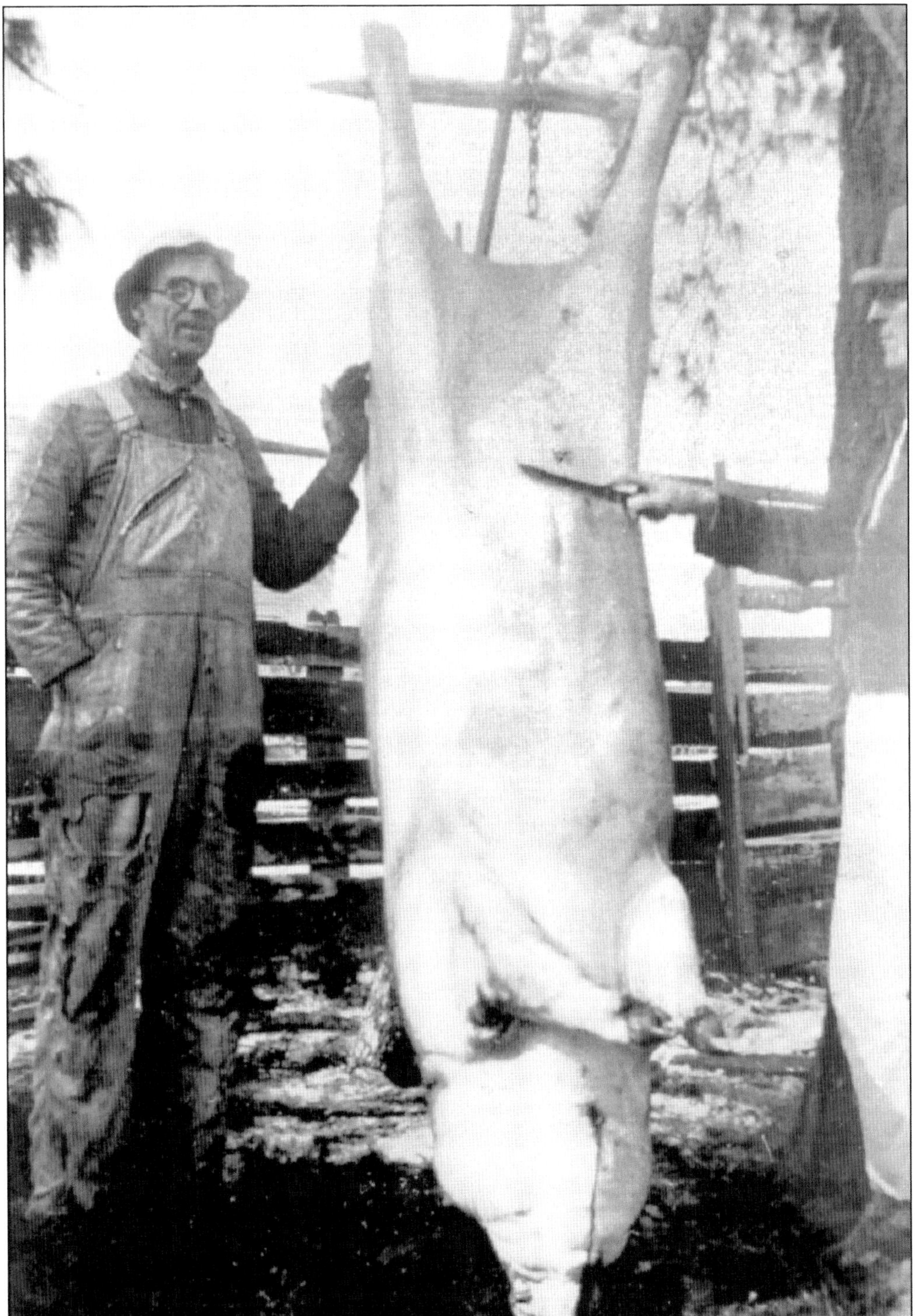

Victor Penny (left) observes as Rufus M. Johnson (right) prepares to butcher this 1,000-pound hog on the Johnson farm in Pleasant Grove Township in the 1930s.

Six

By Land, Air, and Sea

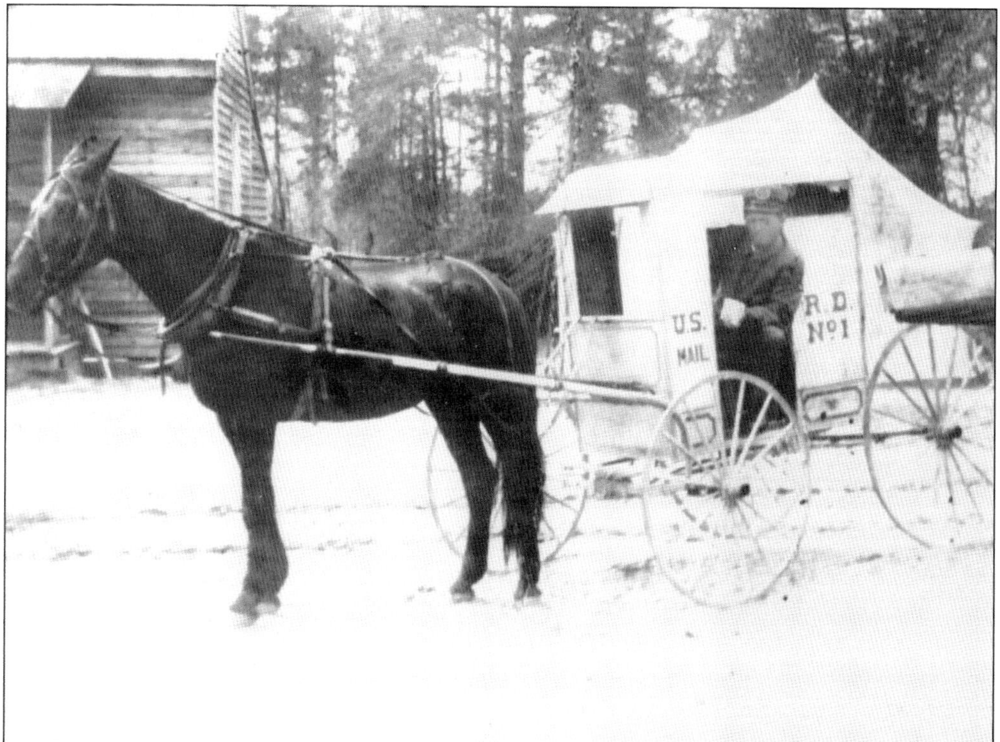

Benson rural mail carrier Jesse Stephenson prepares to stuff a mailbox sometime between 1910 and 1920. (Courtesy of Benson Museum of Local History.)

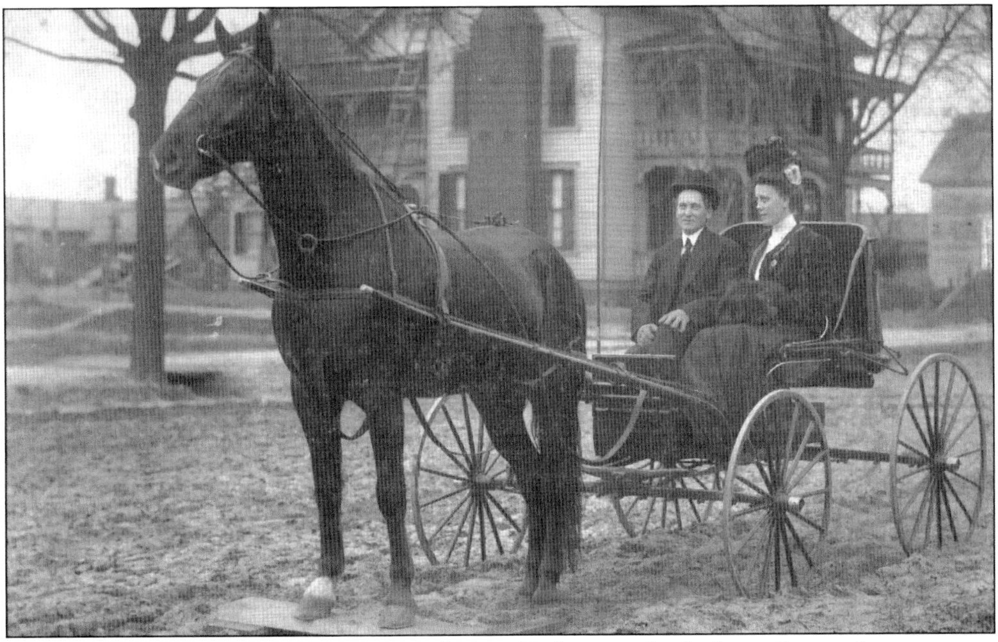

Smithfield merchant Ed F. Boyette Sr. and Mary Hickman, who had a millinery shop in town, pose with horse and buggy on one of Smithfield's dirt streets in the early 1900s. Their eyes seem fixed on the horse, with front hooves on a posing stand.

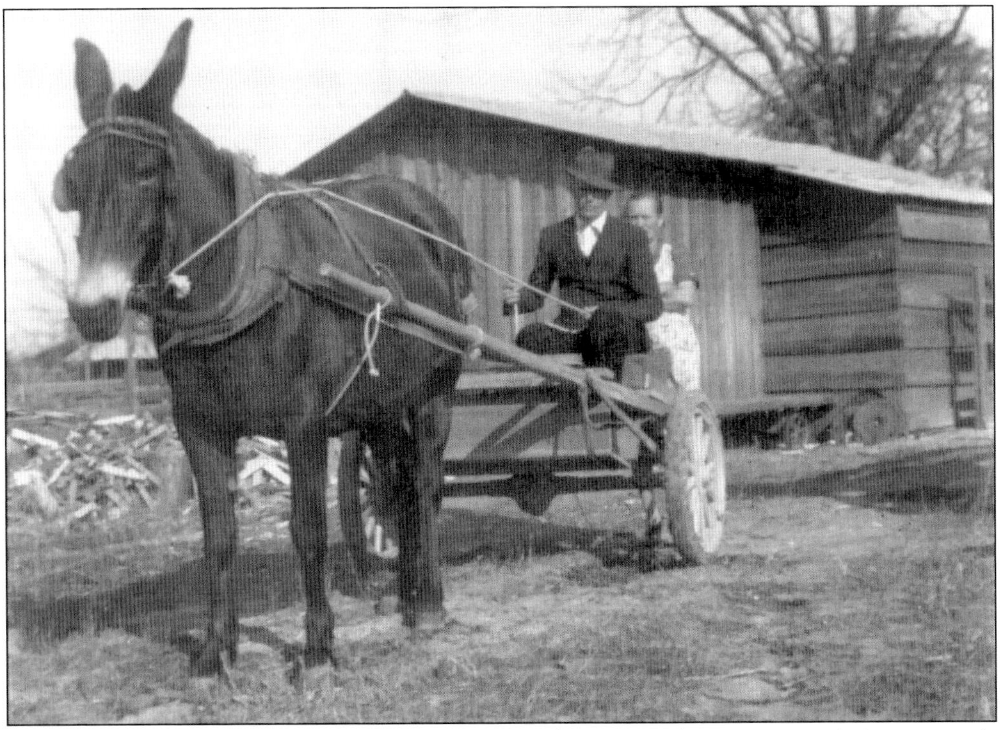

Fred Grice's aunt Lillie sees him off as he ventures out in his courting/going-to-town clothes on a mule and cart from the family's Ingrams Township farm in 1940. Many small farmers saved money during the Great Depression by traveling with work animals rather than gas-powered transportation.

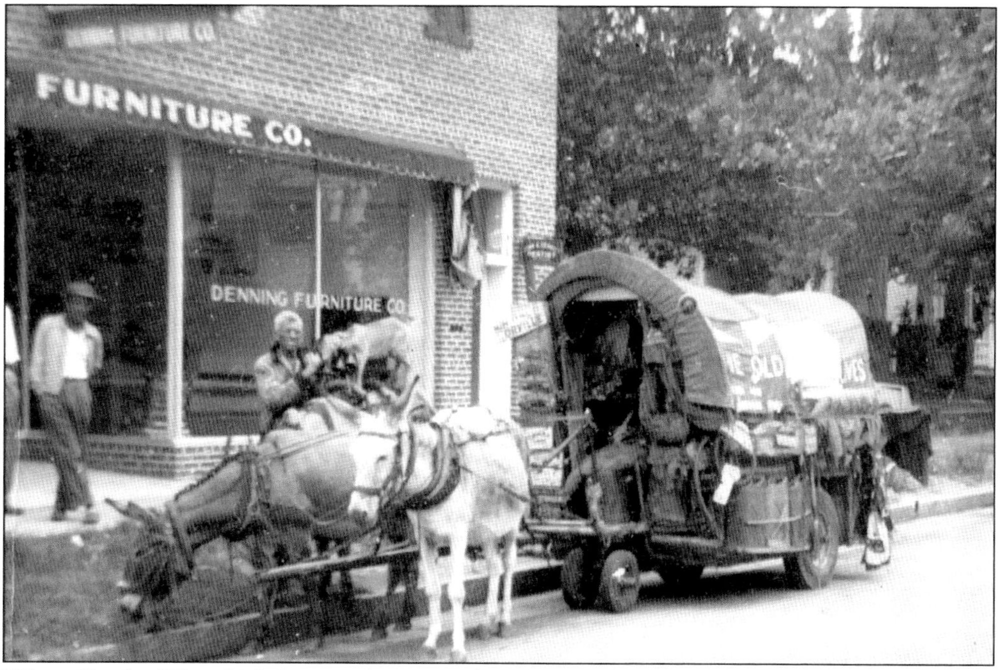

When Charles "Chess" McCartney, known as the "Goat Man," rolled into town on his horse-drawn covered wagon in the 1950s, people gathered around and cameras flashed. These photographs show him on South Third Street at Denning Furniture Company. The below image also shows the R.P. Holding residence. (Both, photograph by Reuben Johnson.)

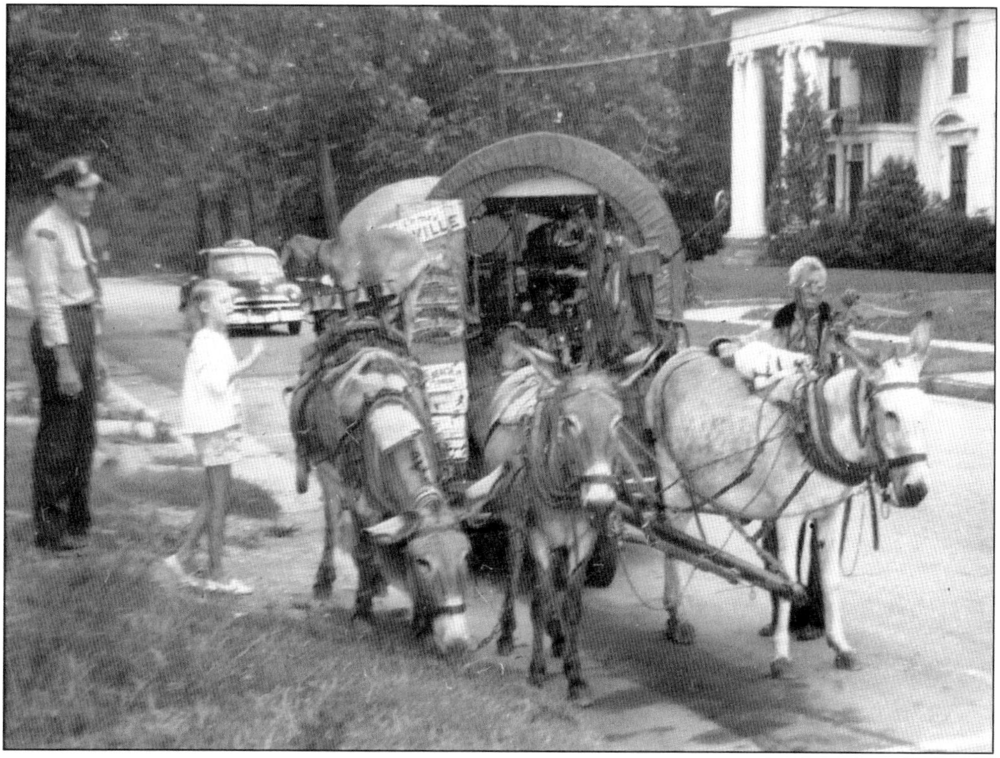

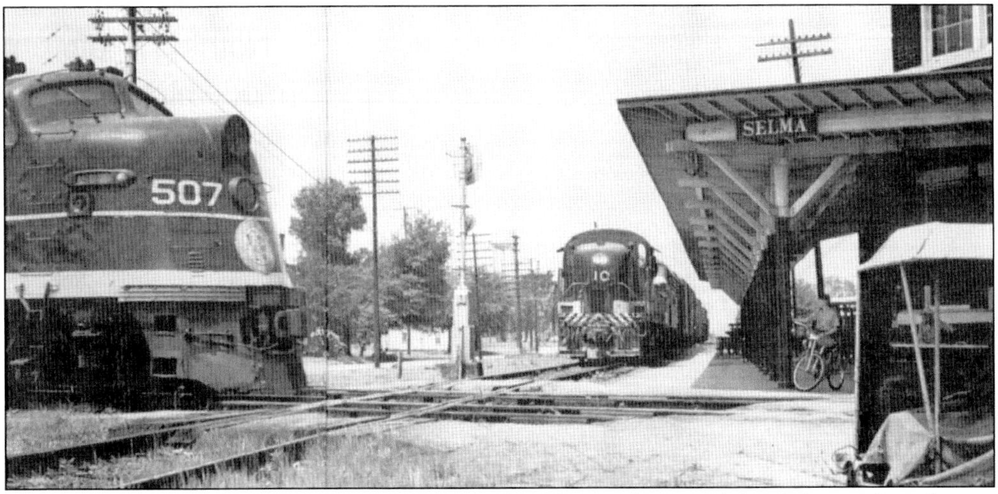

This 1962 image shows the spot were two railroads—the Southern and the Atlantic Coastline—meet near Selma's Union Station.

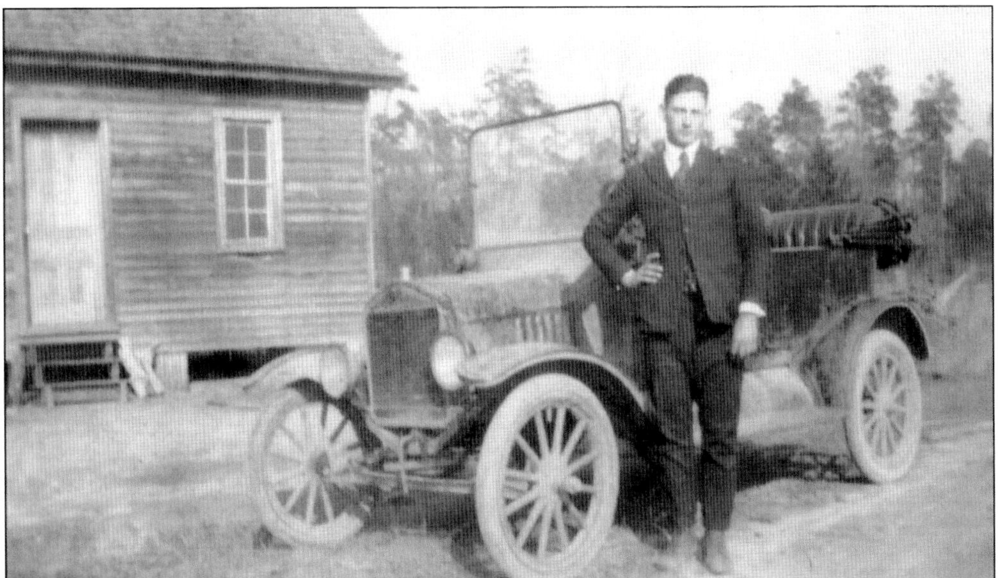

Erastus Barefoot of Meadow Township poses proudly with his Ford Model T sometime in the 1920s. (Courtesy of Michael Wheeler.)

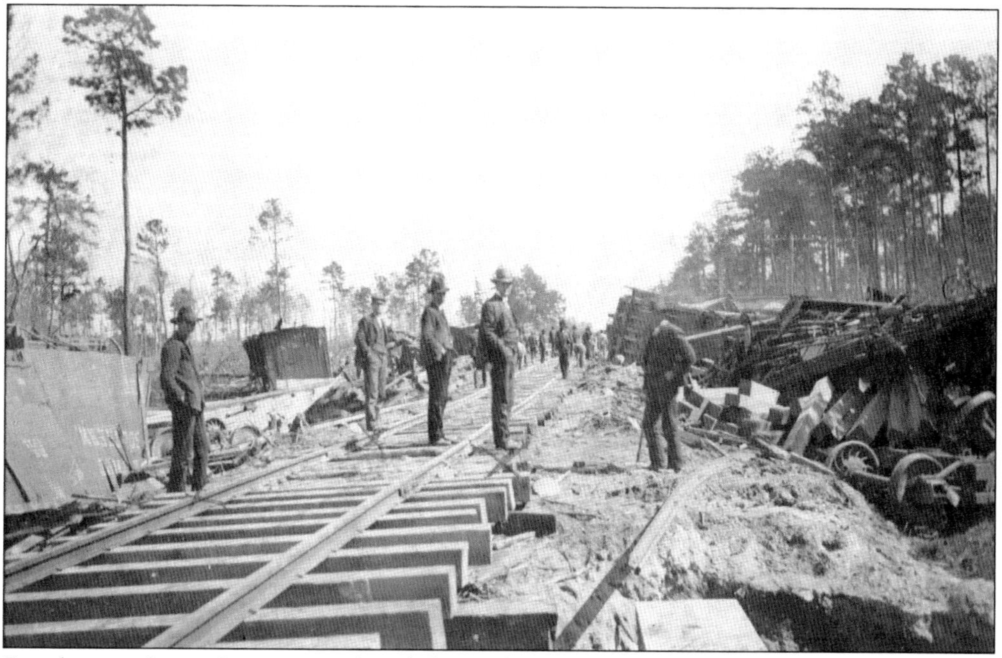

Standing on the tracks at center, from left to right, Hunter Ellington, Jim Woodall, and George Potter survey damage from a train wreck on the Atlantic Coastline Railroad, south of Smithfield near the A.J. Heath place.

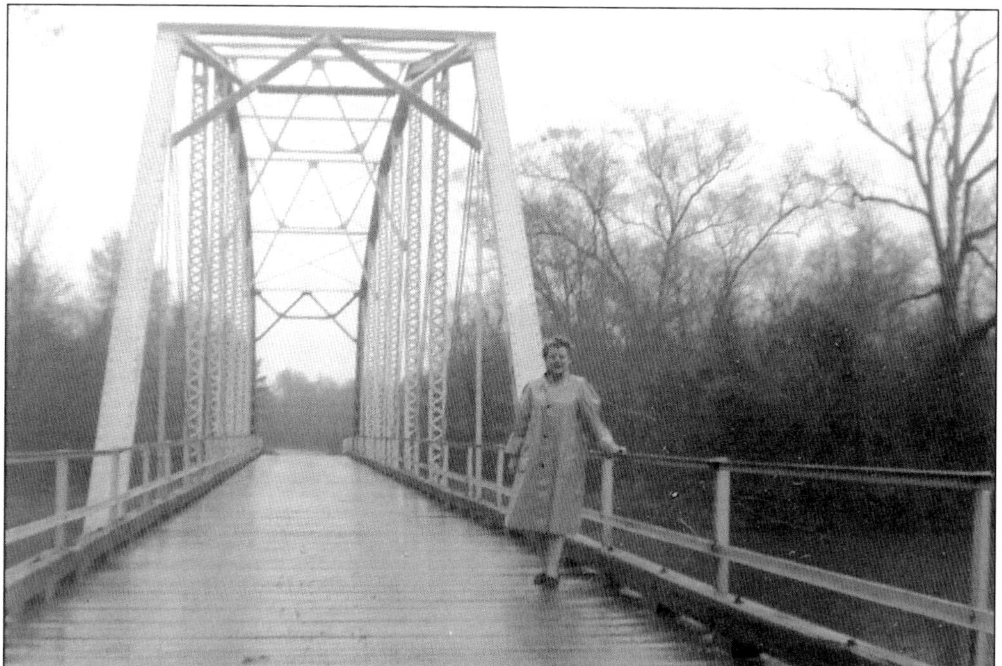

County bookmobile librarian Betsy Sanders snapped this photograph of the old Richardson Bridge over the Neuse River near Princeton while she was delivering books and goodwill in 1952. This was one of several steel bridges over the Neuse River built in the early 20th century and one of the last ones standing at the time this photograph was taken. The woman is unidentified.

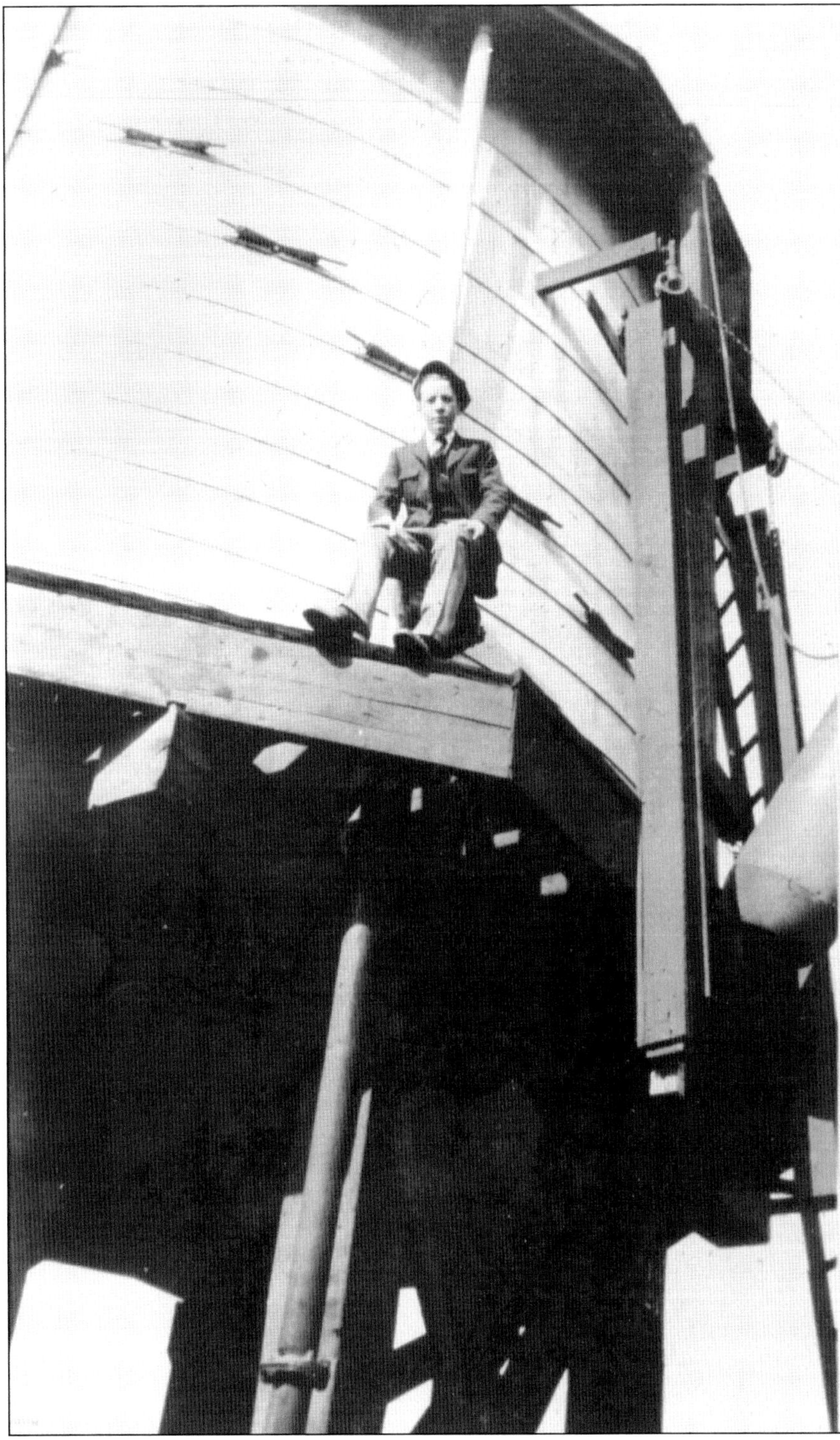

An unidentified well-dressed thrill seeker is shown perched on the Atlantic Coastline Railroad's water tank at Mingo, near Benson, sometime around 1910. (Courtesy of Benson Museum of Local History.)

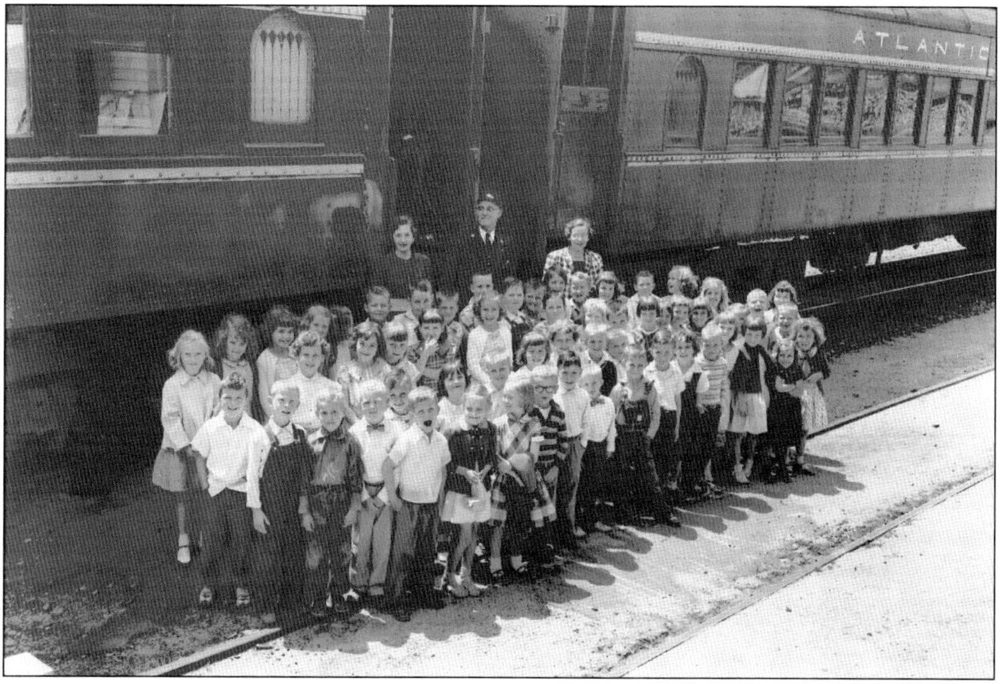

These first and second graders from Glendale School posed during an exciting, albeit short, train excursion on the Atlantic Coastline Railroad in May 1956. One of the teachers is Eula Godwin. (Photograph by Reuben Johnson.)

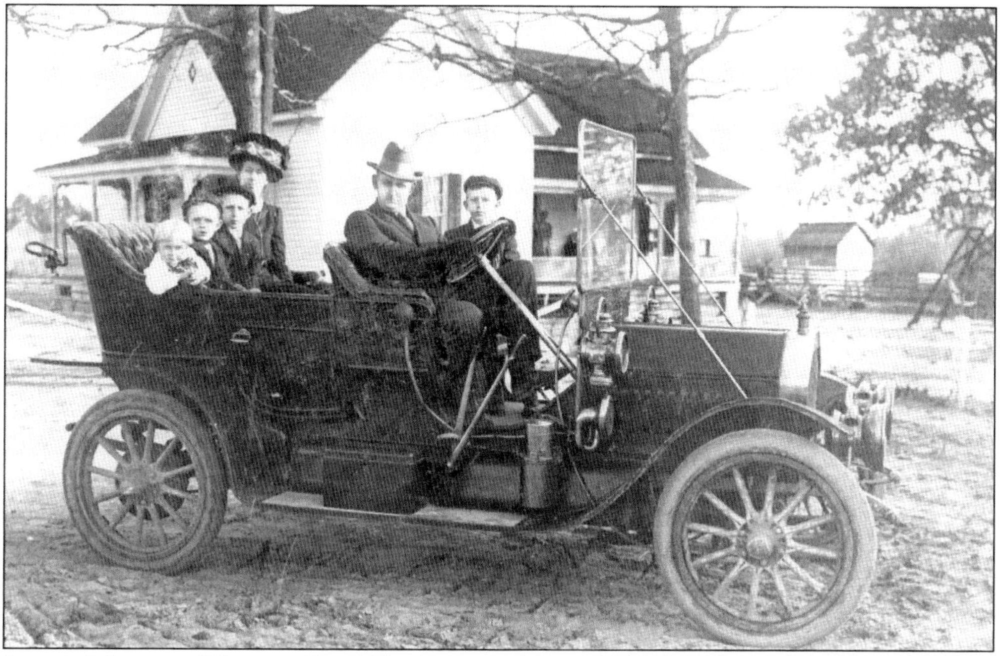

John L. Johnson of Pleasant Grove Township had a small photography studio in his yard when he captured this image of the Kemp B. Johnson family of Fuquay Springs on a jaunt through the countryside in their 1912 Buick. K.B. Johnson was a lumberman who had timber interests in the Pleasant Grove area.

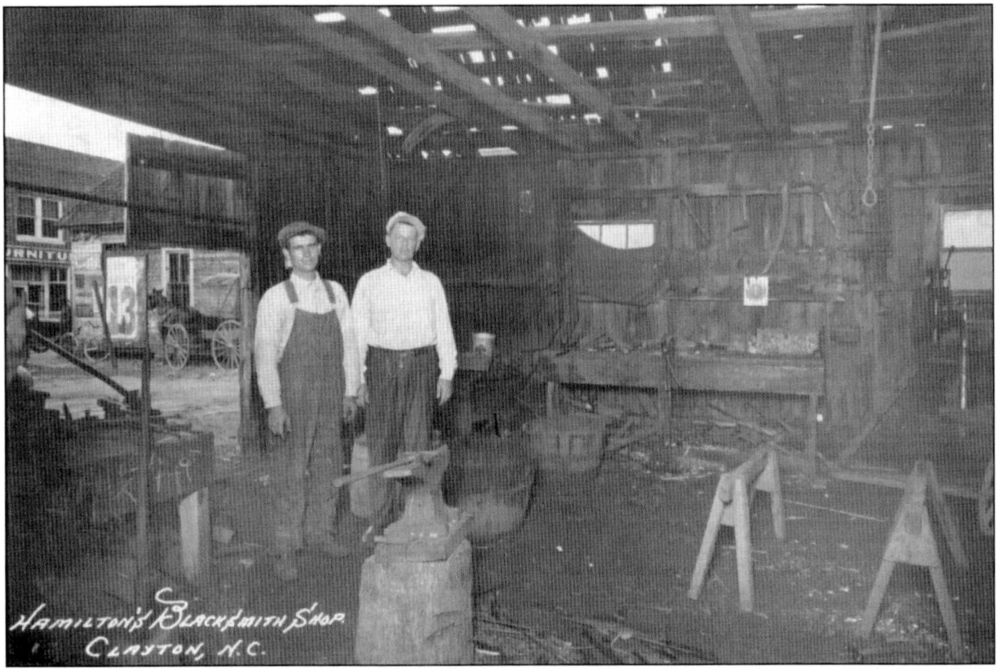

Colon Hamilton and Ashley Horne II are shown in Hamilton's Blacksmith Shop in Clayton about 1920. Scenes such as this were quickly becoming obsolete, as the automobile replaced the horse-drawn conveyance. (Courtesy of the Hocutt-Ellington Memorial Library.)

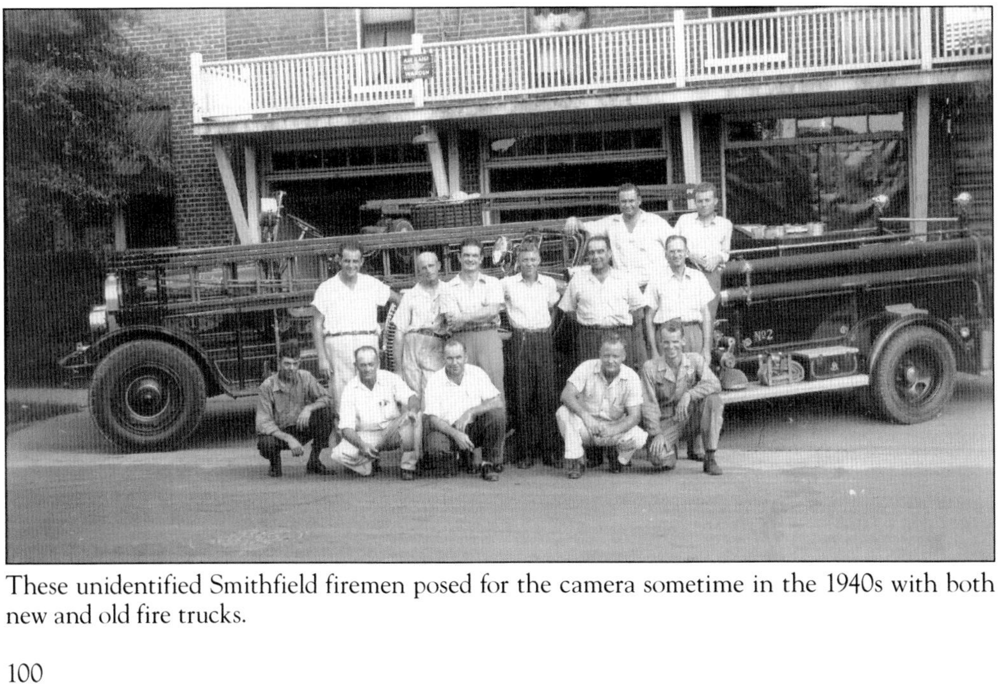

These unidentified Smithfield firemen posed for the camera sometime in the 1940s with both new and old fire trucks.

Pictured here in 1935 are, from left to right, Four Oaks pioneer firemen Henry Johnson, John Bandy, Newitt Williams, and Hubert Massengill. Massengill organized the town's fire department in 1930, and the 1.5-ton 1930 Chevrolet truck shown here was purchased from the Howe Fire Apparatus Company of Anderson, Indiana. It is parked on South Railroad Street beside the railroad depot.

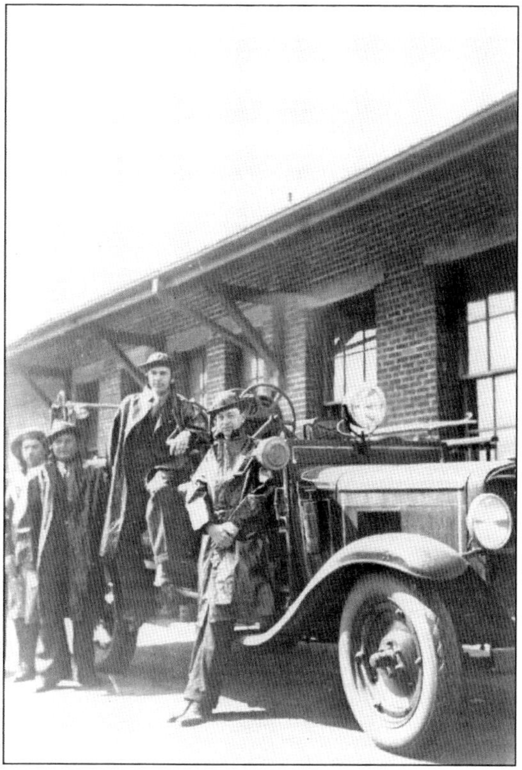

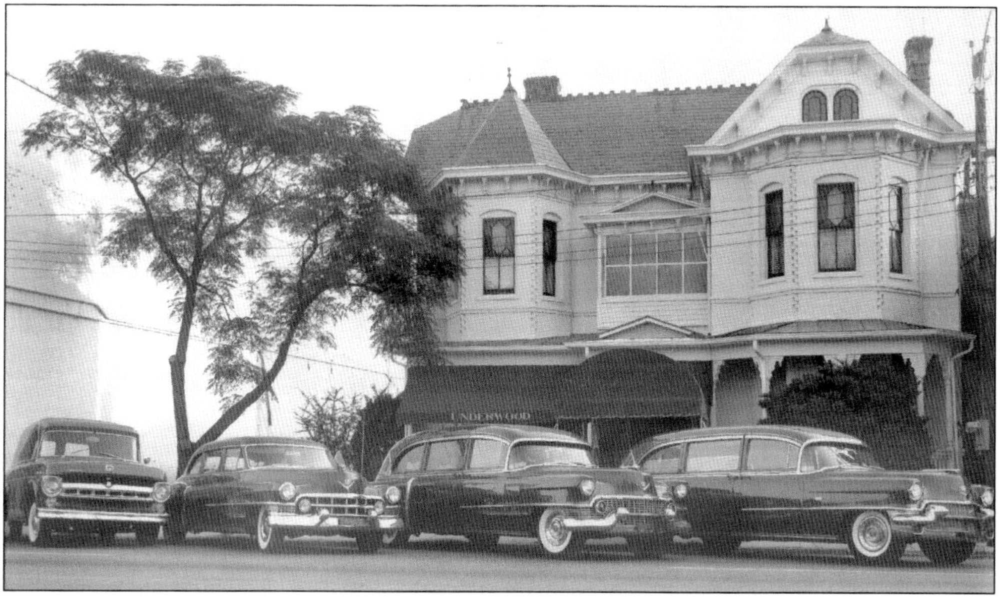

These Underwood Funeral Home cars date from the 1950s. The funeral home facility was previously the home of Ashley and Lina Smith, former slaves who were among Smithfield's wealthiest residents in the early 20th century. Their home included stained-glass windows and hand-carved woodwork throughout. The exterior brick walls were 16 inches thick, such that when Underwood sold the property to Hudson-Belk in the 1960s, the house was demolished because it was too heavy to move. (Photograph by Reuben Johnson.)

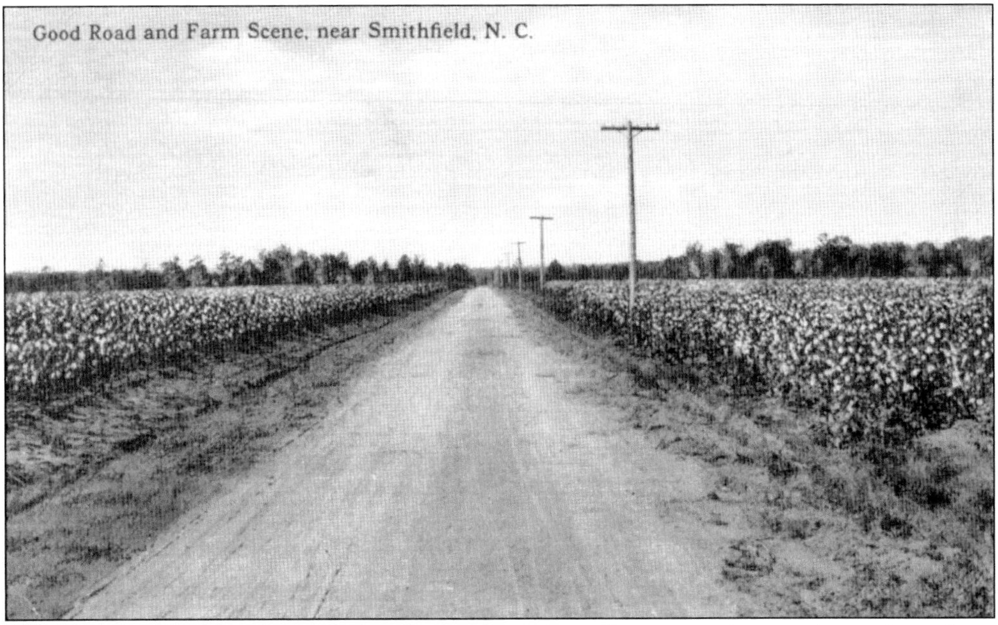

Not all unpaved roads were bad, according to the title on this postcard image dating from about 1915. Telephone poles and wires were already in place in the countryside, but it would be a number of years before electricity would come to most rural areas of Johnston.

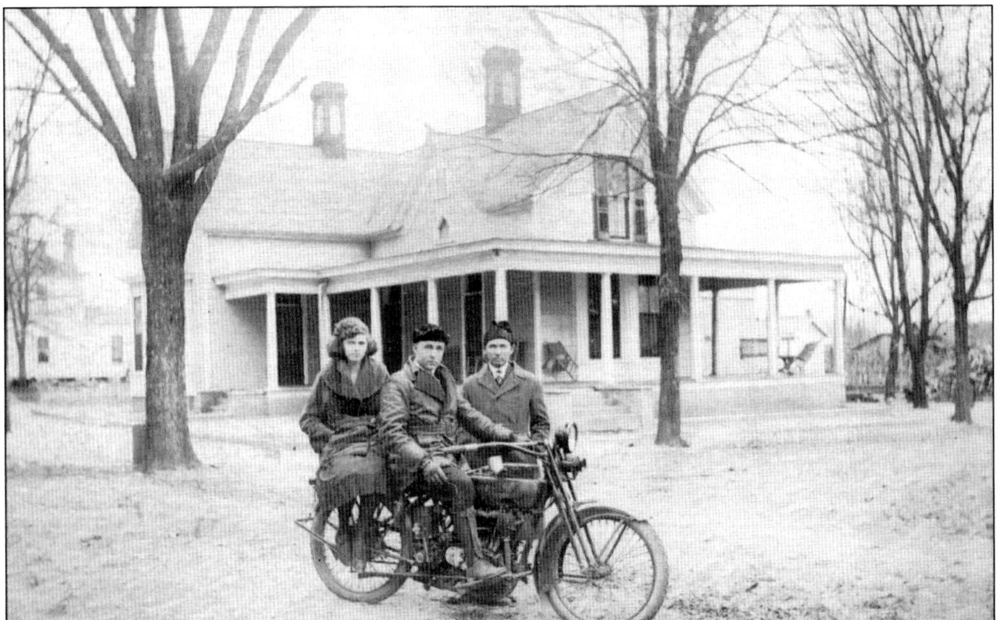

Three unidentified people with an early motorcycle pose in front of the J.W. Sanders home in Four Oaks in the early 1920s. It appears that sitting sidesaddle carried over from riding horses to riding motorized vehicles.

The Johnston County Library's first bookmobile in the summer of 1946 includes a banner with the previous year's circulation statistics.

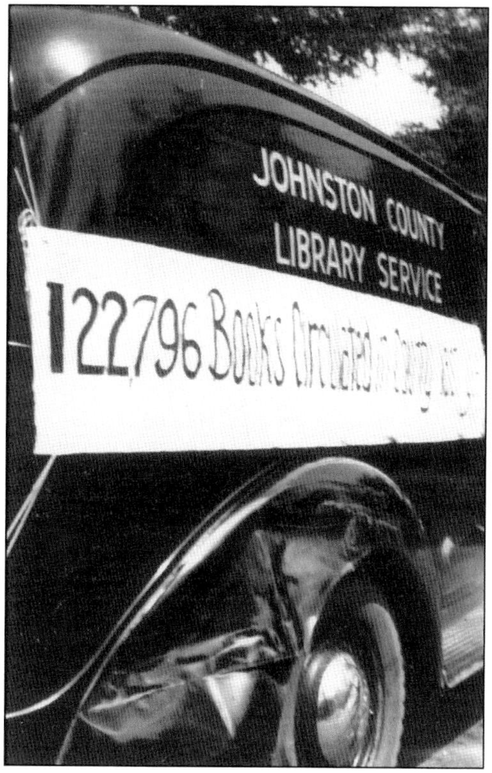

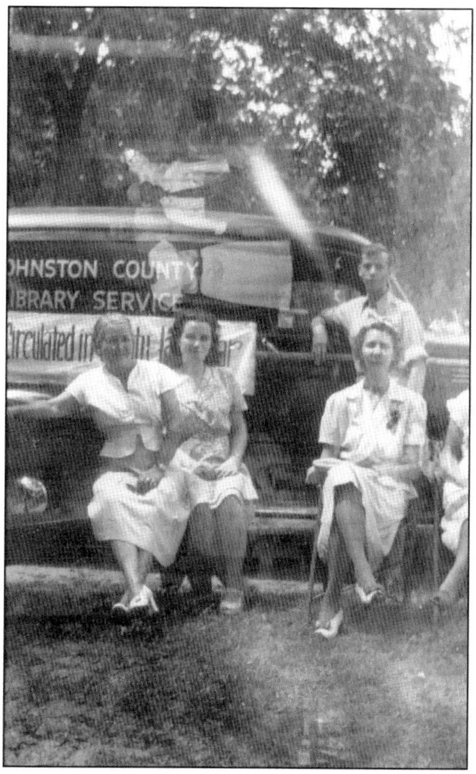

Bookmobile librarian Willye Wright (left) and county librarian Virginia Williamson (right) enjoy summer reading program festivities in 1946 with summer employees, thought to be Hortense Boomer of Swan Quarter and Ed Thompson of Pine Level. Williamson participated in a librarian exchange program and switched places with Margaret Scoffield of Rawdon, England, for 13 months in 1949–1950. Only weeks after her return in February 1950, Williamson was killed in a car accident near Garner after reportedly driving on the left side of the road.

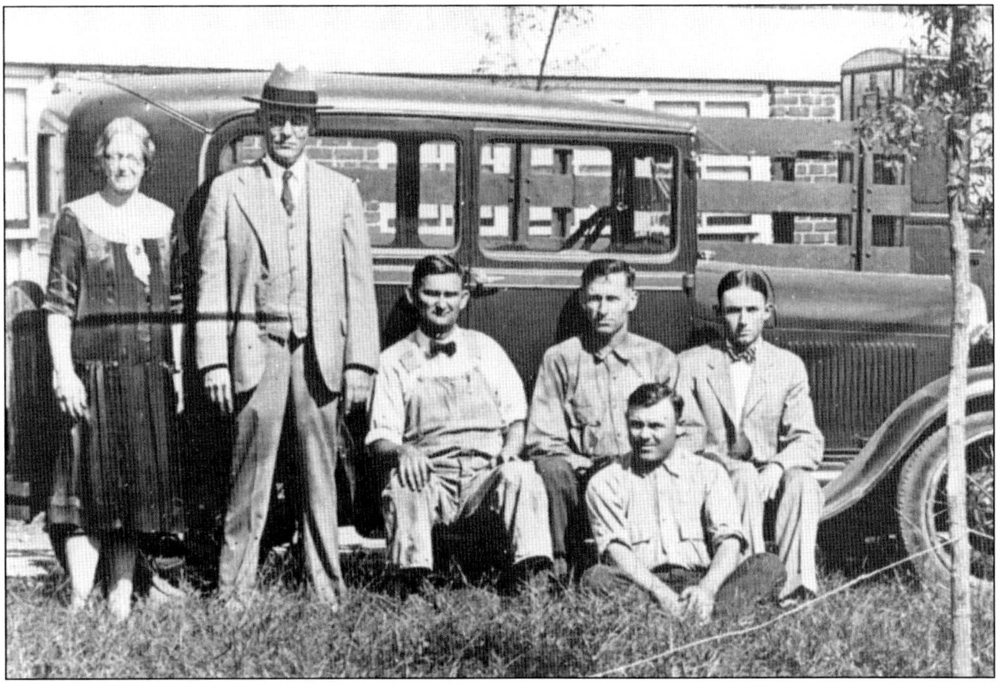

The school consolidation movement of the 1920s would not have been possible without a large fleet of buses. Pictured here are the people who were instrumental in getting students safely to school and keeping the school buses running in the 1930s: Mary E. Wells (administrative assistant), H.B. Marrow (school superintendent), William Avery Williams (head of transportation), John Massengill, Preston Collier, and Madison Hodge.

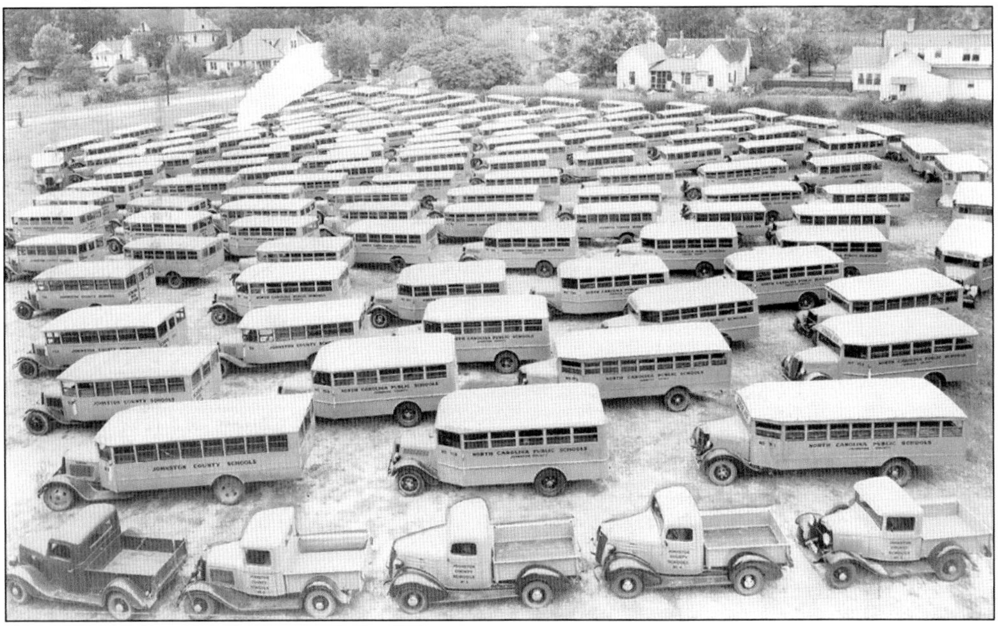

It took many buses to get students from farm to school. This 1937 fleet, captured on camera from an upper floor of Smithfield's elementary school building on Rose Street, was touted in the *Smithfield Herald* on October 12, 1937, as the "Largest in North Carolina."

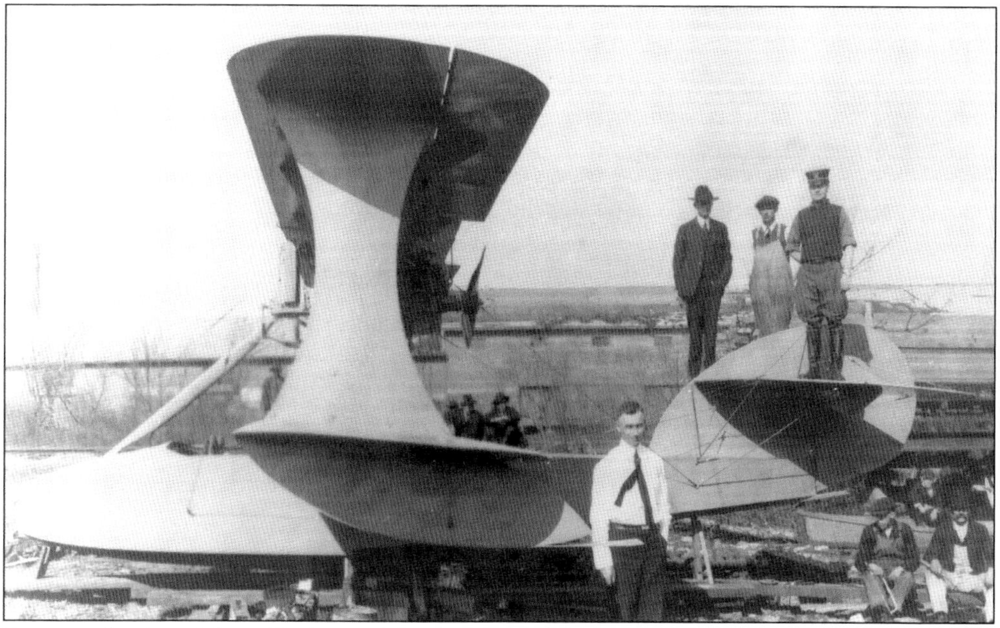

Renowned aviator Harry N. Atwood (wearing white shirt, standing on the ground) shows off a seaplane he built for the US Navy at his Carolina Aircraft plant near Smithfield in 1919. This photograph was taken in Morehead City, where he attempted unsuccessfully to fly the plane for a federal inspector. The machine was too heavy for sustained flight because Atwood modified the Navy's specifications, and the inspector returned to Washington in disgust. (Courtesy of the Museum of Flight, Seattle, Washington.)

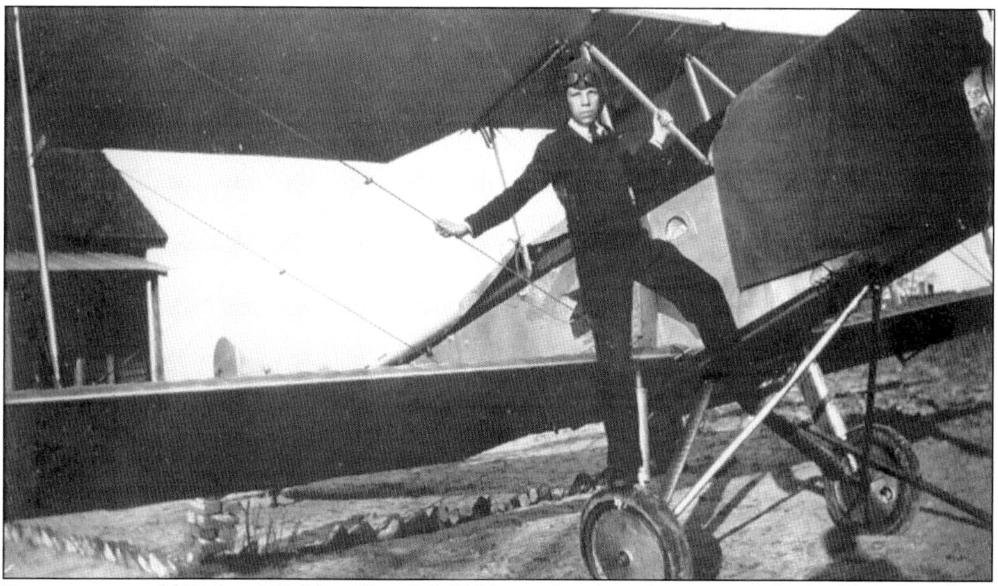

Fourteen-year-old Richard Noble of Smithfield (shown here) took turns with his buddy Jeff Wallace posing with a Navy plane whose pilot made an emergency landing on the Wellons farm south of Smithfield around 1930. Noble recalled there was a basketball game going on in the gymnasium, so they invited the pilot to attend. The gym soon filled up with curious spectators.

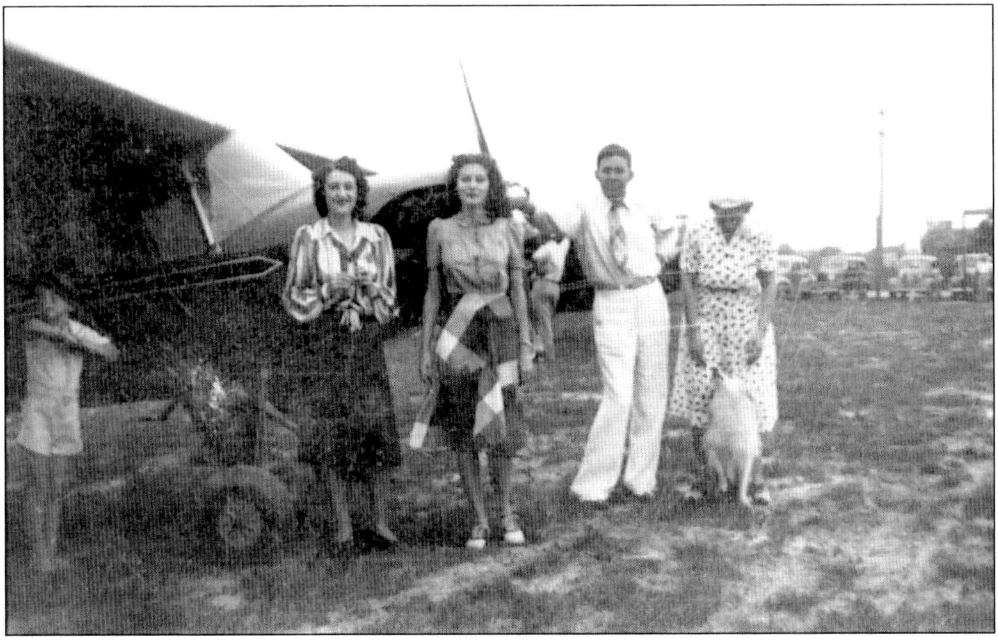

Ava Gardner, third from right, poses with sister Bappie, Bappie's ex-husband William Godwin, and her mother, Mollie Gardner, at the Selma Airport about 1940, shortly before signing a contract with Metro-Goldwyn-Mayer and going off to Hollywood. Godwin was the developer of the airport in 1937 and gave Ava her first of many plane rides. (Courtesy of the Ava Gardner Museum.)

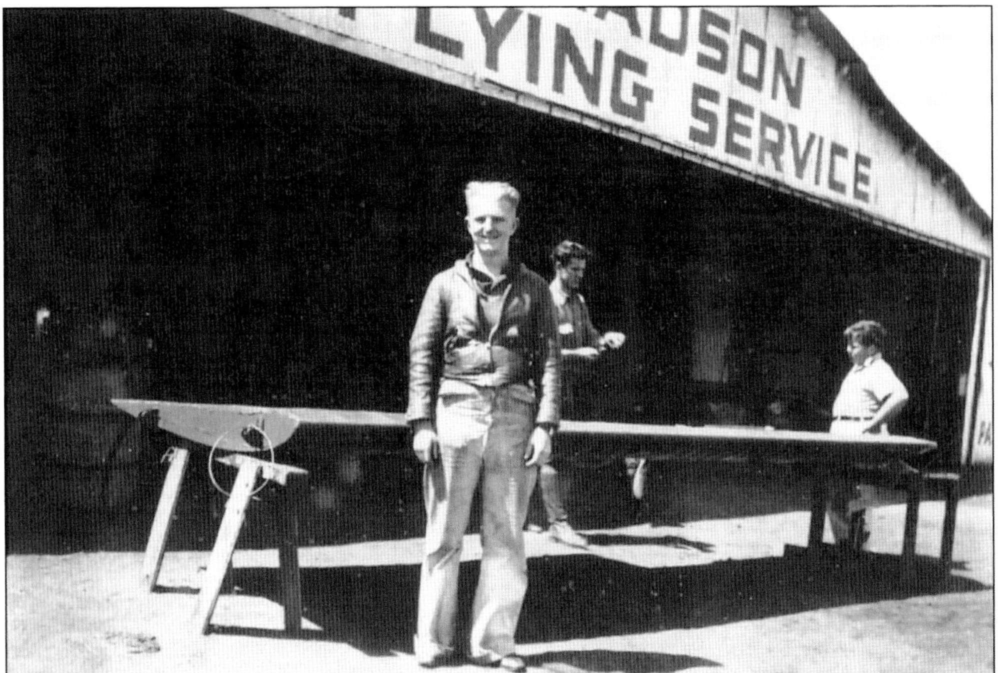

This unidentified pilot repairs a wing at the Selma Airport's lone hangar in the late 1940s or early 1950s. (Courtesy of Bradley Sasser Jr.)

Alonzo Clifton snapped this photograph of his grandparents John and Susan Jones around 1919 with his new Brownie camera. The Joneses had just paid a visit to their daughter Alice Clifton in Elevation Township.

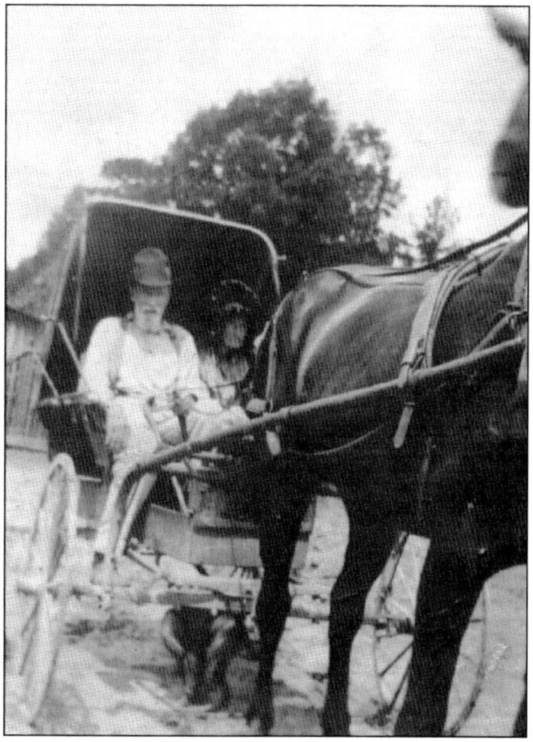

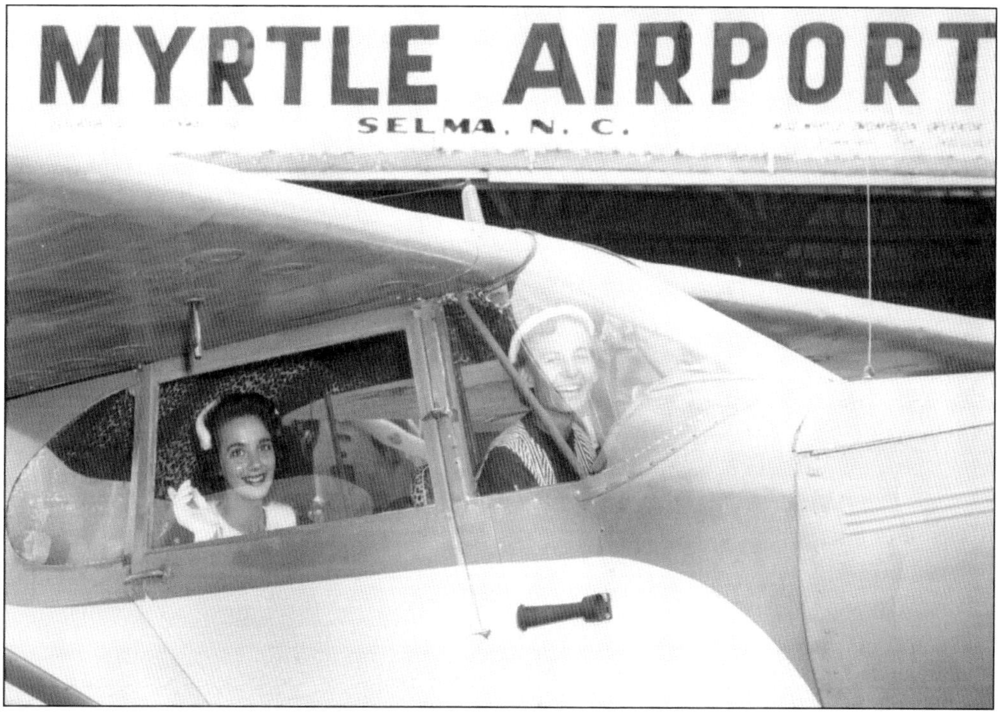

Myrtle Thompson prepares for take-off with Shirley Bagwell, the Selma Chamber of Commerce's golden queen, in this Reuben Johnson photograph taken in 1956. The Selma Airport was known as Myrtle Airport when Myrtle Thompson ran it.

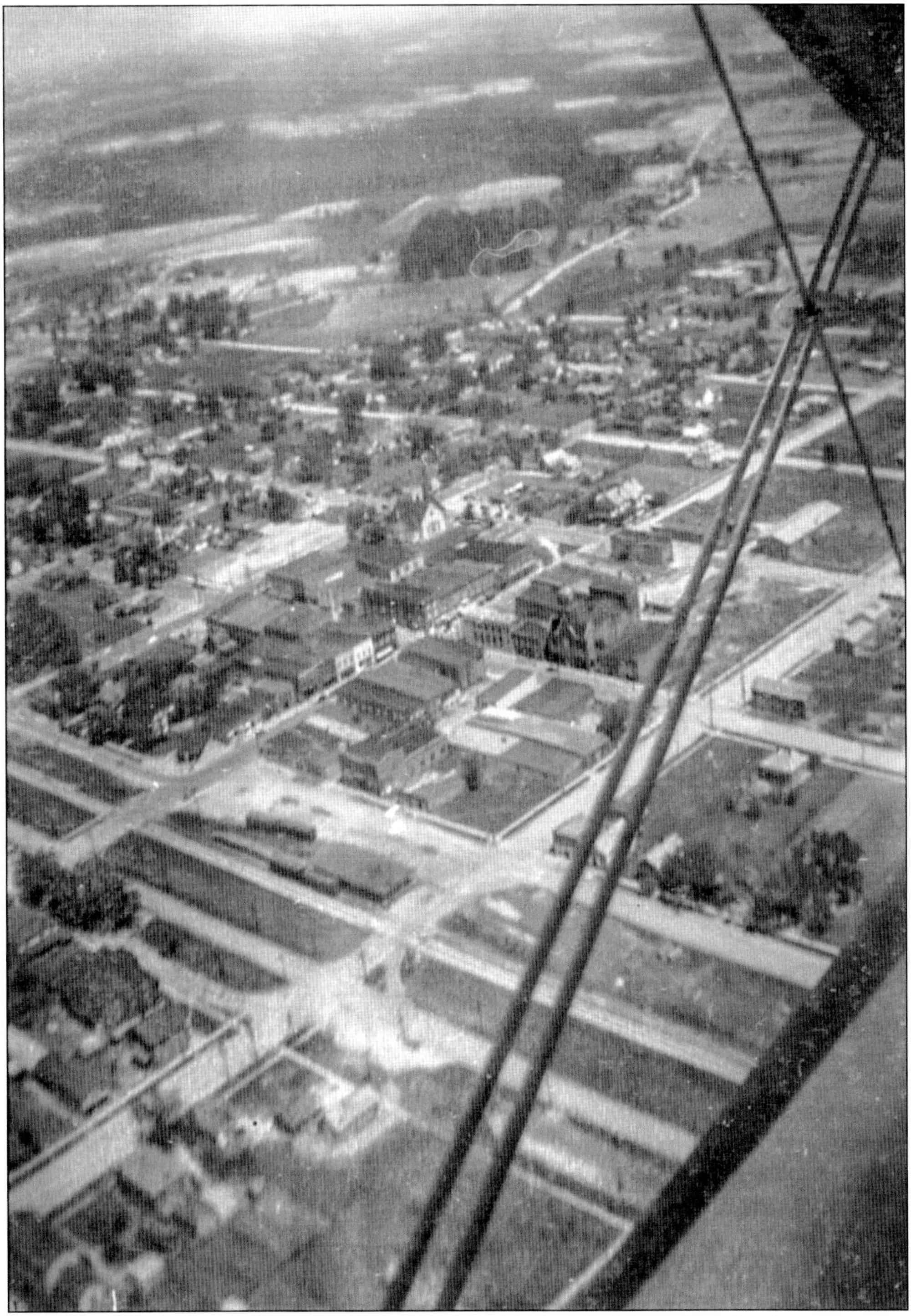

Bradley Sasser Sr., owner of the Selma Airport in the late 1940s, is believed to have shot this aerial view of downtown Selma. (Courtesy of Bradley Sasser Jr.)

Seven

JUST FOR FUN

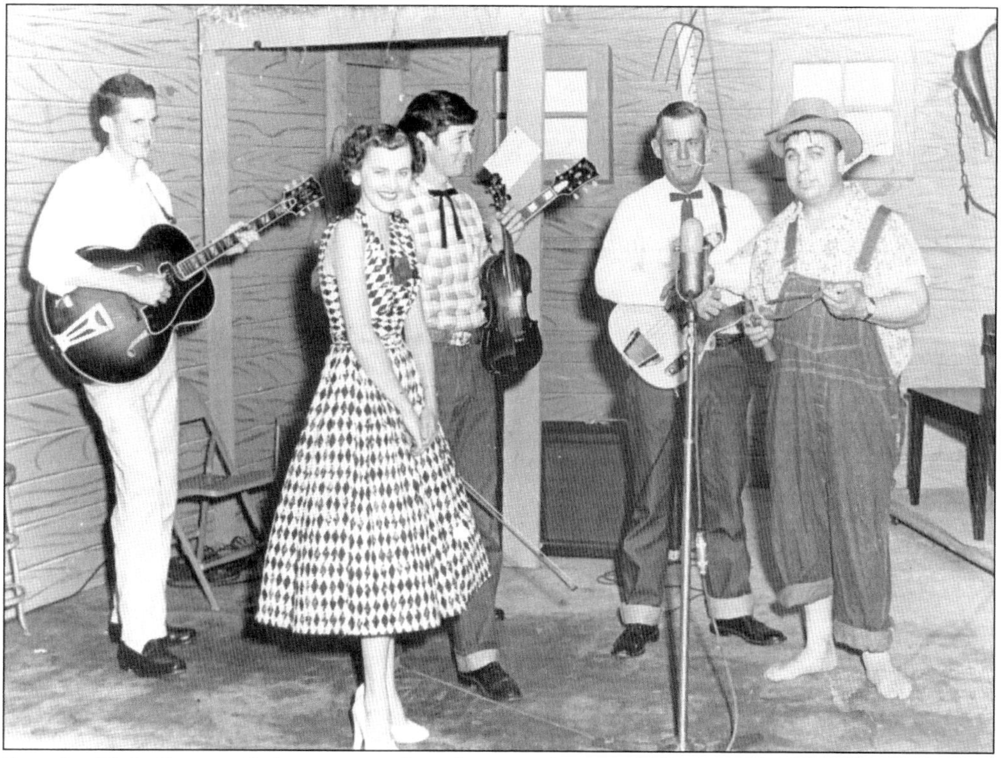

Saturday Night Country Style was a popular television show in the 1950s and early 1960s. Broadcast from WTVD in Durham, it featured Benson's Jim Thornton, barefoot and wearing overalls, best remembered for his vivid and sometimes embarrassing tales about the people of Broadslab, a southern Johnston County section with nebulous boundaries, and advertising (and eating) Yellow Rose Dog Food on the air. Shown here are, from left to right, soon-to-be country music legend George Hamilton IV, Mozelle Phillips, Gerald Young, Hayden Ivey, and Thornton. (Courtesy of Benson Museum of Local History.)

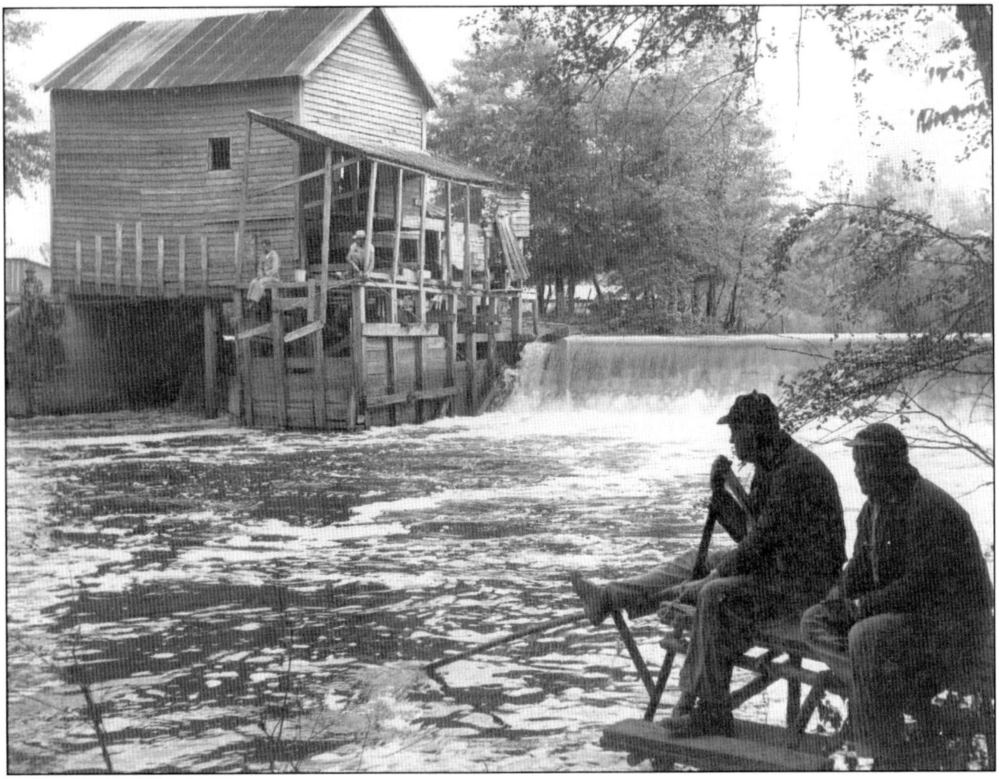

Jack Dermid took this photograph of Barber Mill in Cleveland Township sometime before a freshet washed it away about 1958. The B.T. and Sarah Tomlinson Barber family operated a gristmill here beginning in 1879. Farmers came to grind corn and wheat, and fishermen came from near and far in the spring for shad when the fish left the ocean and ventured up the fresh waters of Swift Creek to spawn.

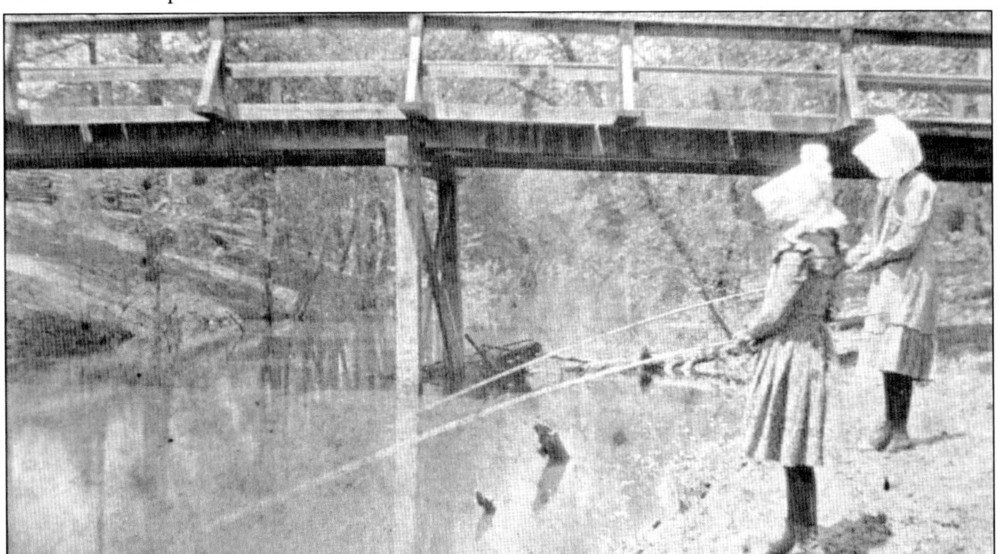

The faces of Mattie and Mary Sanders are hidden by their bonnets as they fish by the Walter Moore Bridge over Middle Creek in Cleveland Township about 1900.

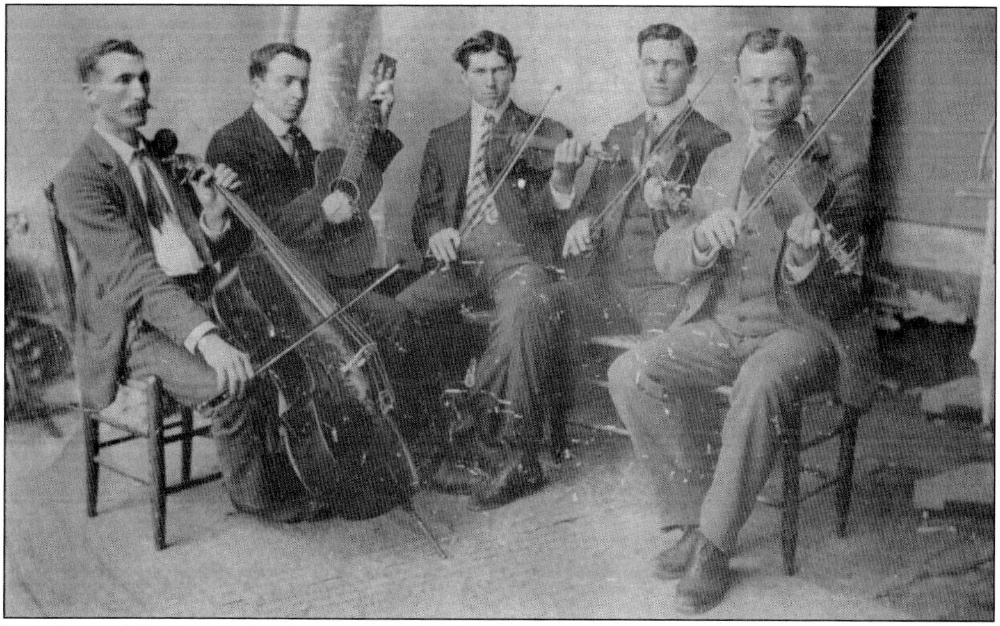

Members of this string band from Four Oaks include John Ruffin Stanley (cello), Dave Sanders (guitar), Preston Massengill (violin), David Lassiter (violin), and J. Percy Smith Sr. (first violin and band leader). They were in great demand for parties and other social functions where lively music was essential.

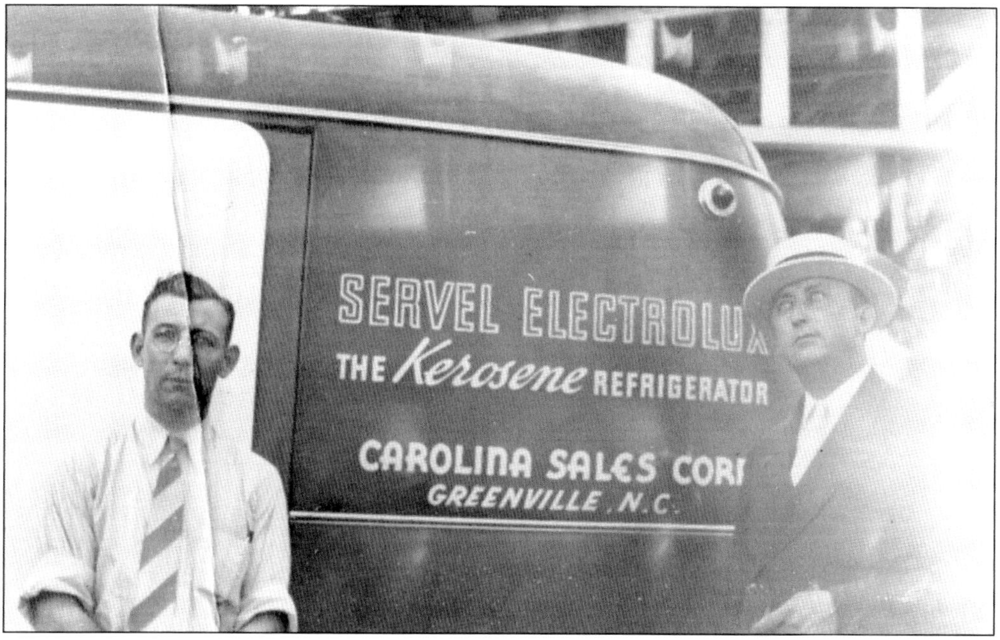

J. Hiram Rose (left) was a longtime Benson funeral director and director of the Benson Sing when this photograph was taken in the late 1930s. He and Decker Creech are shown with the van containing sound equipment loaned for the annual singing convention in June. (Courtesy of Benson Museum of Local History.)

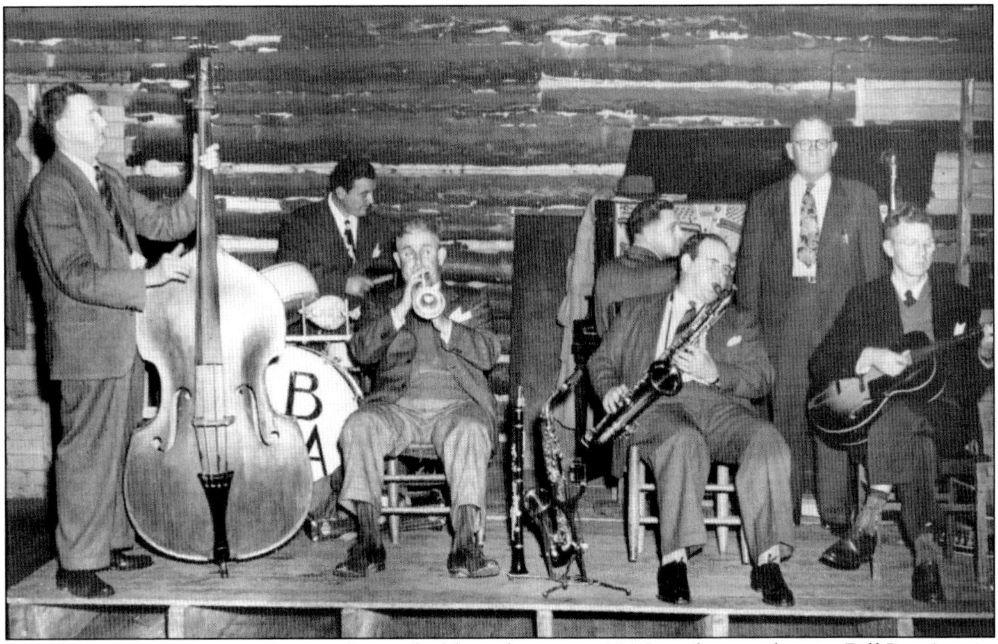

The American Legion in Benson began holding dances in 1945, with saxophonist Bill Joe Austin and his band providing the music. Shown here that year are Skin Jackson (bass fiddle), Rainey Norton (drums), Walt Lassiter (trumpet), Pete Shell (piano), Austin (saxophone), Allen Johnson (organizer and caller of square dance figures), and Tommy Jackson (guitar).

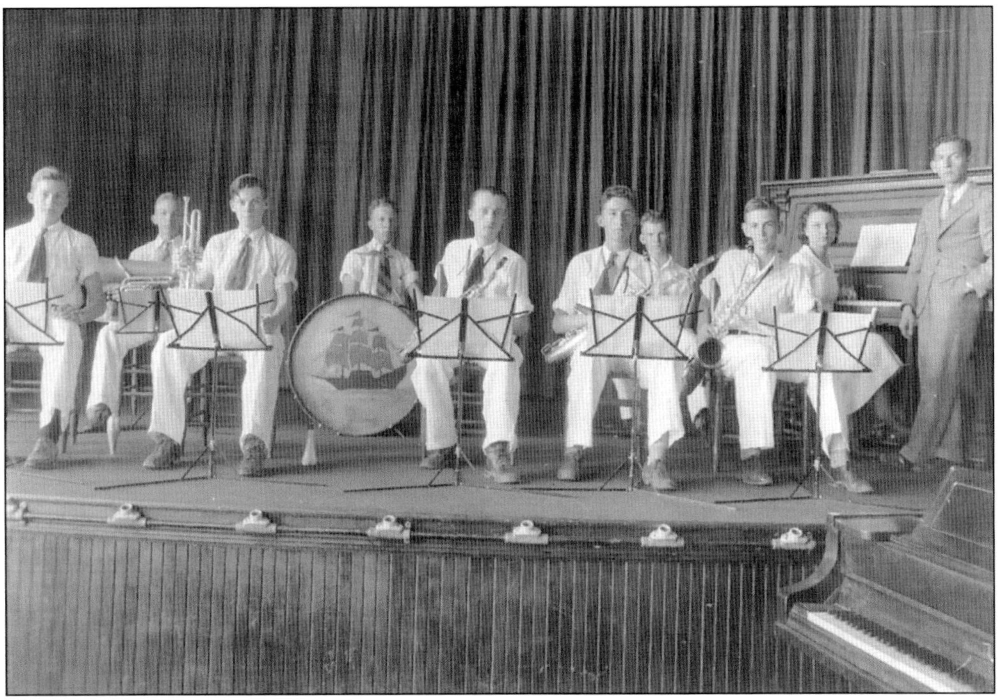

The Smithfield High School Orchestra and their leader are pictured here in 1931. From left to right are Edwin Broadhurst, Ben Grimes, Lynwood Perkins, Richard Noble, Walt Sellers, Paul Johnston, Lemuel Creech, William Norman Holt, Elizabeth Scher, and teacher Mr. Groves.

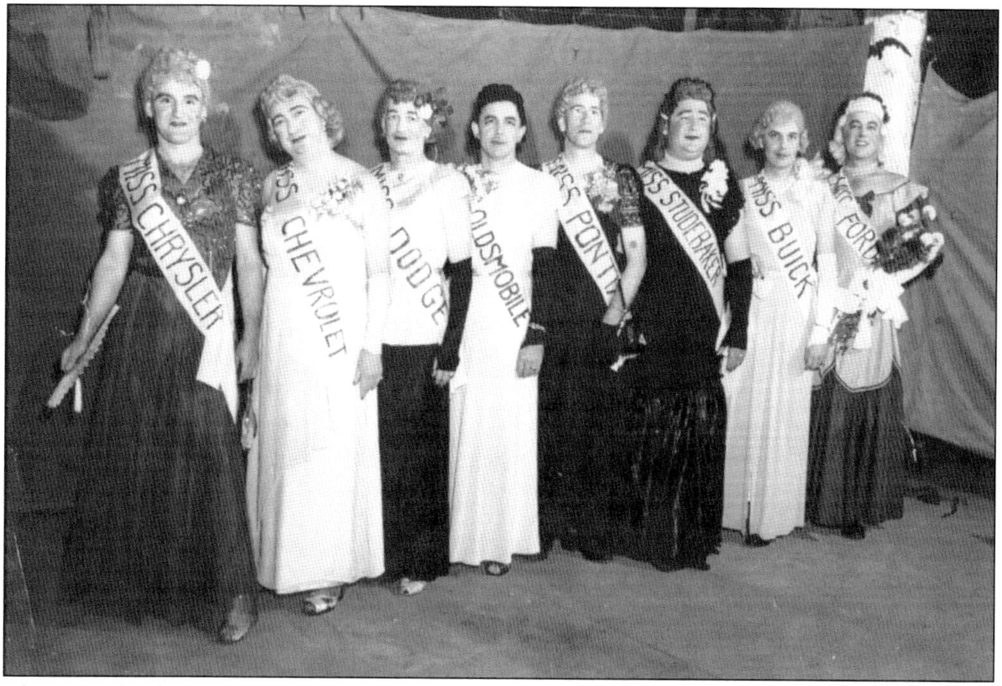

This "Parade of 1950 Models" included local car dealers dressed up for the Smithfield Automobile Dealers Association Dance. The gentlemen are, from left to right, Haywood Stanley, Audy Baggett, Arthur Gardner, Claude Pippin, Carl Little, W.O. Buie, Newitt Williams, and Brack Wilson.

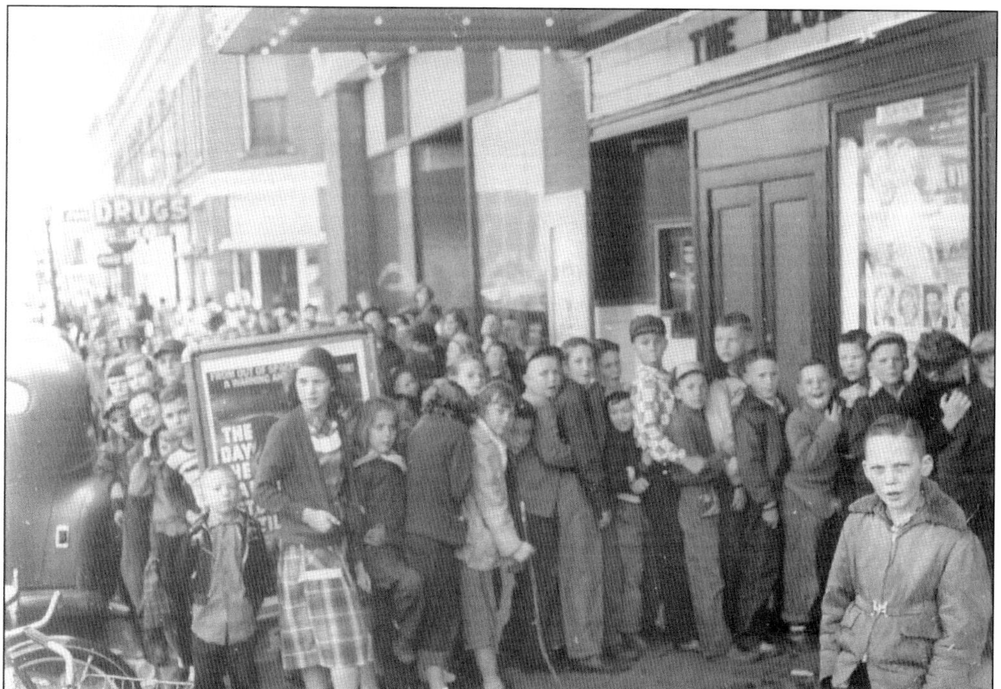

Many children anxiously stand in line to see the thriller *The Day The Earth Stood Still* at the Princess Theatre in Benson in 1951. (Courtesy of Benson Museum of Local History.)

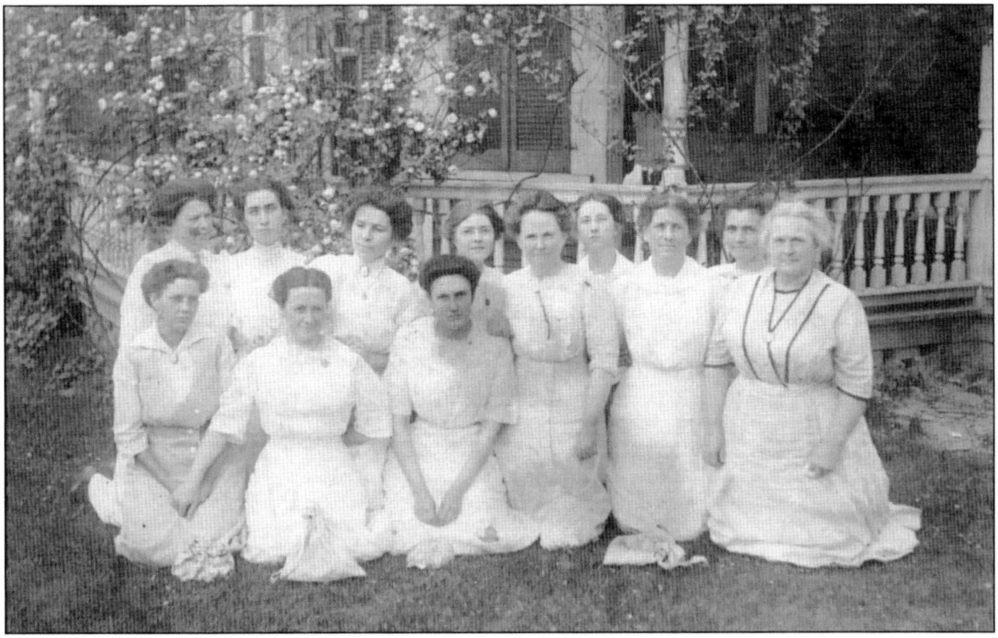

Members of Kenly's Priscilla Club are shown here about 1920. Organized in 1919, they included, from left to right, (first row) Cleva Bowman, Nettie Darden, Martha Woodard, Mary Kirby, Pattie High, and Ida Bailey; (second row) Genie Sauls, Emma Renfrow, Maude Snipes, a Mrs. Nobles, Eva May Broughton, and Loula Alford. (Courtesy of the Kenly Historical Association.)

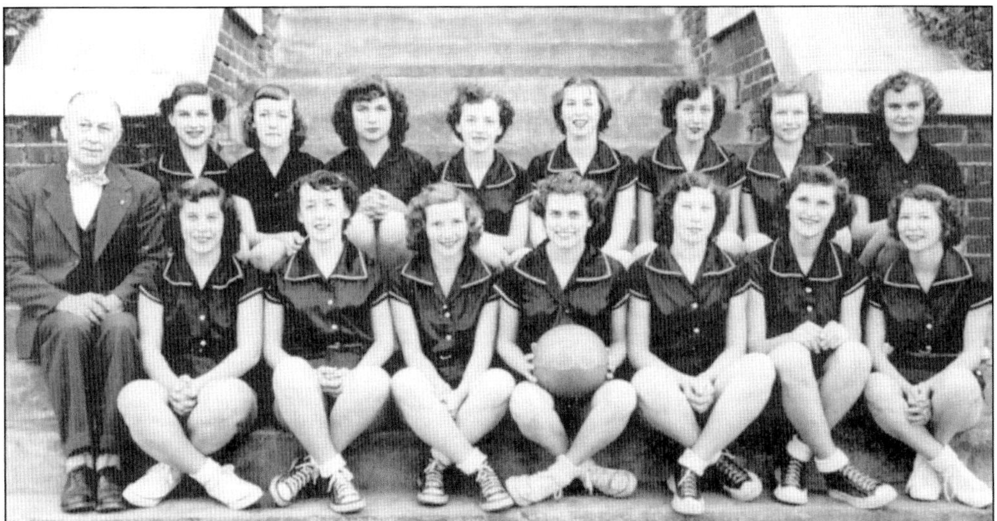

According to the 1950 Meadow High School yearbook, these girls, who played on the school's basketball team in 1949–1950, operated under the motto that physical education and sportsmanship are more important than points. Shown here are, from left to right, (first row) coach C.H. Aderholdt, Edna Lou Adams, Evelene Tart, Katie Godwin, Agnes Lee, Mavis Parker, Edna Ruth Johnson, and Annie Ruth Lawhon; (second row) Joan Johnson, Mary Barefoot, Martha Johnson, Peggy Westbrook, Sally Bryan, Charlotte Fields, Geraldine Kinsey, and Shirley Wood.

The Johnston County Library sponsored this float in a 1950s Farmer's Day parade to encourage children to read.

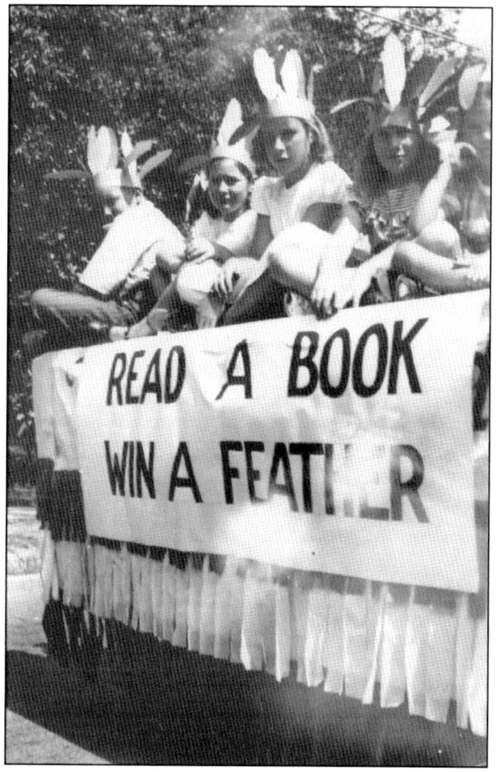

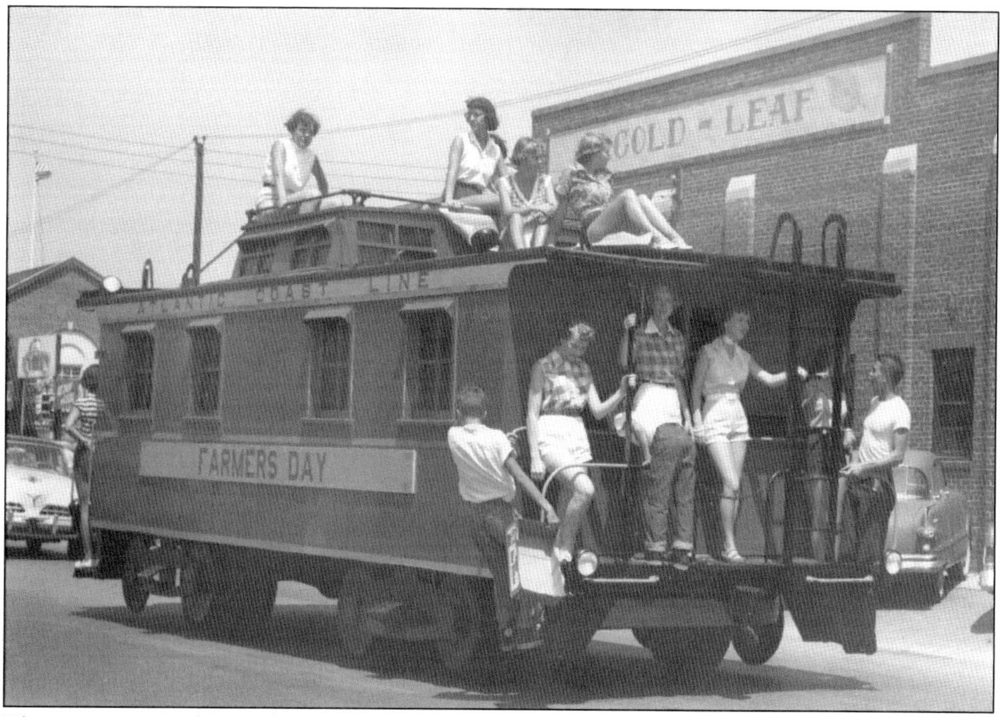

These young people are all aboard the little red caboose in a 1950s Farmer's Day parade lineup on Market Street near the old post office. (Photograph by Reuben Johnson.)

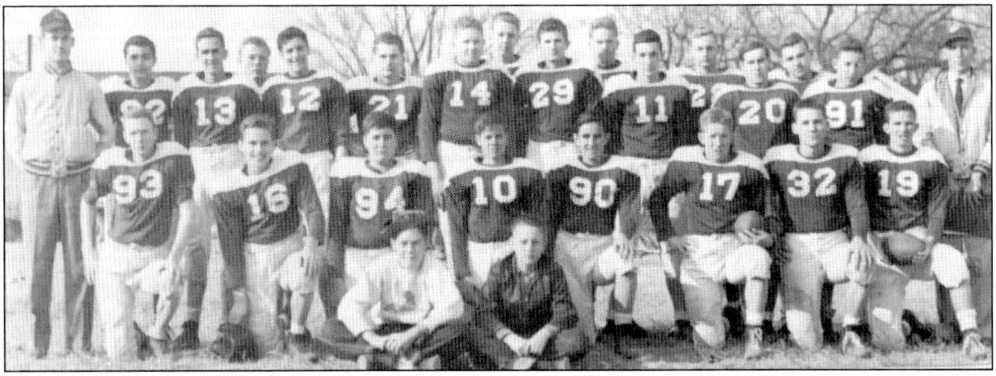

The Clayton High School football team won the State Six Man Football Championship in 1952. Players pictured here include William Bagley, Raymond Capps, Bobby Dodd, Lamar Lee, Clark Davis, Kenneth Edwards, Charles Gordon, Winfred Hall, Jimmy Moore, Allen Stewart, Bobby Turner, Eugene Capps, Nelson Coats, Larry Johnson, Raeford Underwood, Jerry Capps, Bucky Coats, Al Cole, Douglas Dean, Jennings Gower, Bobby Hamilton, Eugene Healon, and Thomas Woodell. Coaches were Joe Hicks and Tom Benton. Jack Gulley and Robert Adams were managers.

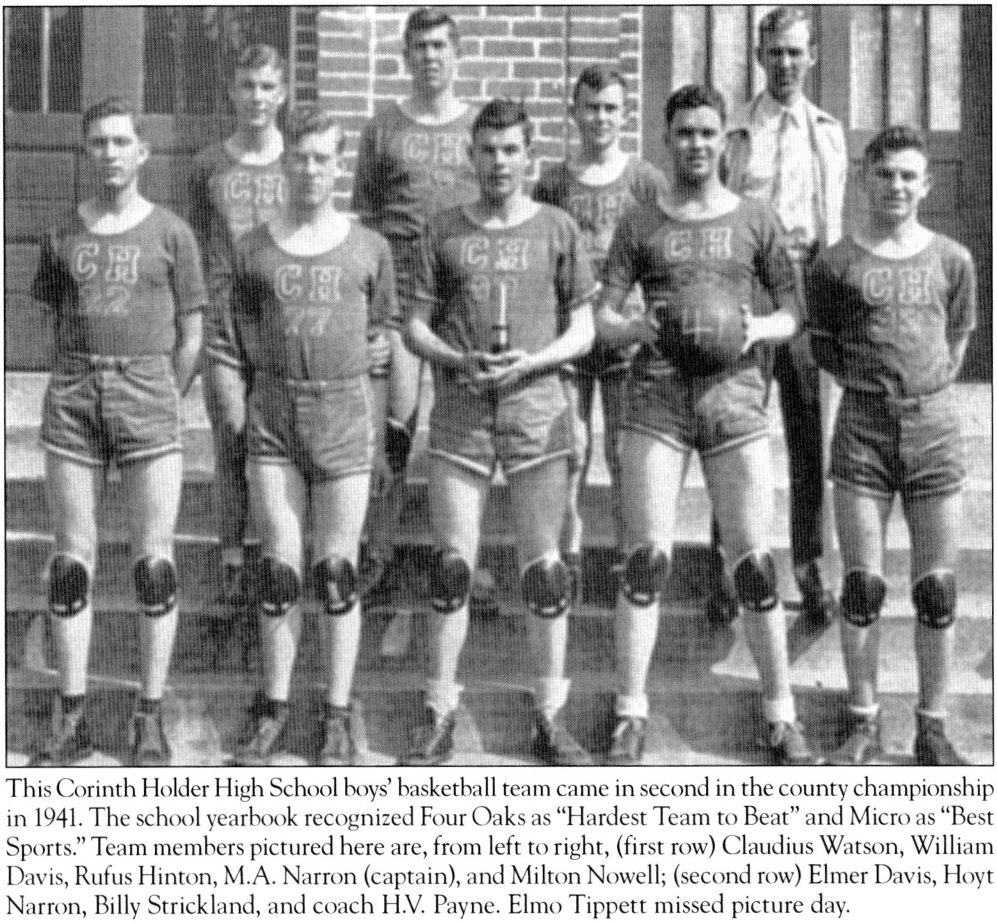

This Corinth Holder High School boys' basketball team came in second in the county championship in 1941. The school yearbook recognized Four Oaks as "Hardest Team to Beat" and Micro as "Best Sports." Team members pictured here are, from left to right, (first row) Claudius Watson, William Davis, Rufus Hinton, M.A. Narron (captain), and Milton Nowell; (second row) Elmer Davis, Hoyt Narron, Billy Strickland, and coach H.V. Payne. Elmo Tippett missed picture day.

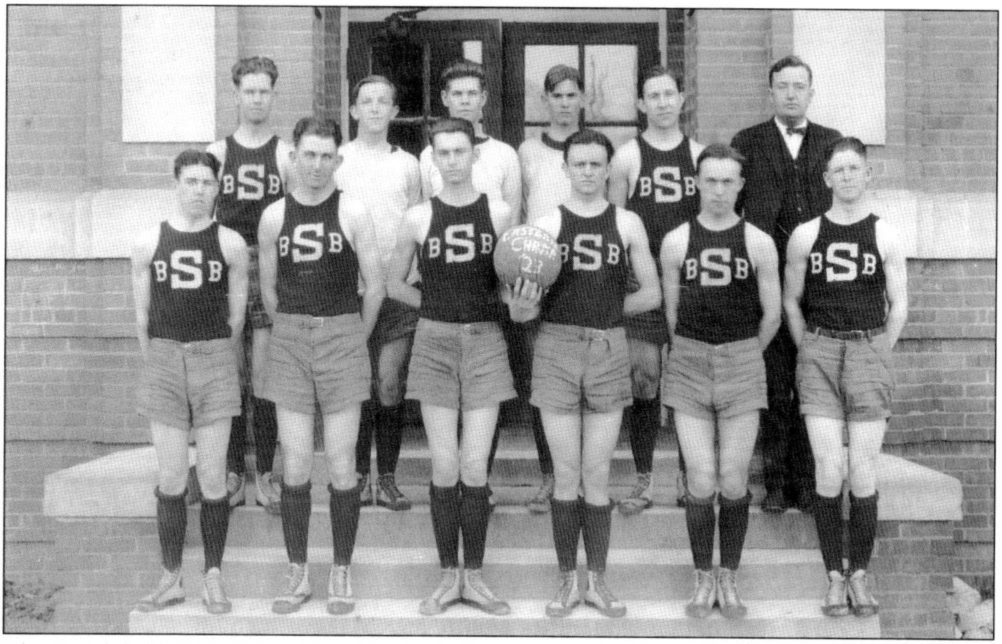

The Smithfield High School boys' basketball team was the Eastern North Carolina champion in 1923. Pictured here are, from left to right, (first row) Frank Skinner, James Hill, Raymond Stephenson, Norwood Holland, Delma Brown, and Leon Hill; (second row) John Caudill, unidentified, Gene Caudill, Clarence "Snoxie" Stephenson, Moses Godwin, and Coach Parks.

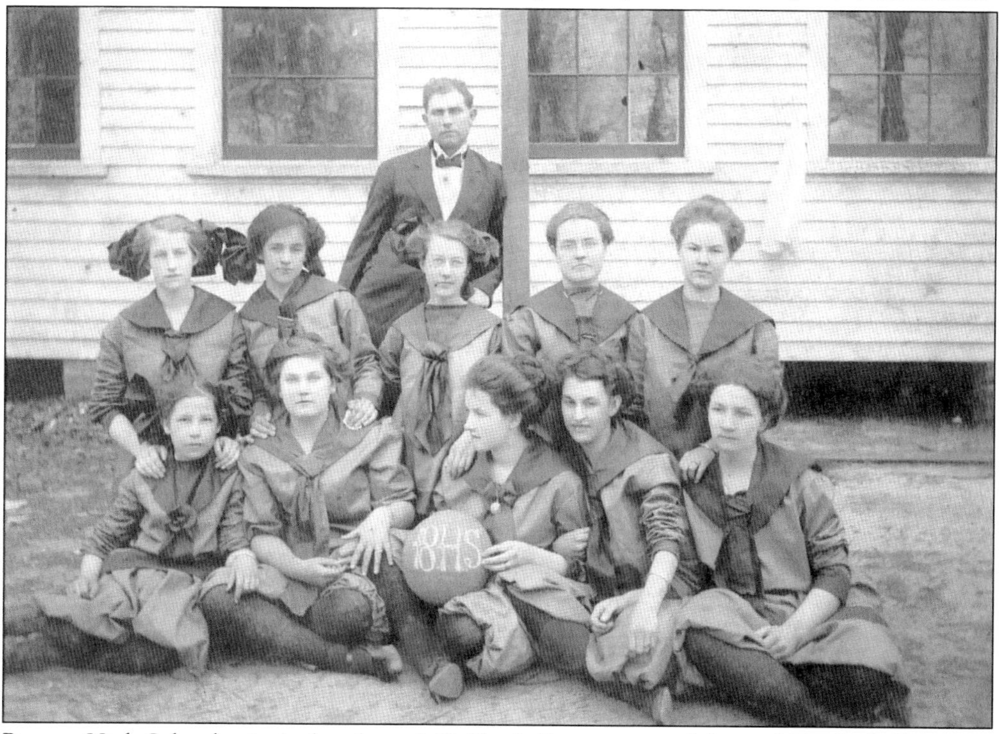

Benson High School principal and coach Z. Hardy Rose poses with his girls' basketball team in about 1910.

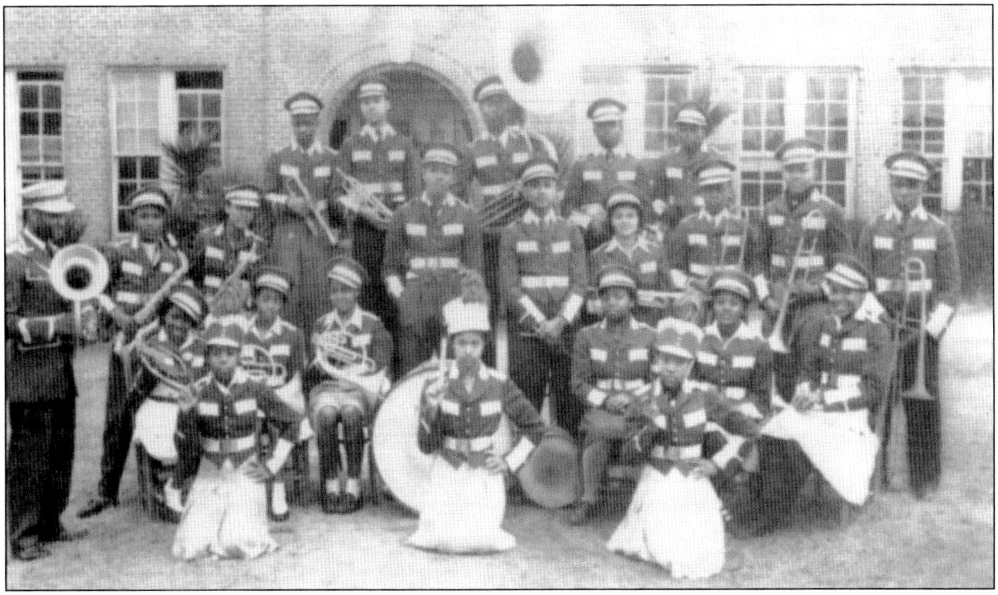

This photograph shows the 1946 band of Cooper High School in Clayton, directed by J.A. Holden. Majorettes are Rose Marien McNiel, Ann Ruth Bryant, and Evelyn Dodd. Band members are Ethel Sanders, Earnest Lamberth, John Whitley, Gordon Hinton, Royestine Rand, Harriet Goodson, Hazel Morgan, Gwendolyn Smith, Lois Tomlinson, Rayford Earp, Henry Goodson, Grover Sanders, Helen Peacock, Parthenia Hood, Elizabeth Tomlinson, David Price, Lee Earl Horton, and Frank Emory.

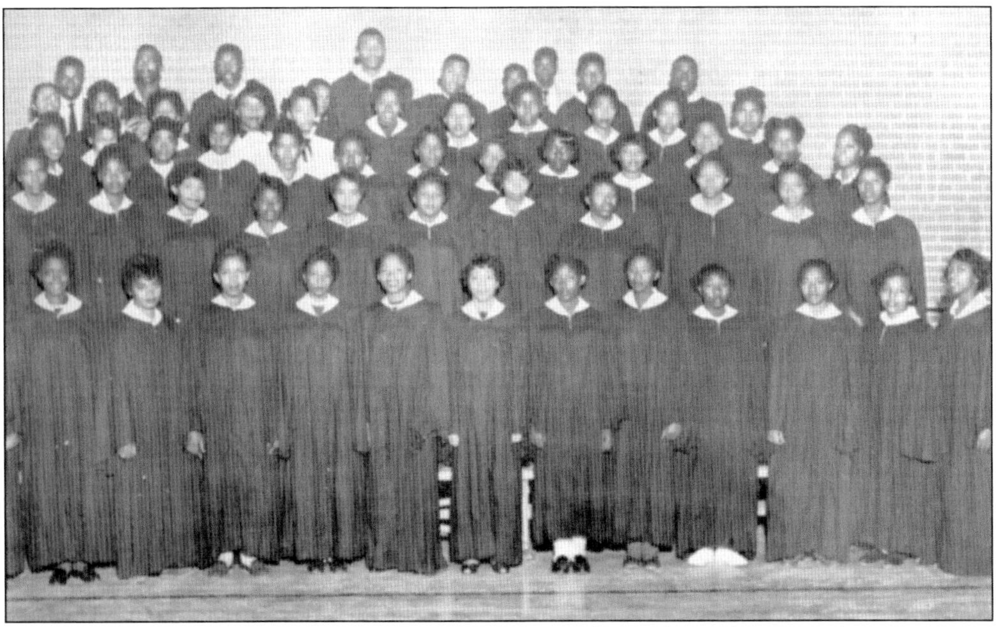

The Richard B. Harrison High School Choral Club in Selma is shown here in 1956. Georgianna McLean is in the first row, sixth from left. She also taught at Smithfield High School and Smithfield-Selma Senior High School and is still much loved by all the students she inspired.

Johnston County Training School's boys' basketball team in 1926 included, from left to right, (first row) Charles Forte, Emanuel Dancy (captain), and Charles McEachin; (second row) Thomas Morgan, Samuel Woodard, and Robert Smith; (third row) coach F. D. Marshall and Ernest Morgan.

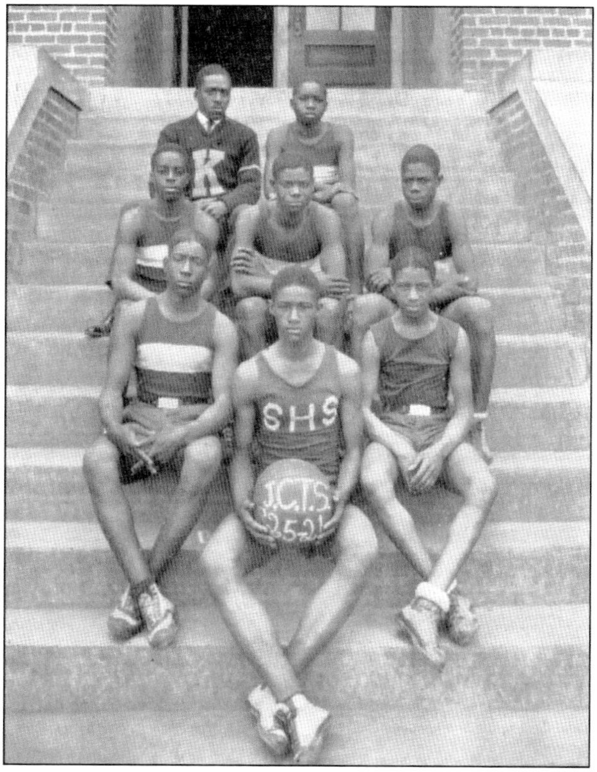

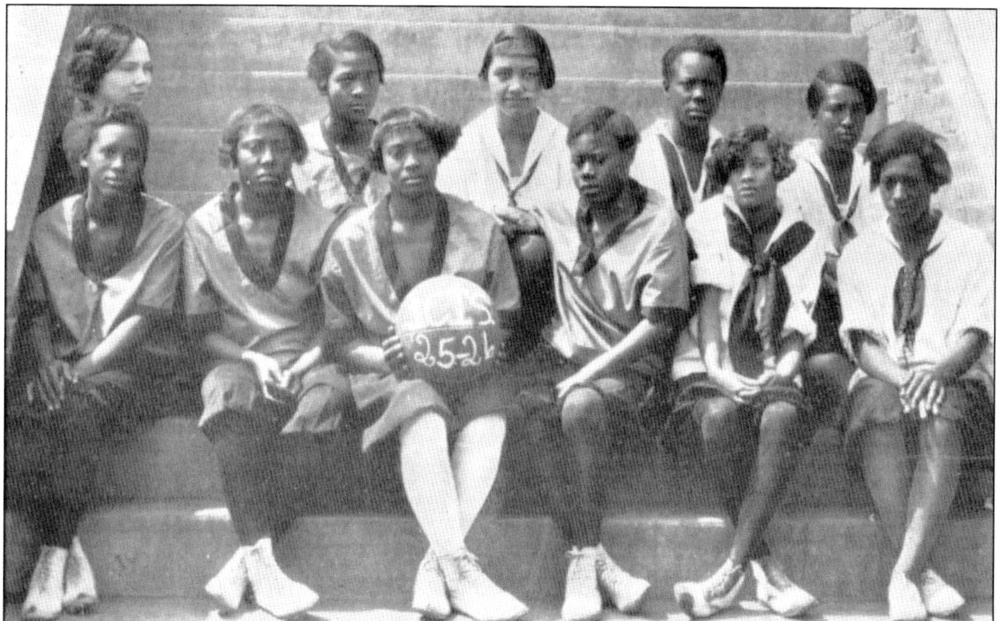

The 1926 girls' basketball team of Johnston County Training School is pictured here. From left to right are (first row) Goldia Bridges, Ellen Sanders, Eddie Dora Mitchener (captain), Lurienda Dublin, Lorien Bridges, and Annie Lue Beckwith; (second row) coach I.D. Banks, Leasie Ann Smith, Lina Mae Smith, G. Murphy, and Annie Mae Forte.

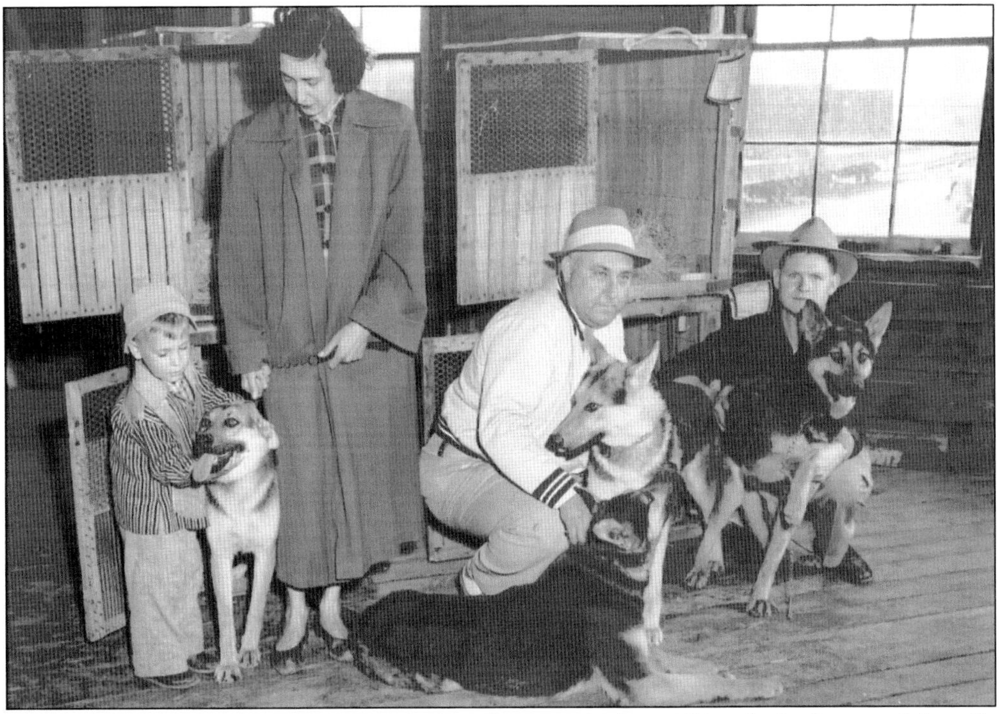

Nathan Lassiter (kneeling, third from left) is photographed in 1956 with the large and friendly German shepherds he loaned for military guard duty. According to son Tom (boy at left), Lassiter brought the parents, Kandy and Kaiser, back from England, and they had several pups. The dogs lived with the Lassiters at Holt Lake while not in service and later went to live on a farm on Devil's Racetrack. (Photograph by Reuben Johnson.)

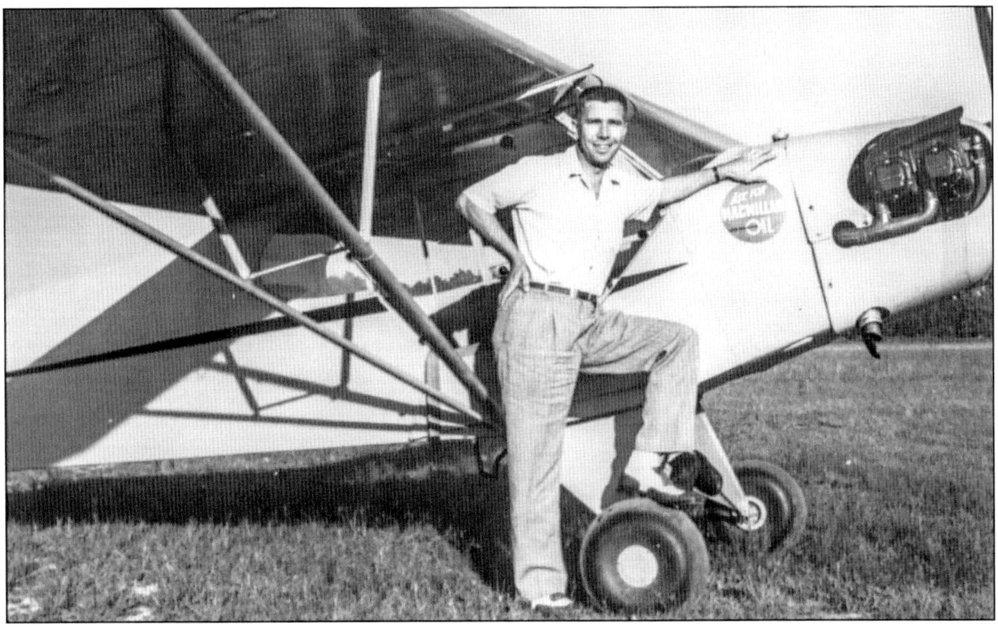

This unidentified flyer was photographed at the Selma Airport sometime in the late 1940s or early 1950s. (Courtesy of Bradley Sasser Jr.)

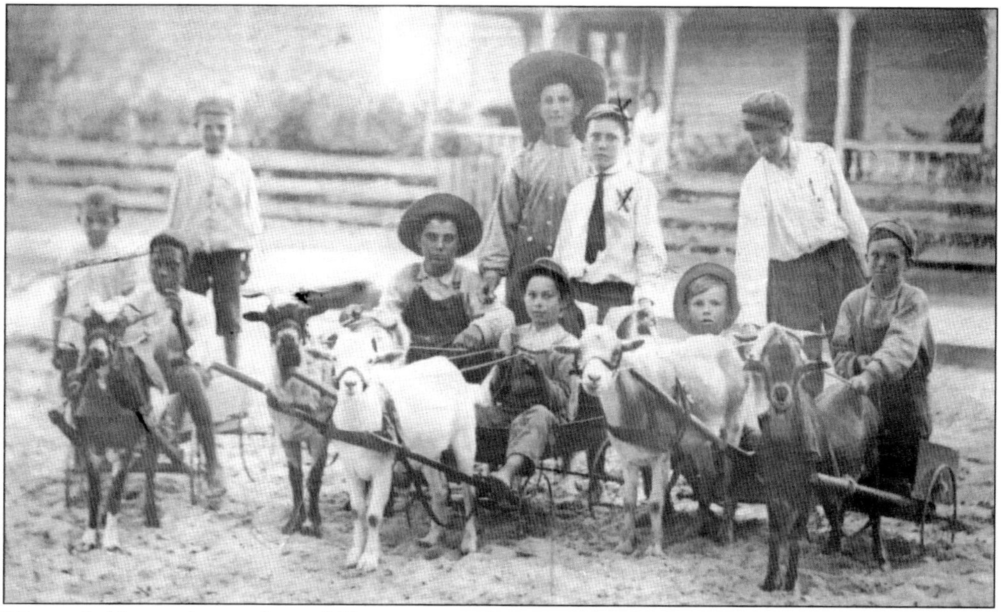

These children, who easily could have inspired an episode of *The Little Rascals*, look ready for a goat cart race. This postcard photograph is labeled "Clarence Fulford at Four Oaks 1911."

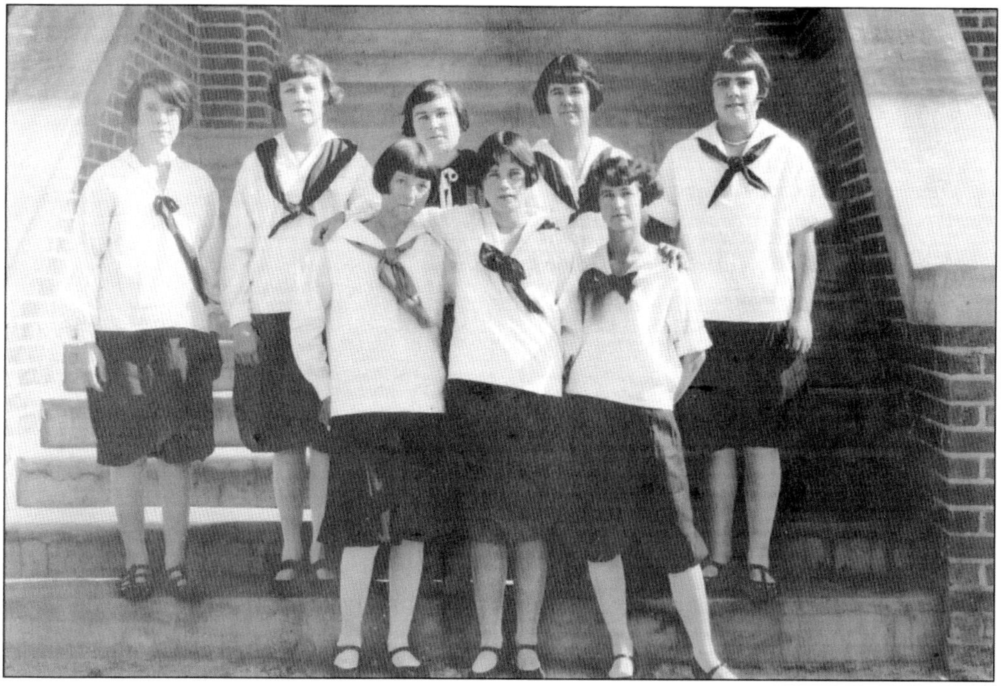

Louise Moser included this photograph of the Micro High School girls' basketball team of 1925–1926 in her "School Friendship Book." Pictured here are, from left to right, (first row) Letha Hatcher, Debbie Broadwell, and Loma Brown; (second row) Lola Starling, Eula Hines, coach Sudie Wellington, Willie Brown, and Nettie Wall. "They have not lost a game," she wrote, "because they have not played but two or three . . . If they can't do anything else, they can sure beat Archer Lodge, 20-0."

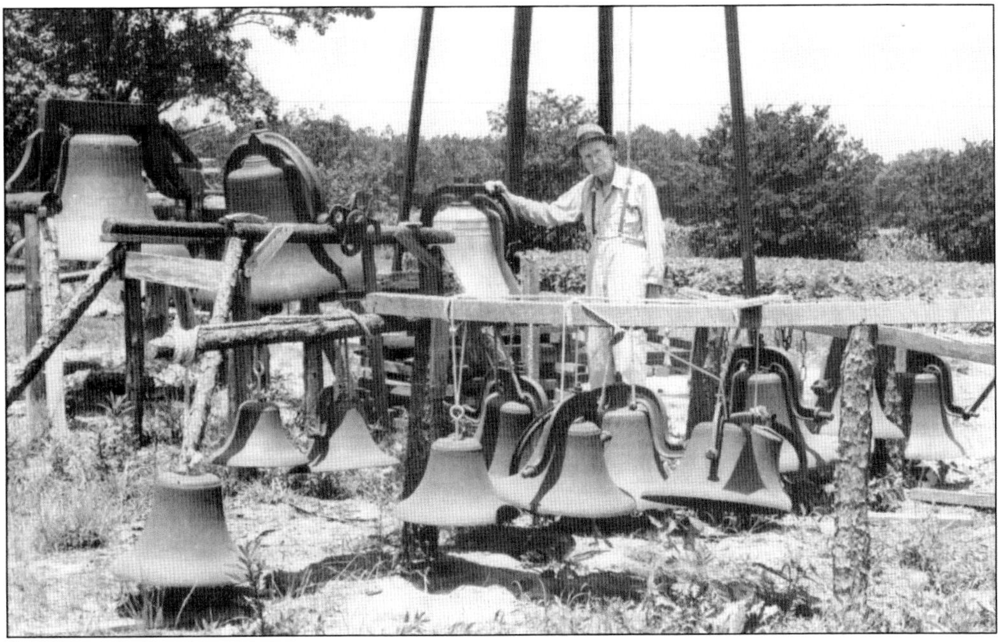

Robert F. "Tink" Coats is shown here in 1965 with his collection of bells from across the country. They were used to build a bell tower, which is one of the major attractions at the Coats Country Museum near McGee's Crossroads in Pleasant Grove Township. They are rung every Fourth of July.

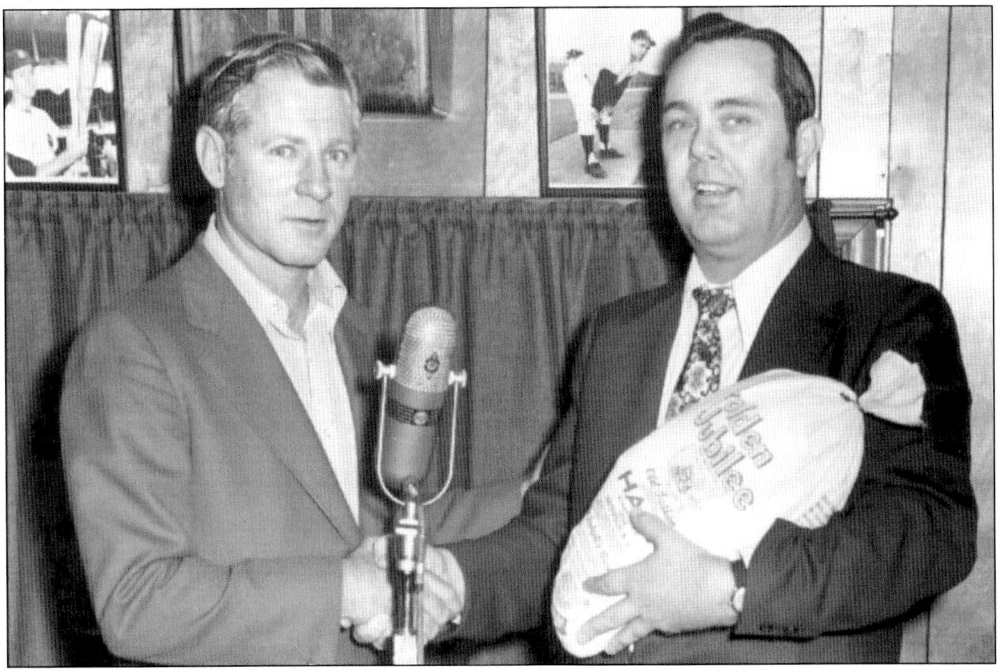

Carl Lamm of WMPM Radio accepts a locally produced sugar-cured ham from a guest in his radio station about 1960. A photograph of Johnston's Major League Baseball player Sam Narron adorns the wall in the background. Lamm continues to be a champion of anything of, by, or for Johnston County. (Photograph by Reuben Johnston.)

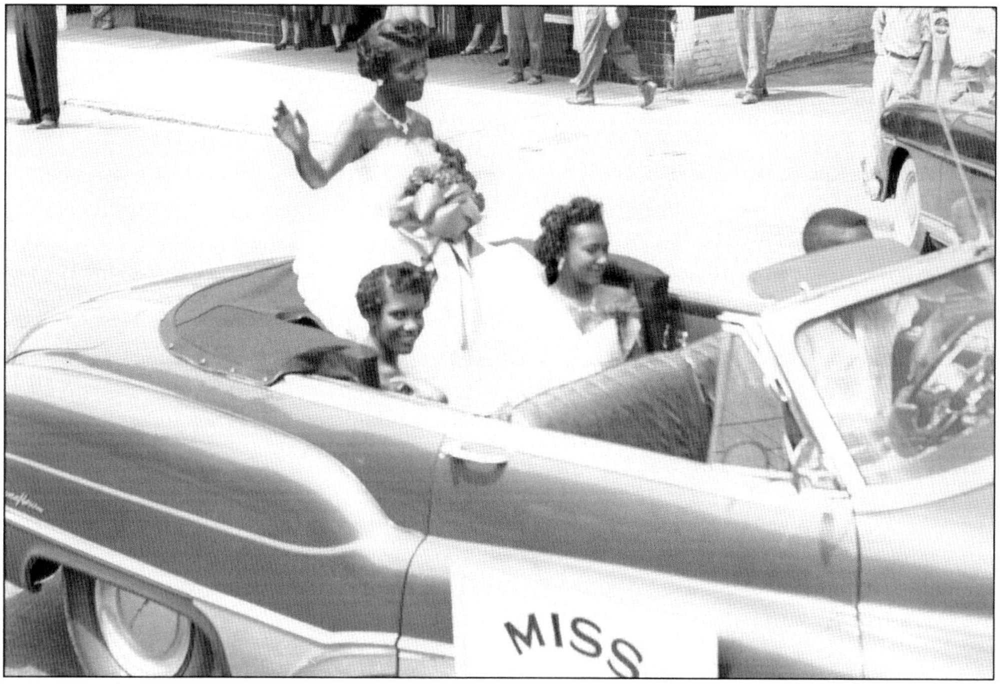

Julia Mae Dublin, Miss Johnston County Training School of 1955, is shown in the school's homecoming parade in downtown Smithfield. Grace Walker (left) and Dorothy Jean Nixon (right) are her attendants. (Photograph by Reuben Johnson.)

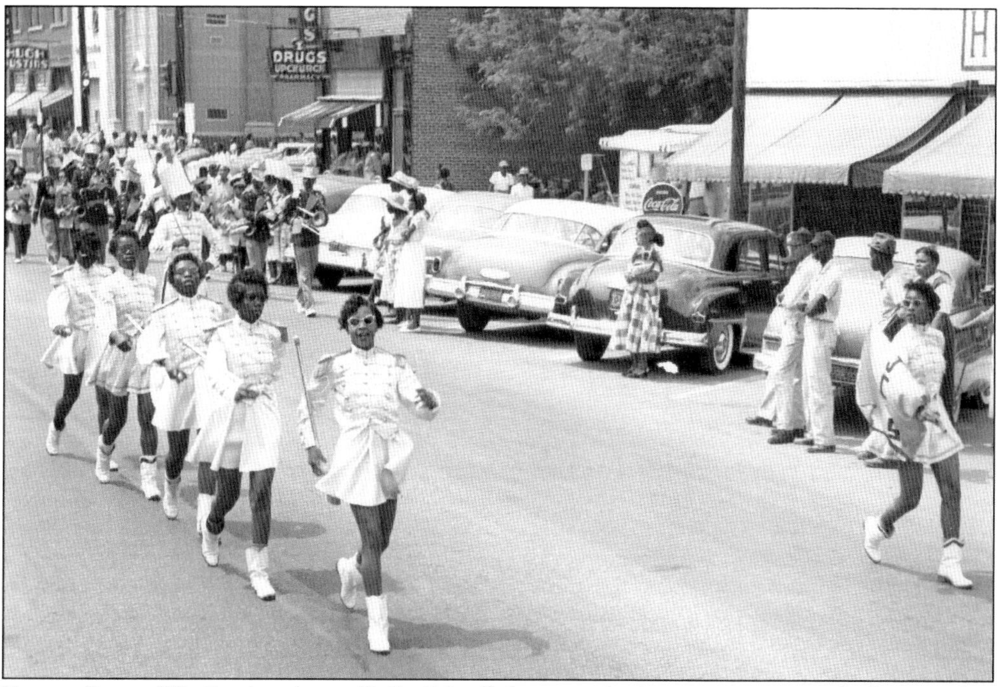

Yvonne Eason, Ella Sanders Avery, Della Carroll Avery, and other majorettes march along Market Street during a 1950s Johnson County Training School homecoming parade. (Photograph by Reuben Johnson.)

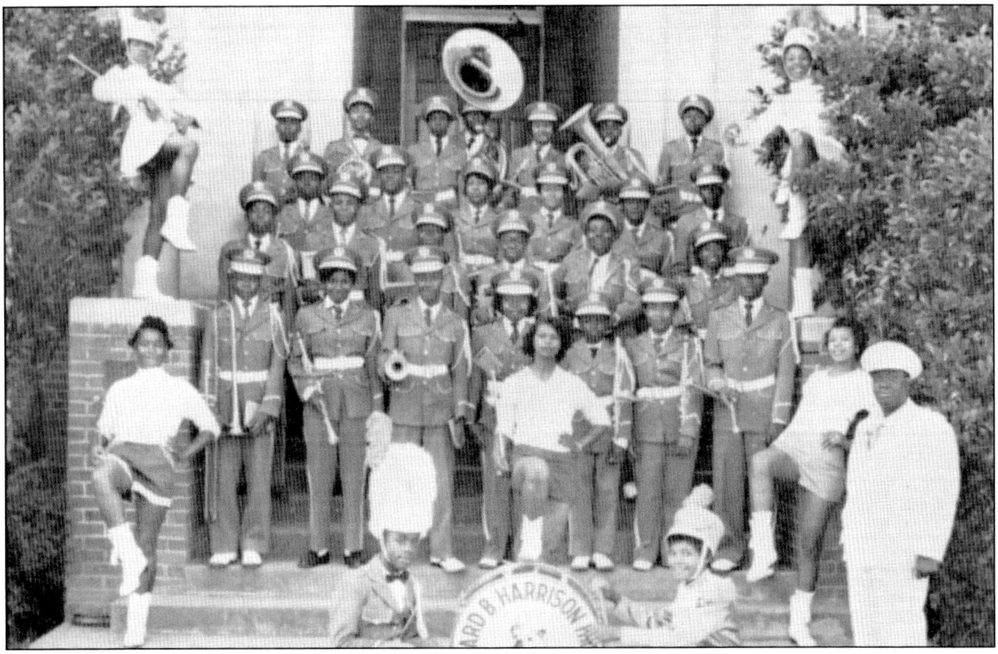

Band director Paul E. Watson (far right) and drum major Robert Lassiter (first row, second from left) are the driving forces behind this Richard B. Harrison High School band, pictured here in 1956. Unfortunately, the school yearbook does not name all the band members.

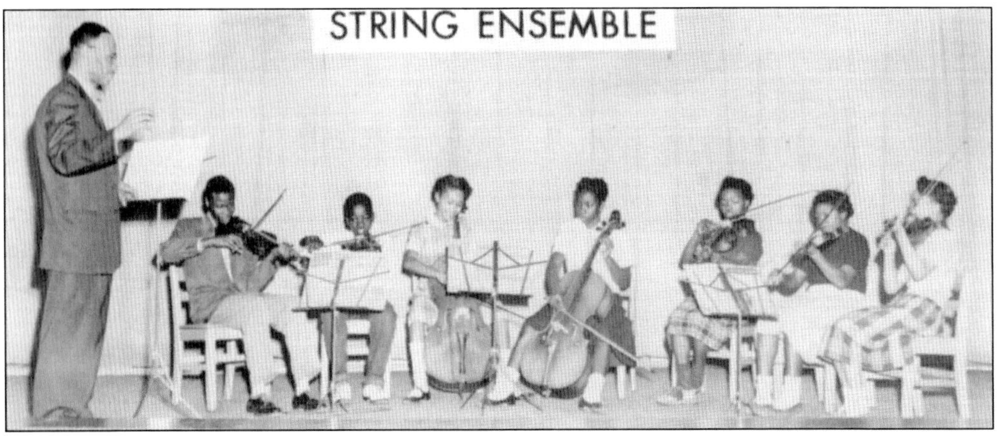

In addition to marching band and chorus, the diverse student body of Clayton's William M. Cooper High School also had a string ensemble in 1956. Principal Nixon L. Cannady (left) was the conductor.

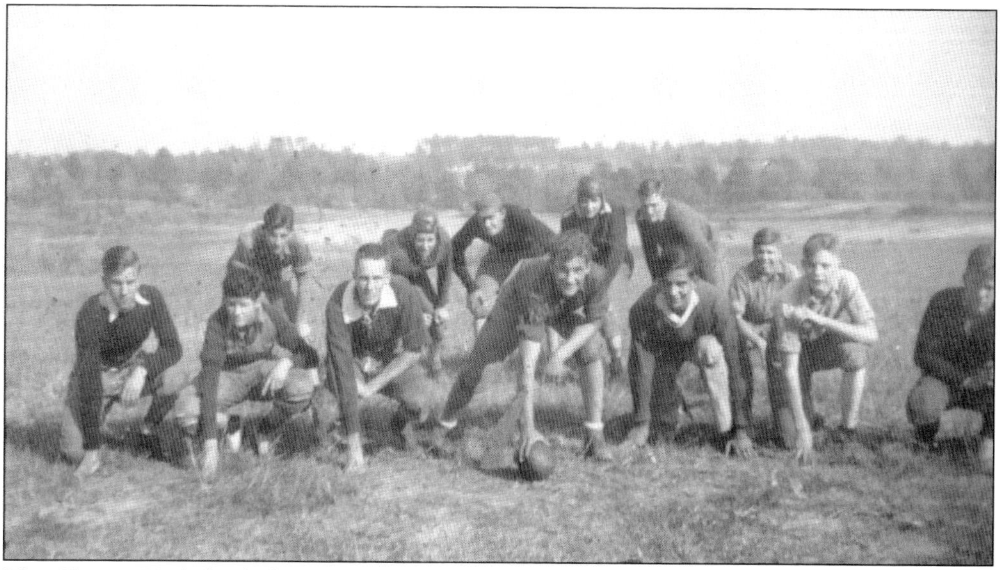

The Clayton High football team faces Four Oaks in this image from the late 1930s. (Courtesy of the Hocutt-Ellington Memorial Library.)

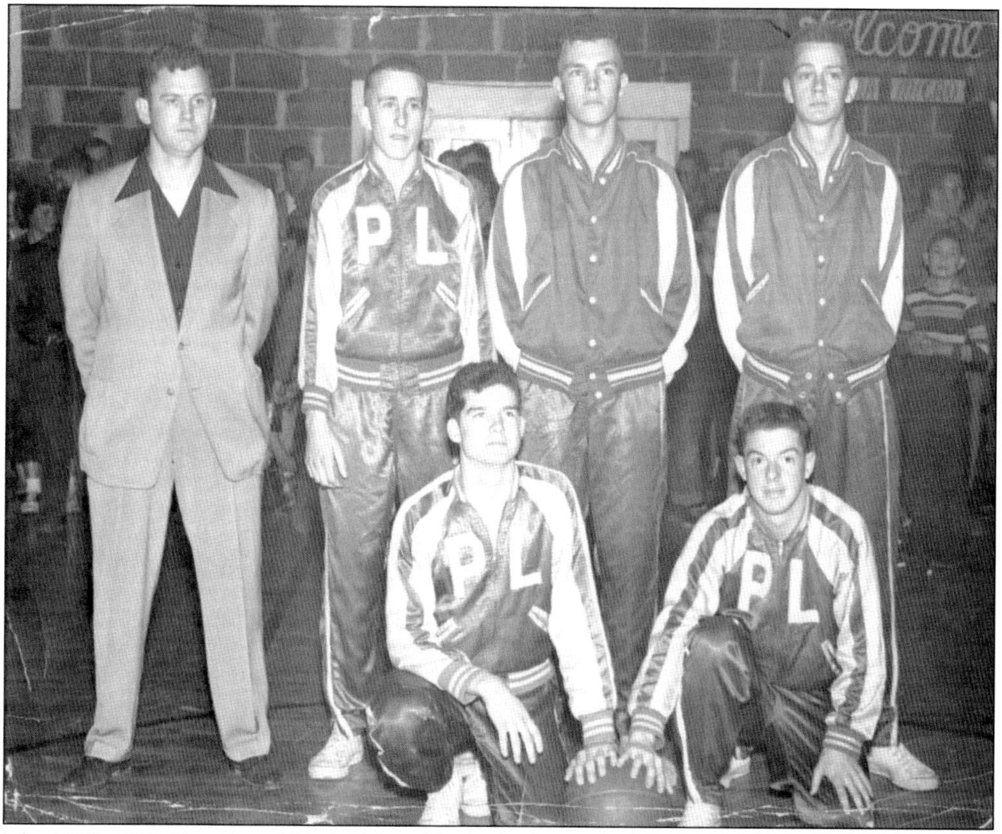

The 1951–1952 Pine Level High School basketball team's first string players pose with coach Bobby Stott (second row, left). Team members included Bobby Harold Stallings, Royster Parker Gaskill, Waverly Jones, Jr., Donald Ray Crumpler, and Junius Jones.

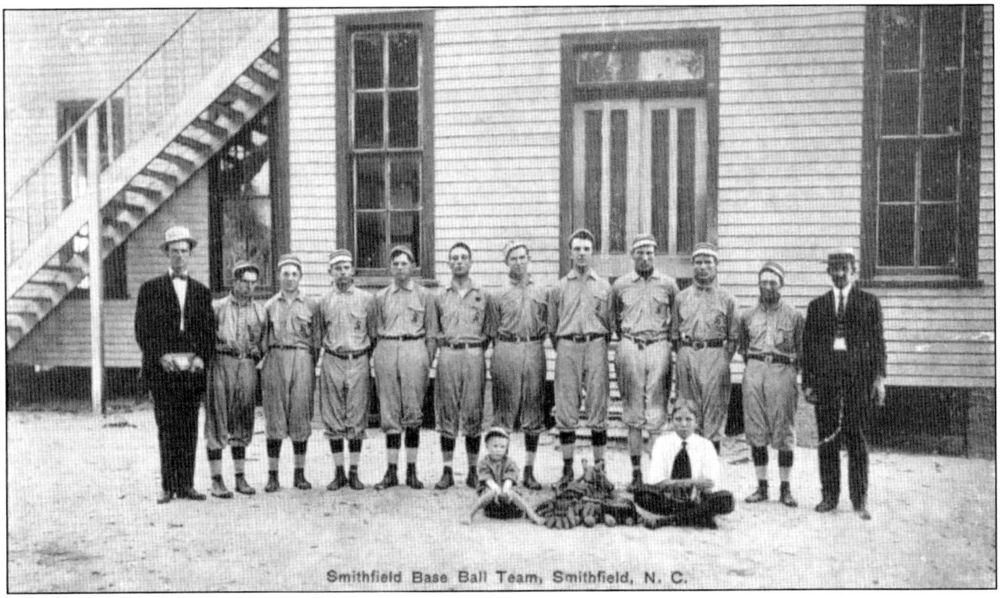

Turlington Graded School's baseball team is pictured on a postcard from 1908. From left to right are (first row) Edward "Pat" Patterson and Milton McGuire; (second row) Seth Myatt, unidentified, Ransom Sanders, Oscar Rand, Marvin Winstead, Abe Rose, Bill Holt, Albert Noble, Leon Stevens, Walter Grantham, Howard Radford, and H.L. Skinner, captain. This image is one of the oldest sports photographs in the Johnston County Heritage Center's collection.

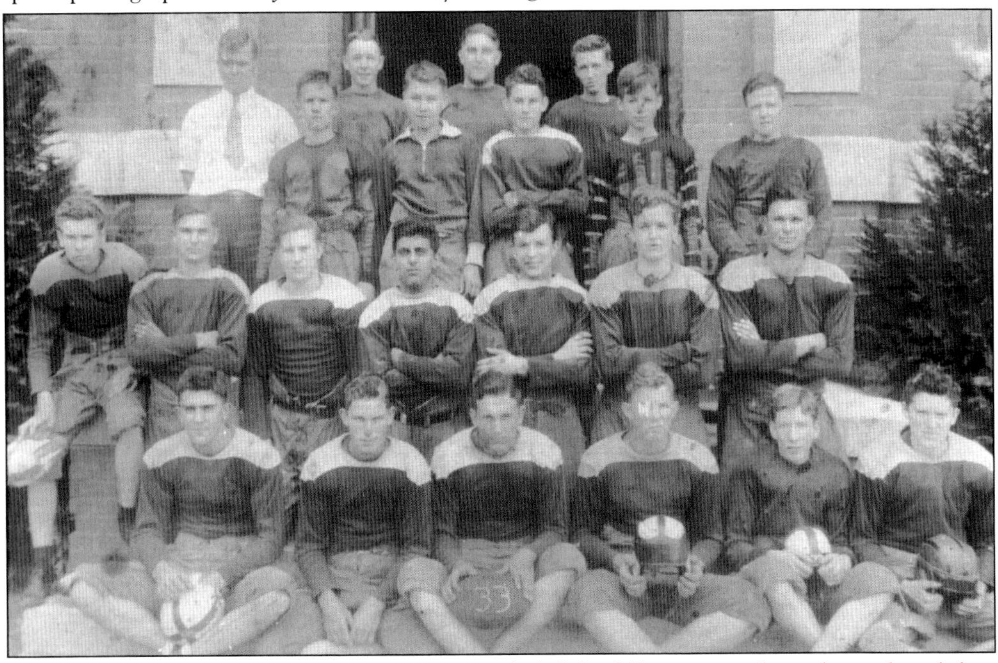

Smithfield High School's football team in 1933 included the following members, shown from left to right: (first row) John K. Davis, Pistol Creech, Aaron Lassiter, Fred Gardner, Charlie Parrish, and Cullen Hooks; (second row) Edwin Matthews, Seavy Page, unidentified, Alec Ziady, Bill Hood, Rainey Norton, and John Rose; (third row) coach Norris Jeffrey, Thel Ragsdale, Ottis Higgins, Rudolph Howell, Nathan Lassiter, Eddie Perkins, Ed Daughtry, Sefton Stevens, and unidentified.

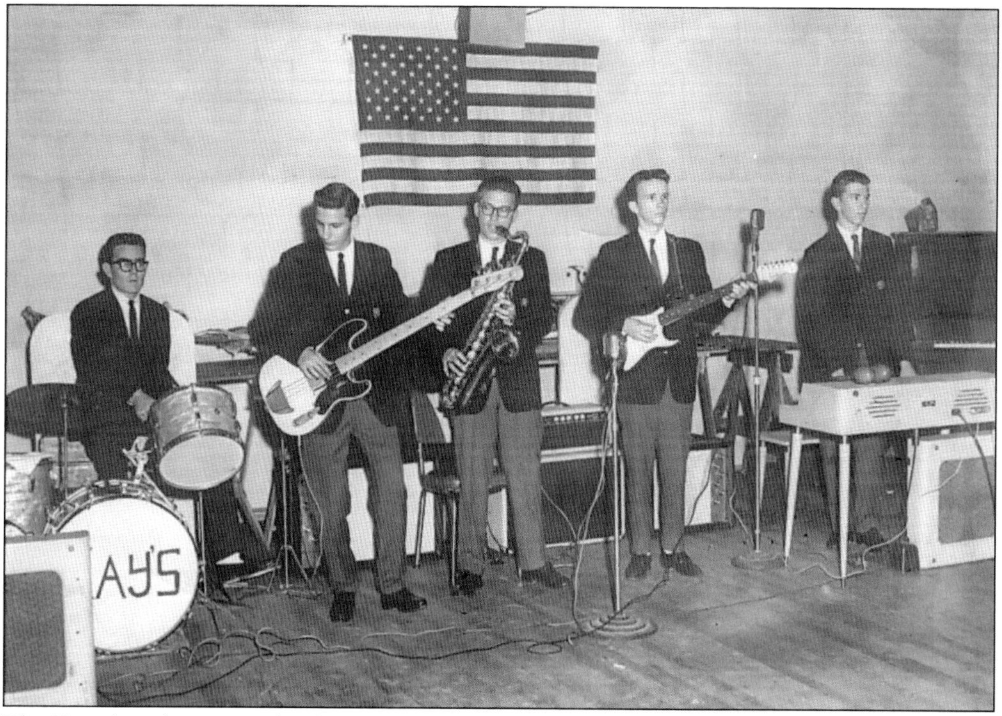

The Kays, later known as the O'Kaysions, gained national attention in 1968 when their hit song, "I'm a Girl Watcher," climbed to No. 5 on the pop charts. Band members Steve Watson, Jimmy Hinnant, Gerald Toler, Wayne Pittman, and Donnie Weaver, shown here in 1961, all hailed from Kenly. (Courtesy of Kenly Historical Association.)

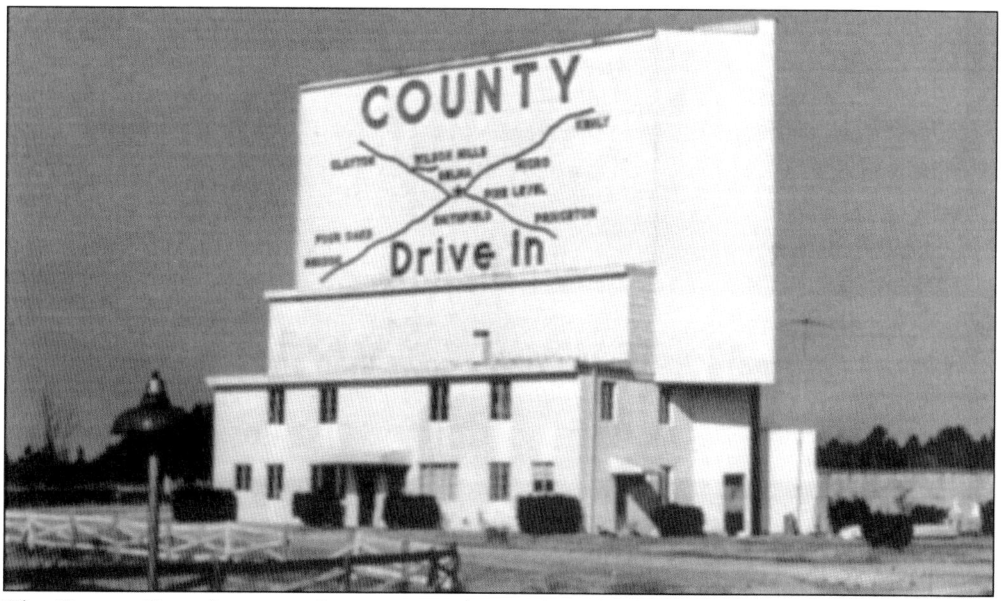

The County Drive-In movie theater opened in 1952 and ushered in a new era of moviegoing. The drive-in concept eventually lost favor, and this site is now home to Smithfield's Walmart Supercenter.